FIFTY KEY POSTMODERN THINKERS

Postmodernism is an important part of the cultural landscape which continues to evolve, yet the ideas and theories surrounding the subject can be diverse and difficult to understand. *Fifty Key Postmodern Thinkers* critically examines the work of fifty of the most important theorists within the postmodern movement who have defined and shaped the field, bringing together their key ideas in an accessible format. Drawing on figures from a wide range of subject areas, including literature, cultural theory, philosophy, sociology and architecture, those covered include:

- John Barth
- Umberto Eco
- Slavoj Žižek
- Cindy Sherman
- Jean-François Lyotard
- Charles Jencks
- Jacques Derrida
- Homi K. Bhabha
- Quentin Tarantino

Each entry examines the thinker's career, key contributions and theories, and refers to their major works. A valuable resource for those studying postmodern ideas at both undergraduate and postgraduate level, this text will appeal across the humanities and social sciences.

Stuart Sim is Professor of Critical Theory and Long Eighteenth-Century English Literature at Northumbria University. His previous publications include *The End of Modernity: What the Financial & Environmental Crisis Is Really Telling Us* (2010), *The Routledge Companion to Postmodernism*, 3rd edition (2011), *The Lyotard Dictionary* (2011) and *Addicted to Profit: Reclaiming Our Lives from the Free Market* (2012).

FIFTY KEY POSTMODERN THINKERS

Stuart Sim

Routledge
Taylor & Francis Group

LONDON AND NEW YORK

First published 2013
by Routledge
2 Park Square, Milton Park, Abingdon, Oxon OX14 4RN

Simultaneously published in the USA and Canada
by Routledge
711 Third Avenue, New York, NY 10017

Routledge is an imprint of the Taylor & Francis Group, an informa business

British Library Cataloguing in Publication Data
A catalogue record for this book is available from the British Library

Library of Congress Cataloging in Publication Data
Sim, Stuart.
Fifty key postmodern thinkers / Stuart Sim.
pages cm. – (Routledge key guides)
Includes bibliographical references.
1. Postmodernism. I. Title.
B831.2.S56 2013
149'.97–dc23
2012049726

ISBN: 978-0-415-52585-5 (hbk)
ISBN: 978-0-415-52584-8 (pbk)
ISBN: 978-0-203-48597-2 (ebk)

Typeset in Bembo
by Taylor & Francis Books

MIX
Paper from
responsible sources
FSC
www.fsc.org   FSC® C013056

Printed and bound in Great Britain by
TJ International Ltd, Padstow, Cornwall

CONTENTS

ALPHABETICAL LIST
OF ENTRIES

CHRONOLOGICAL LIST
OF ENTRIES

ACKNOWLEDGEMENTS

My thanks go to the editorial team at Routledge for all their help and encouragement over the course of this project. Brett Wilson provided useful comments on the science entries, and, as always, Dr Helene Brandon was unfailingly supportive throughout the entire process.

Special thanks go to Alistair Jenkins, whose brilliant surgical skills made writing the latter part of the book a far easier exercise than the earlier had been.

INTRODUCTION

Postmodernism has been part of the cultural landscape for quite some time now, but with many of the major theorists identified with it having died in the last few years (Jean Baudrillard, Jacques Derrida, Jean-François Lyotard, for example), the time seems ripe for a reassessment of their work as well as a reconsideration of who should be included in any survey of the phenomenon's history. Modernity itself as a socio-economic movement is under considerable strain since the credit crisis of 2007–8, which has thrown into doubt its ability to go on delivering the socio-economic progress that is its driving force and the major basis of its public appeal. That makes it all the more topical to look again at those figures who were critical of modernity's stranglehold on world culture, and of the 'Enlightenment project' in general, in the decades leading up to what is still as I write an unresolved crisis seriously threatening the global economy. *Fifty Key Postmodern Thinkers* therefore concentrates on figures working in a wide variety of fields in the later twentieth century, when postmodernism as it is now understood came to have a high profile in popular culture and the public consciousness.

There are forty-six standard-length entries (*c.* 1,900–2,000 words), and two longer; the latter to accommodate thinkers best known for their collaborative work, but who also have substantial bodies of work published under their own name – namely, Ernesto Laclau and Chantal Mouffe, Gilles Deleuze and Félix Guattari. Each entry will include the following: an exposition of the thinker's key concepts; references to their main works and consideration of their impact; a select bibliography of their main works (ten maximum in order not to curtail the coverage of the entry unduly); plus a list of references of other texts mentioned in the entry. The entries are alphabetically arranged, from Adorno through to Žižek.

The volume ranges across philosophy, politics, social theory, psychology, anthropology, religion, feminism, science and the arts in general, to demonstrate the scope of postmodernism as a movement

1

of ideas and the inspiration it gave to cultural critique in the later twentieth century and then on into the twenty-first. The aim is to show that the critique offered by the movement's major figures is as relevant today as it was when it first broke into the public domain back in the 1970s and 1980s, and that it was always far more than a short-lived cultural trend that has now run its course. Indeed, the ideas of those thinkers covered represent an important contribution to the history of scepticism as a cultural phenomenon, with its notably anti-authoritarian, counter-cultural bias from the days of classical Greek philosophy onwards (for more on postmodernism's debt to scepticism, see Sim 2001, 2006). Above all else, postmodernists are sceptical in attitude and spirit: sceptical towards the claims of modernity and modernism to be the best, indeed only, method of organising society; sceptical of the claims made by authorities in general and determined to bring these to public attention wherever possible.

The figures covered here have been chosen to represent their particular fields and by no means exhaust those who could be included under the heading of the postmodern: many other names are mentioned over the course of the volume, but clearly a selection had to be made and this has been done in the first instance on chronological principles. Theodor W. Adorno is the furthest back in the past the selection goes, as his ideas, especially in his later career, strikingly prefigure the postmodern and indeed have set some of the terms of debate amongst theorists there. Adorno, along with his Frankfurt School colleague Max Horkheimer, specifically called into question the Enlightenment's influence and achievements in *Dialectic of Enlightenment* (1944), setting the tone for what was to become a concerted critique of it by the poststructuralist and postmodernist theorists in the later twentieth century. Adorno's *Negative Dialectics* (1966) also stands as a key work in the development of post-Marxism by what is effectively its deconstruction of one of the most basic building blocks of Marxism as a system of thought, a teleological dialectic: it seems entirely appropriate, therefore, that it is Adorno who leads off the entries.

The decision was made to concentrate on the twentieth century and not to go further back than Adorno, since earlier figures who have also strongly influenced postmodern thought – Immanuel Kant, Karl Marx and Friedrich Nietzsche spring most readily to mind in this context – properly speaking belong to other intellectual traditions. To include such as those in the present volume would have been to weaken the specifically postmodern slant of the project at the expense of influences whose work has often been substantially reinterpreted by postmodern thinkers to fit their own objectives. Postmodern theorists are generally more post-Marxist than Marxist in their philosophical and political orientation, and Kant would hardly have approved of his ideas being appropriated, as they have been by the postmodern community, to undermine rather than reinforce the role of reason in human affairs. Everyone given an entry can claim a direct role in helping to form what we now call postmodern thought, although reference will also be made, where appropriate, to the sources of their ideas in cultural history. The second principle of selection has been to cast the net as widely as possible over academic, intellectual and artistic disciplines in order to demonstrate the very considerable breadth of postmodern thought, the implications of which soon became apparent across the entire cultural spectrum from those working in the arts through to those in the sciences. The artists, musicians and writers chosen for inclusion here are to be considered as leading examples of their fields, rather than as isolated figures who happen to display some characteristics of the postmodern aesthetic in their work.

It is a point worth making, too, that many of the figures here rejected the label of 'postmodernist', and that there is no such thing as a defined postmodernist movement − except perhaps in the field of architecture (as I will explain in more detail below; readers are also referred to the Charles Jencks entry). There is, however, a definable condition of postmodernity, and all the figures included in the volume have contributed significantly to our understanding of this phenomenon, and stand in some kind of critical relation to its predecessor, modernity. It is that critical relation I take to be most important, and through their articulation of it these thinkers have, in their varied ways, helped to shape what we mean by postmodernity and the postmodern, hence their inclusion. Every effort will be made to cross-reference between these thinkers, to show the connections that can be made between them that do suggest a common set of concerns running throughout their work.

Defining and contextualising the postmodern

Although the notion of the postmodern has been around since the later nineteenth century, it is only in the latter part of the twentieth that it comes to take on its current meaning of a reaction against modernity and modernism, to the extent of constituting an anti-modernism in some respects. Earlier uses had generally meant by it something more like ultra-modern, often with the connotation that this was an undesirable cultural development that was not in the public's best interests to have occurred. Thus for the historian Arnold Toynbee postmodernity signalled cultural decline (see Toynbee 1954); for the theologian Bernard Iddings Bell it signalled spiritual decline (see Bell 1926, 1939). By the mid-twentieth century, however, it was taking on more favourable connotations within the field of architecture, although it still implied a condition of ultra-modernity, as it did for such as the architect and academic Joseph Hudnut, for whom it was the face of the future in the brave new world following World War Two. This was to be a world where houses would be the product of 'a collective-industrial scheme of life' (Hudnut 1949: 119) that their owners fully supported.

It was within the field of architecture that postmodernism's current meaning of a reaction against a particular style and cultural formation eventually took shape. Charles Jencks was one of the major theorists of this architectural turn, recommending adoption of the concept of 'double-coding' (Jencks 1991: 12), whereby architects would make a conscious effort to appeal to the general public rather than just to their architectural peers, designing buildings which contained something of interest to both constituencies. This tended to take the form of a self-conscious eclecticism, by which styles old and new were freely mixed, often in a humorous and more than somewhat ironic fashion, and it is the style of architecture currently holding sway within the profession, with examples of it multiplying throughout the world's major cities and urban areas. Pastiche became a term of praise for postmodern architectural practitioners, whereas it would have been regarded as a pointed criticism instead by their modernist predecessors, for whom it would have signalled creative laziness because of a failure to break away from tradition. And indeed it can still generate complaint on that latter score: 'I have read that under the name of postmodernism, architects are getting rid of the Bauhaus project, throwing out the baby of experimentation with the bathwater of functionalism' (Lyotard 1984: 71). The complainant in this instance is the famed author of *The Postmodern Condition*, Jean-François Lyotard, whose relationship to the postmodern is admittedly never less than complex, but it does indicate an unease about any possible demonisation of the new in the emerging postmodern aesthetic.

Despite the reservations of Lyotard, and of others like the literary theorist Brian McHale, who argued that the term 'late modernist' (McHale 1992: 206) would more accurately describe texts that would qualify as postmodernist under Jencks's theory, double-coding soon spread into the other arts to become a major element in postmodern aesthetics. Creative artists took it to require setting up a dialogue with the past, and a great many of them plunged into the method with enthusiasm. Modernist aesthetics, on the other hand, tended towards a rejection of past styles in the name of originality and experimentation, which were considered to be central to the individual artistic vision. Postmodernist artists were actively encouraged to revive and imitate older styles, again often with a humorous and ironic touch to show that they were aware that times had changed and that it was not just a case of straight imitation on their part. Pastiche was much in evidence, with styles being freely juxtaposed with each other to make apparent the artist's double-coding credentials. The goal was the same as in architecture, however, that is to widen the reach of the artist's work by offering the general public something familiar with which they could readily identify. It was to be in the way that forms were mixed and handled that the creative artist's appeal to their peers would now lie, rather than in the creation of new and original, and to a general audience often mystifying and incomprehensible, forms.

But the postmodern was much more than just an aesthetic movement: it resonated through pretty well all areas of life in the West, and came to take on a specific political meaning of challenging authority and the power that it claimed to have. It is entirely possible to speak of a distinctively postmodern form of politics, in which Lyotard's idea of the 'little narrative' (Lyotard 1984: 60) looms large. Little narratives were Lyotard's answer to the question of how concerned individuals could set about resisting the overweening power of 'grand narratives' or 'metanarratives' (Lyotard 1984: xxiii, xxiv), with their entrenched institutional power bases. The latter constituted centres of ideological power that set the rules and regulations by which societies operated; the former were loosely organised groupings which protested against the abuse of power by grand narratives, and were conceived of as temporary rather than permanent formations, designed for specific short-term rather than long-term objectives. Again, what is to be recognised is the rejection of centralised authority on sceptical grounds, a demand that power be more generally devolved down the social chain and be open to challenge and debate at all times, not assumed as of right according to traditional norms.

Some theorists, however, have argued that the postmodern was no more than a passing cultural fancy and that its time has come and gone; perhaps even that it can now be declared officially dead (see, for example, Kirby 2006). But while this may be true as an artistic style, where it is fair to say that it is has become somewhat hackneyed and predictable, it is manifestly not so when it comes to ideology. The credit crisis can be interpreted as a failure, not just of neoliberal economics, but of modernity as a project, and most particularly of the authorities behind modernity running back through the 'narrative of emancipation' (Lyotard 1984: 37) that is the foundation of the Enlightenment project (this is a topic discussed in detail in Sim 2010 and Bourriaud 2009). As Lyotard so boldly put it in *The Postmodern Condition*, we can 'no longer have recourse' (Lyotard 1984: 60) to such metanarratives; their credibility has to be called seriously into question. Given the ongoing trials of the global economy the critique offered by postmodernism continues to resonate, and certainly the work of the fifty figures highlighted in this volume still does so to great effect throughout their respective fields. The postmodern condition is still with us, therefore, although it has proved to be even more fraught with problems than Lyotard envisaged in his essentially optimistic vision of it as the basis for a new and fairer world ideological order. The sceptical outlook for which Lyotard became such a high-profile standard bearer in *The Postmodern Condition* is still very much needed in a situation where politicians cannot quite seem to shake off their faith in modernity's progress-based programme as the only way to proceed. As long as that remains the case, then postmodern thought will have an important contribution to make in the wider cultural arena.

I would emphasise again the factor of diversity when dealing with the postmodern. Except in terms of aesthetics it has never been a movement with a precise agenda, being more of a reaction to a world in which ideology (for which read grand narrative) has become a repressive mechanism dedicated to maintaining the political status quo. While there are common features that emerge from this reaction, that does not mean there is agreement between these various thinkers as to how to bring about cultural change: there is a diffuseness about the postmodern that has to be acknowledged. Just as there were 'modernisms', so we have to realise that there are 'postmodernisms', and that there will be subtle differences in their agenda and methods in reacting to modernity and modernism. Nevertheless, the reaction is very real and all the thinkers are united in their dislike of authoritarianism and the system that enforces this. Bearing all that in mind, we can now consider how fifty prominent figures have addressed this issue within their own particular fields of interest in the last few decades – and why they have felt the need to do so.

References

Adorno, Theodor W., *Negative Dialectics* [1966], trans. E. B. Ashton, London: Routledge and Kegan Paul, 1973.

Adorno, Theodor W. and Max Horkheimer, *Dialectic of Enlightenment* [1944], trans. John Cumming, London: Verso, 1979.

Bell, Bernard Iddings, *Postmodernism and Other Essays*, Milwaukee, WI: Morehouse, 1926.

——, *Religion for Living: A Book for Postmodernists*, London: John Gifford, 1939.

Bourriaud, Nicolas, 'Introduction', *Altermodern: Tate Triennial*, London: Tate Publishing, 2009, pp. 11–24.

Hudnut, Joseph, *Architecture and the Spirit of Man*, Cambridge, MA: Harvard University Press, 1949.

Jencks, Charles, *The Language of Post-Modern Architecture* [1975], 6th edition, London: Academy Editions, 1991.

Kirby, Alan, 'The Death of Postmodernism and Beyond', *Philosophy Now*, 58 (November/December, 2006), pp. 34–7.

Lyotard, Jean–François, *The Postmodern Condition: A Report on Knowledge* [1979], trans. Geoff Bennington and Brian Massumi, Manchester: Manchester University Press, 1984.

McHale, Brian, *Constructing Postmodernism*, London and New York: Routledge, 1992.

Sim, Stuart, *Contemporary Continental Philosophy: The New Scepticism*, Aldershot and Burlington, VT: Ashgate, 2001.

——, *Empires of Belief: Why We Need More Doubt and Scepticism in the Twenty-First Century*, Edinburgh: Edinburgh University Press, 2006.

——, *The End of Modernity: What the Financial and Environmental Crisis Is Really Telling Us*, Edinburgh: Edinburgh University Press, 2010.

Toynbee, Arnold, *A Study of History*, vols I–IV, abridged by D. C. Somervell, New York and Oxford: Oxford University Press, 1954.

FIFTY KEY POSTMODERN THINKERS

THEODOR W. ADORNO (1903–69)

Adorno was one of the leading figures in the Frankfurt School of Social Research, a Marxist-influenced grouping based at Frankfurt University, which flourished in Germany during the 1920s and 1930s until it relocated in America after Adorno and his associates found themselves forced to flee the country by the Nazi takeover in 1933. After World War Two the School returned to Germany, although another key member, Herbert Marcuse, chose to remain in America, where he soon became a focal point for a new generation of political radicals through works such as *One Dimensional Man*. The School developed an analytical method known as 'critical theory', a blend of philosophy and sociology which they applied across the cultural spectrum: in effect, they were pioneering what has subsequently become known as 'cultural studies'. Adorno's writing, for example, comprises philosophy, social theory and aesthetics, often in colla-boration with his Frankfurt School colleague Max Horkheimer. Much of Adorno's later work is highly critical of Marxism, and could be described as post-Marxist in orientation, making him an inspiration for early poststructuralist and postmodernist thinkers (Jacques Derrida as a case in point), who picked up on Adorno's deep distrust of authoritarian political systems and the absolutist philosophical bias of Marxism. Such anti-authoritarianism and anti-absolutism were to become intrinsic to the postmodern outlook, which progressively has distanced itself from Marxism, regarding it as having been superseded by historical events. The point made by Martin Jay that it could be argued that 'Adorno was an ambitious failure, at least from the per-spective of those who want solid and unequivocal answers to the questions they pose' (Jay 1984: 163), is precisely what marks him out as a critical source for the postmodern.

Adorno and Horkheimer's most famous collaboration is *Dialectic of Enlightenment*, written during World War Two. It is a book which is, not surprisingly, highly critical of the state of the world, and in par-ticular the authoritarian socio-political systems which had developed between the two world wars, such as fascism and communism. These are claimed to represent the logical conclusion of the Enlightenment project of continual human progress, and as the authors acidly remark: 'In the most general sense of progressive thought, the Enlightenment has always aimed at liberating men from fear and establishing their sovereignty. Yet the fully enlightened Earth radiates disaster triumphant' (Adorno and Horkheimer 1979: 3). Effectively, that constitutes the opening salvo in what is to become a sustained poststructuralist and postmodernist campaign against the way the Enlightenment project has developed, and in particular the 'grand narratives' (or ideological systems) that have emerged from its cumulative influence in Western culture since the eighteenth century.

For Adorno and Horkheimer the commitment to liberation and progress had led instead to totalitarianism, with its belief that it knew best how to achieve those goals on behalf of humanity (more specifically perhaps, that its leaders, such as Hitler and Stalin, knew best and could force compliance with their programmes on those grounds). Neither are Adorno and Horkheimer much more sanguine about the alternative offered by Western liberal democracy, treating this as little better than a mirror-image of those authoritarian systems in its insistence that it constituted the ultimate answer to all our socio-political needs, an all-purpose grand narrative in its own right. All such systems demanded complete commitment and adherence to the cause from their followers and dismissed the claims to validity of all others: 'The choice by an individual citizen of the Communist or Fascist ticket is determined by the influence which the Red Army or the laboratories of the West have on him. ... The person who has doubts is already outlawed as a deserter' (Adorno and Horkheimer 1979: 205). Such an outcome was hardly what the proponents of Enlightenment had envisaged when they set out to undermine the oppressive *ancien régime* in eighteenth-century Europe, but a similarly negative view of the Enlightenment project is to become a defining feature of postmodern thought. Eventually, Adorno is to hold the Enlightenment responsible for 'Auschwitz'; the term standing for all the horrors perpetrated in the Holocaust.

Auschwitz becomes deeply symbolic of the Enlightenment project for Adorno, demonstrating the degree of inhumanity, up to outright barbarism, that its latter-day proponents are capable of inflicting in pursuit of their objectives. After an event of this magnitude, he suggests, it is all but impossible to engage in activities such as the creative arts; it is as if the higher ideals of humanity have been irretrievably compromised and it would be false to pretend that we can go on as before: 'Cultural criticism finds itself faced with the final stage of the dialectic of culture and barbarism. To write poetry after Auschwitz is barbaric. And this corrodes even the knowledge of why it has become impossible to write poetry today' (Adorno 1981: 34). Auschwitz has left a permanent mark on Western civilisation, to the extent that Adorno can even find himself wondering 'whether one can *live* after Auschwitz' (Adorno 2003: 435). He goes on to insist that steps have to be taken to prevent a recurrence of such barbarism: 'The premier demand upon all education is that Auschwitz not happen again. Its priority before any other requirement is such that I believe I need not and should not justify it' (Adorno 2003: 19). (Lyotard is later to reach a similar conclusion about the impact of the Holocaust in works like *Heidegger and 'the Jews'*, arguing that it would be an act of bad faith ever to allow oneself to 'forget' such an event had occurred, and that many Germans were indeed guilty of just this sin – notably, from Lyotard's perspective, the philosopher Martin Heidegger, a critical influence on postwar French philosophy.)

Adorno also wrote extensively on aesthetic matters, particularly music, as in his *Philosophy of Modern Music*, in which he strongly defended the musical style of Arnold Schoenberg against that of other contemporary composers such as Igor Stravinsky. Schoenberg's compositional style, serialism (or 'twelve-tone' music, as it is also known), was for Adorno a revolutionary method, whilst Stravinsky's early ballets such as *Petrushka* and *The Rite of Spring* presented a picture of the human race as ontologically, rather than ideologically, alienated, and thus were to be considered reactionary since their story-lines seemed to rule out the possibility of political change (one might question the comparison of a ballet score to Schoenberg's generally more abstract orchestral work, however). In the event, Stravinsky has proved to be by far the more popular of the two composers, and Adorno's defence of serialism, a style deliberately breaking with the Western classical music tradition by refusing to adhere to its system of tonality controlled by seven-note scales, cultivating 'atonality' instead, marks him out as a modernist sympathiser rather than a precursor of the postmodern. (Martin Jay has even defined Adorno's dense and complicated writing, often criticised by commentators, as 'atonal philosophy' (Jay 1984: 56).) Postmodern composers are quite happy to use standard tonality (as in the work of Philip Glass or Steve Reich, for example), and regard this as a way of reconnecting with an audience which never showed much enthusiasm for serialism anyway. Indeed, serialism has all but died out as a musical style and the works of its major composers do not feature very prominently in concert-hall programmes.

Adorno's pro-serialism views also very much differentiate him from the main trends of the time in Marxist aesthetics, such as socialist realism, with its campaign against formal experimentation and insistence on the use of older styles with a more obviously popular impact. To that tradition, Schoenberg's style was elitist and did nothing to further the cause of proletarian revolution, therefore Soviet composers were banned from adopting the serial method and required to use standard tonality in all their works. Any hint of dissonance at all was disallowed by the Soviet authorities, never mind the persistent presence of it in the work of the early serial school – namely, Schoenberg and his composition pupils Alban Berg and Anton Webern. In Adorno's view, however, Schoenberg represented 'progress' (Adorno 1973: 29), having so uncompromisingly broken from traditional musical practice in the West and created an entirely new method of composition. Adorno's Marxism is never less than iconoclastic, and it is not difficult to see why he ultimately feels the need to question some of the theory's most fundamental principles, such as the nature of the dialectic.

The work of Adorno's which more than any other signals towards postmodern thought is *Negative Dialectics*, which is a broadside against Marxism and all other totalising forms of philosophy, prefiguring one of the central concerns of postmodernism. Marxism takes over the concept of totality from Hegelian philosophy and similarly sees the dialectic as having a specific end-goal, although of course this is very different in Marxism than it is in Hegelianism, being materialistically rather than metaphysically inclined: dialectical materialism as opposed to dialectical idealism. So for Hegel the world spirit eventually realises itself in the perfect society (symbolised for him by the Prussian state, in which he was a prominent public official as Professor of Philosophy at Berlin University); whereas for Marx class struggle culminates in the 'dictatorship of the proletariat', the Marxist utopia, when the dialectic's mission is complete. In Adorno's reading, however, the dialectic was open-ended and had no final objective, a notion that proved to be very congenial to poststructuralist and postmodernist thinkers who rejected teleologically oriented systems in general and Marxism in particular. Adorno is adamant throughout *Negative Dialectics* that everything that happens in the world cannot be reduced to a system, or can ever be made to fit into a preconceived system; the 'non-idealistic form', as he pointedly describes it, of dialectics has long 'since degenerated into a dogma' (Adorno 1973: 7). The book turns out to be, as its translator E. B. Ashton puts it, 'an apologia for deviationism' (Adorno 1973: xi) from an ostensibly Marxist thinker.

Without absolute identity, Adorno argued, there could be no teleology of the kind envisaged by both Hegel and Marx, and Adorno dismissed this possibility: 'The principle of absolute identity is self-contradictory. It perpetuates nonidentity in suppressed and damaged form' (Adorno 1973: 318). As far as postmodern thinkers are concerned there is no pattern to be found in history, never mind the inevitable trajectory towards the 'dictatorship of the proletariat' posited by Marxism, and the future is to be considered wholly unpredictable. The critique of the notion of unity that is to be found in *Negative Dialectics* is to resound throughout postmodern thought.

Adorno's major writings

Adorno, Theodor W., *Negative Dialectics* [1966], trans. E. B. Ashton, London: Routledge and Kegan Paul, 1973.

——, *Philosophy of Modern Music* [1948], trans. Anne G. Mitchell and Wesley Bloomster, London: Sheed and Ward, 1973.

——, *Minima Moralia: Reflections from a Damaged Life* [1951], trans. E. F. N. Jephcott, London: Verso, 1974.

——, *Prisms*, trans. Samuel and Shierry Weber, Cambridge, MA: MIT Press, 1981.

——, *Aesthetic Theory* [1970], ed. Gretel Adorno and Rolf Tiedemann, trans. C. Lenhardt, London: Routledge and Kegan Paul, 1984.

——, *The Culture Industry: Selected Essays on Mass Culture*, London: Routledge, 1991.

——, *Critical Models*, trans. Henry W. Pickford, New York: Columbia University Press, 1998.

——, *Metaphysics: Concept and Problems*, ed. Rolf Tiedemann, trans. Edmund Jephcott, Stanford, CA: Stanford University Press, 2001.

——, *Can One Live After Auschwitz?: A Philosophical Reader*, ed. Rolf Tiedemann, trans. Rodney Livingstone *et al.*, Stanford, CA: Stanford University Press, 2003.

Adorno, Theodor W. and Max Horkheimer, *Dialectic of Enlightenment* [1944], trans. John Cumming, London: Verso, 1979.

References and further reading

Jay, Martin, *Adorno*, London: Fontana, 1984.

Lyotard, Jean-François, *Heidegger and 'The Jews'* [1988], trans. Andreas Michel and Mark Roberts, Minneapolis, MN: University of Minnesota Press.

Marcuse, Herbert, *One Dimensional Man: Studies in the Ideology of Advanced Industrial Society*, London: Routledge and Kegan Paul, 1964.

Stravinsky, Igor, *Petrushka*, 1911.

——, *The Rite of Spring*, 1913.

PAUL AUSTER (B. 1947)

Auster is one of the most characteristic of postmodern authors, with works like *The New York Trilogy*, his best-known book and the one that established his reputation, being constructed around typical postmodern concerns and obsessions, such as the nature of identity. He has gone on to explore that theme through a series of critically praised novels that have established him as one of the most distinctive and imaginative voices in contemporary fiction.

The New York Trilogy plays elaborate games with identity over the course of the three novels, while maintaining a detective-story format designed to extend its appeal as much as possible in double-coding fashion. In the first volume, *City of Glass*, the lead character, Daniel Quinn, is an author who has adopted the pseudonym William Wilson as an author of detective stories featuring a private eye called Max Work. Quinn is a reclusive character who keeps his own identity completely secret, even from his publisher and agent, and appears to be a firm believer in the 'death of the author' (Barthes 1977: 148), remarking of his detective fiction that 'he did not consider himself to be the author of what he wrote, he did not feel responsible for it' (Auster 1988: 4). After receiving several mysterious late-night phone calls, he decides to answer the phone and go along with what the caller wants, to see if he can work out why he is being bothered. The caller, it turns out, is trying to get in touch with the Paul Auster Detective Agency, and Quinn pretends to be Auster. Before he knows it he has met the caller and agreed to take on an assignment as a private eye, despite having no knowledge of what this involves except through writing about the exploits of his fictional detective figure Max Work. The sheer randomness of human existence, a theme to which Auster keeps returning, comes across strongly; circumstances are capable of pushing us in strange directions we might never have thought about.

The book becomes even more strange when Auster introduces himself into the narrative as a character. Quinn, in desperation when the case is not going well, looks up Auster's address in the phone book and pays him a visit, explaining that he is seeking out the Paul Auster Detective Agency. Auster is highly amused by this, but assures Quinn that he is a writer, not a detective, and that he cannot really help him out with what is going on. Auster puts in another appearance at the end of the story, when he meets the 'author'. It might sound over-intellectualised, but it does work on the detective-story level and the reader is drawn along by the plot in this regard. Quinn subsequently has a cameo role in the third part of the trilogy, *The Locked Room*, where he is referred to as a private detective, and hired to help one of the characters in the story, Sophie Fanshawe, find her husband, who has disappeared. The disappearance turns to be deliberate, as the narrator, a childhood friend of the husband, later receives a letter from him, emphasising that he does not want to return to his previous life or be tracked down in any way. Although Quinn has officially dropped the case by then, we are to find out at the end that for some unexplained reason he has gone on following Fanshawe for some time after that, only to disappear yet again. The narrator, by then hired by a publisher to write Fanshawe's biography, after struggling to make sense of the details involved, remarks that '[i]n general, lives seem to veer abruptly from one thing to another, to jostle and bump, to squirm' (Auster 1988: 251), and those prove to be the kind of lives that Auster is most interested in relating in his fiction.

The Music of Chance also very much invites metaphorical interpretation, seeming to draw attention yet again to the sheer meaninglessness of human effort and the absurdist nature of existence: there is a flavour of Samuel Beckett and French existentialism about it in that respect (Auster did in fact live in France for a while in the early stages of his career). It might also be seen as a critique of capitalism – therefore of the 'American Dream', *the* grand narrative of American life – and how it enslaves its workers by cunningly seeming to offer them liberation at some future point if they cooperate in the meantime with the system. The sting in the tail is that the liberation is seemingly always being deferred. The story involves two drifters, Jim Nashe and Jack Pozzi, who lose a large amount of money in a card game with two very rich individuals, Flower and Stone, which they are forced to repay through labour on the latter's estate for a period of fifty days building a wall: the epitome of pointless activities. Shortly before their scheduled 'release' they are allowed to hold a party, with a local prostitute being invited in for the night as well as large quantities of expensive alcohol and food being ordered to mark the occasion. They think they are receiving all this as part of their due from their captors, but the cost of this event, plus all their expenses to date on groceries etc., is subsequently added on to their debt, resulting in an extension of their working time by thirty days that all but breaks Pozzi's spirit. Nashe helps Pozzi to escape, only to find his badly beaten-up body dumped outside the door of his trailer the next morning. Pozzi is then ostensibly driven off to hospital, but no record of his admission can subsequently be found and Nashe can only assume that he has died.

When the date of release finally arrives Nashe accepts an invitation to go into town with Murks, the employee detailed to direct Nashe and Pozzi in their building work on the wall, and his son-in-law Floyd (either one of whom could be suspected as Pozzi's killer), to celebrate having completed his spell of imprisonment. On the way back Nashe, despite the increasingly desperate pleas of Murks and Floyd, proceeds to drive faster and faster, intent on crashing the car

17

and thus killing or severely injuring them all in a dramatic act of revenge. On the verge of this event, the novel closes:

> There was no time to stop, no time to prevent what was going to happen, and so instead of slamming his foot on the brakes, he pressed down even harder on the gas. He could hear Murks and his son-in-law howling in the distance, but their voices were muffled, drowned out by the roar of blood in his head. And then the light was upon him, and Nashe shut his eyes, unable to look at it anymore.
>
> (Auster 1991: 216–17)

The film of *The Music of Chance* added an intriguing twist to the end of the story, although an entirely credible one given the games Auster played in *The New York Trilogy*, by cutting from the moment before the car crashed to the morning after. Nashe staggers out of the wreckage having apparently survived the crash, just as a passing motorist in a sports car stops to ask him if he is alright. The driver is played by Paul Auster: at which point the film ends.

Auster has a talent for constructing tortuous plots that seem to fold in on themselves, as can be seen in works like *The Book of Illusions* and *Oracle Night*. In the former a comic silent film star, known as Hector Mann, turns his back on Hollywood at the height of his fame, and eventually ends up making a living by performing live sexual acts with a prostitute he has become acquainted with while drifting around. When his identity is discovered, he simply disappears (a recurrent trope in Auster), later to become a filmmaker who shoots highly sophisticated films at his home that are, however, never released to the general public. Identity here is certainly describable as 'svelte' in the fashion recommended by Jean-François Lyotard; that is, the ability to metamorphose from one role to another as circumstances change around one, constantly to display flexibility in your dealings with others (see Lyotard 1993: 25–9). Framing this inner narrative is one set in contemporary America about an academic, David Zimmer, who writes a study of Mann, and gets drawn into a complicated relationship with the actor's wife that gradually reveals his subject's complicated life-story to him.

In *Oracle Night* a novelist recovering from a severe illness, Sidney Orr, finds his life turned upside down after he purchases a blue notebook in a newly opened store near his apartment in Brooklyn, owned by a mysterious Chinaman called M. R. Chang. Starting a new novel about a New York literary editor called Nick Bowen, Orr has him receive a manuscript, lost since 1927, of a novel called *Oracle Night* by a now-dead novelist, Sylvia Maxwell. In typical Auster style Bowen then decides to disappear, leaving his old life, and marriage, behind him, on little more than a whim; yet another life that 'veers abruptly' from its expected course. The book proceeds from there onwards, abruptly cutting between one narrative and the other. Auster also throws in a series of often quite extended footnotes to the text that provide additional information on both the main character's life and his fictional creation, Nick Bowen. Since these sometimes run over several pages they break up the continuity of the narrative even further, adding yet another layer of complexity to the work: in effect, a narrative within a narrative within a narrative.

The narrator in *The Locked Room*, an author himself, remarks at one point that '[w]e all want to be told stories, and we listen to them in the same way we did when we were young' (Auster 1988: 247), and this brings out something very important about postmodern fiction. Modernist authors very often drifted away from story, trying to dazzle readers instead by the brilliance and ingenuity of their experiments with narrative form, but the attraction of story never goes away altogether and seems to be very deeply rooted in us. Auster's stories may be full of unexpected twists and turns and mysteries that are never quite cleared up, the endings offering little in the way of narrative resolution; but in his books the story-line itself does carry us along in each case, wondering what his characters' fates will be. 'Lives make no sense' (Auster 1988: 250), as *The Locked Room*'s narrator reflects when embarking on a biography of his friend Fanshawe, but it is never less than interesting to follow their erratic course as mapped out by someone like Auster.

Auster's major writings

Auster, Paul, *The New York Trilogy* (comprising *City of Glass*, *Ghosts* and *The Locked Room*), London and Boston: Faber and Faber, 1988.
——, *In the Country of Last Things*, London: Faber and Faber, 1988.
——, *The Music of Chance*, London: Faber and Faber, 1991.
——, *Leviathan*, London and Boston: Faber and Faber, 1992.
——, *The Book of Illusions*, London: Faber and Faber, 2002.
——, *Oracle Night*, London: Faber and Faber, 2004.
——, *The Brooklyn Follies*, London: Faber and Faber, 2005.
——, *Travels in the Scriptorium*, London: Faber and Faber, 2006.
——, *Man in the Dark*, London: Faber and Faber, 2008.
——, *Invisible*, London: Faber and Faber, 2009.

References and further reading

Barthes, Roland, *Image-Music-Text*, ed. and trans. Stephen Heath, London: Fontana, 1977.

Haas, Philip, *The Music of Chance*, IRS Media, Transatlantic Entertainment, 1993.

Lyotard, Jean-François, 'A Svelte Appendix to the Postmodern Question', in *Political Writings*, trans. Bill Readings and Kevin Paul Geiman, London: UCL Press, 1993, pp. 25–9.

JOHN BARTH (B. 1930)

As well as being a major novelist, Barth is one of the first theorists of the postmodern literary aesthetic and how this should be developed as a reaction to what he regarded as the aridity of late modernism, as exemplified by the works of such writers as Samuel Beckett. For Barth, Beckett became symbolic of the end of modernism as his work could hardly be reduced any further in terms of its content: 'Beckett has become virtually mute, musewise. ... [F]or Beckett, at this point in his career, to cease to create altogether would be fairly meaningful: his crowning work, his "last word". What a convenient corner to paint yourself into!' (Barth 1977: 73, 74). Given that in his late career Beckett wrote two mime plays (*Play Without Words, I* and *II*) and a play with neither characters nor action (*Breath*), lasting only around twenty-five seconds, one can appreciate what Barth was getting at. Theatre seems to be vanishing before one's eyes at such points, in an author apparently striving for the kind of purity of vision to be found in such controversial modernist artworks as Kasimir Malevich's painting *White Square on a White Ground* (1918), the work which launched 'monochrome' painting. Barth was writing this in 1967, well before anything like a postmodern aesthetic for literature was being widely discussed, although the beginnings of it can be noted in architectural theory, so this was a call for action on the part of the new generation of authors coming through.

In Barth's view, such writing as Beckett was producing was to be considered the 'literature of exhaustion', or, even more aptly, the 'literature of exhausted possibility' (Barth 1977: 70). To counter this tendency he advocated returning to literature's traditional elements of grammar, punctuation, plot and characterisation, on the grounds that after the experiments of authors like Beckett there was nothing left to experiment with or shed further from the writing process. Even commentators better disposed towards Beckett than Barth agree on this aspect of his work, with Gilles Deleuze noting that 'Beckett's entire oeuvre is pervaded by exhausted series' (Deleuze 1998: 154) of actions that bespeak an exhausted sensibility. While some can find this metaphysically resonant (Deleuze did), Barth's argument is that a particular line of literary development had simply run out with Beckett, and writers would have to think again about how to pursue their art in the aftermath of modernism's apparent implosion.

Although he still admires Beckett, Barth takes his work as a challenge to new generations of writers to come up with something else to break out of the dead end he has worked himself into, citing the work of Jorge Luis Borges as an author of Beckett's generation who has successfully managed to do so. Both Beckett and Borges are working in 'an age of ultimacies and "final solutions" – at least *felt* ultimacies, in everything from weaponry to theology, the celebrated dehumanization of society, and the history of the novel' (Barth 1977: 73). But while Beckett is being rendered 'mute' by such cultural trends, Borges is able to work the concerns they raise into his fiction, as in his story 'Pierre Menard, Author of the Quixote' (Borges 2000). The protagonist, Pierre Menard, a French Symbolist author, finds himself writing Cervantes' *Don Quixote* word-perfectly, so that instead of writing about the difficulty of writing anything original in the era of the 'end of the novel' – perhaps even the 'end of literature' – Borges gives us a protagonist who discovers 'the difficulty, perhaps the unnecessity, of writing original works of literature' (Barth 1977: 76) in such an age. For Barth, that extends the realm of literature rather than closing it down in Beckettian fashion.

Barth can be particularly scathing about some of the other experiments that were coming out of late modernism in the 1960s, arguing that, while

> their wares are lively to read about, and make for interesting conversation in fiction-writing classes, for example, where we discuss Somebody-or-other's unbound, unpaginated, randomly assembled novel-in-a-box and the desirability of printing *Finnegans Wake* on a very long roller-towel. It's easier and sociabler to talk technique than it is to make art.
>
> (Barth 1977: 71)

What is conspicuously being ignored by such experiments is the audience, and also, Barth complains, 'the most traditional notion of the artist: the Aristotelian conscious agent who achieves with technique and cunning the artistic effect' (Barth 1977: 71). Despite its elitist overtones, he aligns himself unashamedly with that notion, and worries about where literature, and the arts in general, will end up if the possibility of that conscious agency is dispensed with by creative artists. Barth is also critical of what he calls the 'intermedia' (Barth 1977: 70) arts that were beginning to become more prominent in the 1960s, such as 'happenings'; these too represented an abdication of conscious agency. In our own day, performance art and installation art might be said to set similar problems – not to mention the opportunities opened up by new media phenomena like YouTube.

The traditional elements Barth pines for had never gone out of use in popular fiction, but they certainly had in more serious fiction, so for Barth to make this suggestion was at the time to sound, para-doxically enough, quite iconoclastic. And it is just such a return, often spiced with a sense of knowing irony on the author's part, that has occurred in postmodern literary fiction, with Barth one of its major practitioners in a series of linguistically exuberant and fantastical works. Plot, characterisation and story are once again very much part of the landscape of serious literature, and authors are unashamed and unapologetic to be reverting to the methods of previous generations: as Barth saw it, there was no other option left for the budding author.

Barth defined this move away from the late modernist tradition as the 'literature of replenishment', and that is largely how postmodern fiction has developed in the interim, building on the models of the past while adding its own distinctive twist to how older forms are appropriated. The aim is to reconnect with the wider audience for literature, who were no longer being catered for by the practitioners of the 'literature of exhaustion', as well as to come up with something more representative of our age than modernism was becoming by the later twentieth century. As Barth expressed it: 'The modernist aes-thetic is in my opinion unquestionably the characteristic aesthetic of the first half of our century – and in my opinion it *belongs* to the first half of our century. The present reaction against it is perfectly understandable and to be sympathized with' (Barth 1997: 202). Barth's 'ideal postmodernist author ... aspires to a fiction more democratic in its appeal' (Barth 1997: 203) than late modernism had been achieving: that, for him, would be the literature of replenish-ment. Charles Jencks's concept of double-coding (outlined in *The Language of Post-Modern Architecture*) actively encourages such a replenishment-based approach, conceiving of it as a way of recaptur-ing the interest of the general public in artistic activity, rather than alienating it by endless formal experimentation purely for the sake of being different from one's peers – the cult that modernism had built up of originality over the course of the twentieth century, inspired in literary circles by the work of such luminaries as James Joyce and Beckett. It is a rather ironic point that Barth is making overall, that plot, characterisation, etc., can count as double-coding, since their use is being recovered from past literary practice. Mocking in tone though his introductory note to *Lost in the Funhouse* is – 'On with the story. On with the story' (Barth 1969: x) – it could well stand as Barth's personal motto as a writer of fiction.

The Sot-Weed Factor provides the reader with a substantial helping of story, plot, characterisation and narrative structure, if in a sprawling and complicated form, which is nevertheless very comic: Barth clearly is heading in the opposite direction from Beckettian minimalism. The plot concerns the exploits of one Ebenezer Cooke, sent out to the colony of Maryland in the late seventeenth century to run his father's tobacco business. The colony turns out to be a hotbed of corruption and debauchery that is signally failing to live up to the ideals it is expected to uphold – the metanarrative of the burgeoning English empire, one might say. *Giles Goat-Boy* is, amongst other things, a satire on the Cold War taking place at the time between the Soviet empire and the West, and the futility of it all. Again, we are presented with a sprawling, labyrinthine plot. In *The End of the Road*, Barth's characters struggle to construct viable selves in a world without absolute values. As one of the lead characters, Joe Morgan, tries to convince his wife, Rennie: 'What I'm trying to say is that you shouldn't consider a value less real just because it isn't absolute, since less-than-absolutes are all we've got' (Barth 1969: 39). 'Less-than-absolutes' prove inadequate to resolving the emotional tangles the three main characters become caught up in, however, and Rennie dies during a botched abortion following an affair with the novel's narrator, Jacob Horner. Farcically complicated metaphysical discussions are brought to a halt by actual human tragedy.

For all that he can provide a programme for novelists to put into effect in the aftermath of modernism, Barth can sound very doubtful about the idea of a postmodern movement itself, describing the label as 'awkward and faintly epigonic, suggestive less of a vigorous or even interesting new direction in the old art of storytelling than of something anti-climactic, feebly following a very hard act to follow' (Barth 1997: 196). He is not alone in feeling this way; Nicolas Bourriaud's assessment of postmodernism as 'the philosophy of mourning' (Bourriaud 2009: 19) for modernism is making a very similar point; all the more reason, Bourriaud feels, to adopt a new term like 'altermodernism' instead and try to capture the best features of the modern aesthetic in one's creative work. Although he sounds more positive about the notion of the postmodern in 'The Literature of Replenishment', Barth seems to have prefigured the notion of the altermodern to some extent, and his work is worth study because of its symbolic significance in showing a shift in literary taste and concerns at the grassroots level of the individual writer.

Barth's major writings

Barth, John, *The Floating Opera*, New York: Doubleday, 1956.
——, *The Sot-Weed Factor*, London: Martin Secker and Warburg, 1961.
——, *Giles Goat-Boy or, The Revised New Syllabus*, London: Secker and Warburg, 1967.
——, *The End of the Road* [1958, 1967], New York: Grosset and Dunlap, 1969.
——, *Lost in the Funhouse: Fiction for Print, Tape, Live Voice* [1968], London: Martin Secker and Warburg, 1969.
——, 'The Literature of Exhaustion' [1967], in Malcolm Bradbury, ed., *The Novel Today: Writers on Modern Fiction*, Manchester: Manchester University Press, 1977, pp. 70–83.
——, *Letters, A Novel*, New York: Putnam, 1979.
——, *The Tidewater Tales*, New York: Putnam, 1987.
——, *The Last Voyage of Somebody the Sailor*, London: Little, Brown, 1991.
——, 'The Literature of Replenishment' [1980], in *The Friday Book: Essays and Other Non-Fiction* [1984], Baltimore, MD and London: Johns Hopkins University Press, 1997, pp. 193–206.

References and further reading

Beckett, Samuel, *Play Without Words, I* and *II*, in *The Complete Dramatic Works*, London and Boston: Faber and Faber, 1986.
——, *Breath*, in *The Complete Dramatic Works*, London and Boston: Faber and Faber, 1986.
Borges, Jorge Luis, 'Pierre Menard, Author of the Quixote', in *Labyrinths: Selected Stories and Writings*, ed. Donald A. Yates and James E. Irby, London: Penguin, 2000, pp. 62–71.
Bourriaud, Nicolas, 'Altermodern', in Nicolas Bourriaud (ed.), *Altermodern: Tate Triennial*, London: Tate Publishing, 2009, pp. 11–24.
Deleuze, Gilles, *Essays Critical and Clinical* [1993], trans. Daniel W. Smith and Michael A. Greco, London and New York: Verso, 1998.
Jencks, Charles, *The Language of Post-Modern Architecture* [1975], 6th edition, London: Academy Editions, 1991.
Joyce, James, *Finnegans Wake* [1939], ed. Robert-Jan Henkes *et al.*, Oxford: Oxford University Press, 2012.
Malevich, Kasimir, *White Square on a White Ground*, 1918.

ROLAND BARTHES (1915–80)

Roland Barthes was one of the major theorists of structuralism until late in his career he started to adopt a more poststructuralist orientation in his work, most notably in *S/Z*, an analysis of Honoré de Balzac's novella *Sarrasine*, which breaks the work down into a series of narrative codes that are capable of yielding a multiplicity of interpretations. Barthes might be considered to form a bridge between these two theoretical traditions, showing how structuralism could move on from what had come to seem to a new generation of critical and cultural theorists like Jacques Derrida as a rather formulaic, even facile, method of analysis whose universalist pretensions deserved to be challenged (Umberto Eco was later to perform a similar function to Barthes in this respect). Structuralism, for thinkers like Derrida, had exhausted itself and was philosophically questionable anyway. While Barthes's structuralist roots are still apparent in *S/Z* (in the use of codes, for example), Derrida was already in the process of engineering a complete break from that tradition into full-blown poststructuralism (see, for example, Derrida 1978).

Prior to *S/Z* Barthes produced some of the most detailed and influential works on structuralism as a cultural ethic, ranging from the arts through advertising and fashion, drawing extensively on the linguistic theories of Ferdinand de Saussure, whose work in this area formed the basis of semiotics, the theory of signs, which underpinned structuralist analysis (see Saussure's *Course in General Linguistics*). For Saussure, language was made up of signs, consisting of a signifier (word) and signified (concept) which combined to form a sign that the listener or reader recognised and could respond to appropriately. These signs were organised within a grammar which specified what the nature of the interactions between the relevant signs should be. This formed the basis of the so-called 'linguistic model' which then came to be so widely applied across the spectrum of academic disciplines, even being drawn into other theoretical traditions such as Marxism in the 'structural Marxism' of Louis Althusser and his followers (see, for example, Althusser and Balibar 1970).

What was critical to Barthes in each area of discourse was the particular grammar that applied there, and his analyses are centrally concerned with demonstrating what elements go to make up that grammar and how they work as a system, outlining how we are supposed to 'read' the various signs involved in their interactions. His essay 'Structural Analysis of Narratives' (published in English in the collection *Image-Music-Text*) outlines some general principles by which we can decode the grammar of any narrative put in front of us – and Barthes argues that the world is full of narratives awaiting our study:

> The narratives of the world are numberless. Narrative is first and foremost a prodigious variety of genres, themselves distributed amongst different substances. ... [N]arrative is present in myth, legend, fable, tale, novella, epic, history, tragedy, drama, comedy, mime, painting (think of Carpaccio's *Saint Ursula*), stained glass windows, cinema, comics, news item, conversation. ... [N]arrative is present in every age, in every place, in every society.
>
> (Barthes 1977: 79)

Barthes's researches into the grammar of systems seemed to hold out the hope of being able to pin down exactly what these numerous narratives meant, providing an interpretative key that could lay bare their inner workings, the 'deep structure' that was postulated by structuralists to lie behind all of them awaiting discovery by the vigilant reader. This deep structure worked across other texts in any given area, linking them together by means of the common features they displayed. Claude Lévi-Strauss, for example, found such common features across a range of myths, as in the creation theme, such that we could see these as expressions of a deep structure within human culture (see Lévi-Strauss 1963).

Structuralism had unmistakable universalist pretensions, with practitioners conceiving of it as a theory of everything, and it has been applied to most areas of human affairs at one point or other. Yet even in his high structuralist phase Barthes had hinted at the possibility of a freer style of analysis than the high structuralist norm favoured, as in his concept of the 'death of the author', whereby the meaning of the text comes to reside in the individual reader rather than with the author. As Barthes proclaims it, 'the birth of the reader must be at the cost of the death of the Author' (Barthes 1977: 148). This opens up the way to plurality of meaning: 'We now know that a text is not a line of words releasing a single "theological" meaning (the "message" of the Author-God)' (Barthes 1977: 146). Such plurality of meaning inevitably raises questions about the validity of criticism, which becomes just one more interpretation amongst many and therefore can have no claim to any particular authority on its own. Derrida's attacks on structuralist method take off from just such a point as this, emphasising plurality even more strongly and being resolutely opposed to the notion of a theory of everything. Structuralism is for Derrida an attempt to impose order and pattern where none can really be said to exist, emphasising apparently common features – as the analyst perceives them to be anyway – over those that do not fit the assumed pattern, and that is to be considered an authoritarian act. Signs are never as straightforward to interpret as most structuralist theorists and critics seem to think.

Barthes makes a sharp distinction between what he calls a 'readerly' and a 'writerly' text. The former forces a particular reading on the reader, who, as Barthes puts it, 'is left with no more than the poor freedom either to accept or reject the text: reading is nothing more than a *referendum*' (Barthes 1975: 4). We might think of most nine-teenth-century novels as falling into the readerly category, with their authors adopting a position of control with regard to their readers, pushing them towards the particular reading of their narrative they consider to be paramount. Writerly texts, however, demand active participation on the part of the reader, their goal being 'to make the reader no longer a consumer, but a producer of the text' (Barthes 1975: 4). Broadly speaking, modernist texts would qualify as writerly, since they require a lot more work and imagination on the part of the reader in interpreting them (James Joyce's *Finnegans Wake* being an outstanding example of this), there being more gaps to ponder on in the narrative line. For Barthes, the writerly text offers itself up to an infinity of interpretations:

> In this ideal text, the networks are many and interact, without any one of them being able to surpass the rest; the text is a galaxy of signifiers, not a structure of signifieds; it has no beginning; it is reversible; we gain access to it by several entrances, none of which can be authoritatively declared to be the main one; the codes it mobilizes extend *as far as the eye can reach.*
>
> (Barthes 1975: 4–5)

Given such a multiplicity of possible interpretations, and scope for reader contributions (a more recent version of this might be found in Nicolas Bourriaud's theory of 'relational aesthetics'; see Bourriaud 2002), Barthes feels moved to insist that 'there is never a *whole* of the text' (Barthes 1975: 6). This is a sentiment which consistently informs poststructuralist and postmodernist discourse, with their commitment to pluralism rather than absolutism. It is a logical conclusion to be drawn from the death of the author notion that there can be no definitive meaning attached to any text, merely one more in a chain of interpretations stretching out into the future, as long as the text continues to be read. 'To read is to find meanings', as Barthes observes, but these meanings generate, or call to mind, others in an endless pattern of 'becoming' (Barthes 1975: 11). To be caught up in such an unfolding sequence of becoming is to preclude the possibility of wholeness.

Whether 'writerly' texts really are as open-ended and free from an authorial controlling hand as Barthes suggests is, however, very much open to question. It is the author who decides where to place any of the 'gaps' to be found in the text after all, and that is bound to push the reader towards some interpretations more than others; even Derrida, ironically enough, has complained about the misappropriation of his own texts on some occasions. Equally, 'readerly' texts cannot close interpretation off entirely, and in fact many ostensibly 'readerly' texts from the past are interpreted in a very different way now than they were in the author's lifetime: a process which is likely to continue as long as the texts have an audience. To take just one example, John Bunyan's religious allegory *The Pilgrim's Progress* (1678) is now widely read as a political allegory that tells us a great deal about ideological conflict in the seventeenth century during the Restoration period. Readerly/writerly is the kind of binary distinction that post-structuralists like Derrida delight in subjecting to deconstruction, demonstrating that they are in fact entangled with each other and can never be pure enough to function as intended. But the shift to the reader as the main generator of meaning is a significant one that does introduce a degree of indeterminacy into the situation that at least points in a poststructuralist direction.

S/Z is a *tour de force* which breaks *Sarrasine* down into a range of codes; namely, hermeneutic, semic, symbolic, proairetic and cultural, although Barthes emphasises that a code is not to be thought of as a 'list' but rather as 'a perspective of quotations, a mirage of structures' (Barthes 1975: 20). To point up intertextuality in this way is to problematize the notion of wholeness – and that would go for 'readerly' no less than 'writerly' texts, even if the author is actively trying to achieve that state of closure of interpretation in the former style. 'Good narrative writing', Barthes contends, is marked by its quality of 'undecidability' (Barthes 1975: 178), and it is this factor that keeps the text open to continued interpretation and reinterpretation. As long as there is assumed to be that degree of openness and indeterminacy as to meaning, then we are in a poststructuralist frame of reference.

Barthes's major writings

Barthes, Roland, *Writing Degree Zero* [1953], trans. Annette Lavers and Colin Smith, London: Jonathan Cape, 1967.

——, *Elements of Semiology* [1964], trans. Annette Lavers and Colin Smith, London: Jonathan Cape, 1967.

——, *Mythologies* [1957], trans. Annette Lavers, London: Jonathan Cape, 1972.

——, *S/Z: An Essay* [1970], trans. Richard Miller, London: Jonathan Cape, 1975.

——, *The Pleasure of the Text* [1973], trans. Richard Miller, London: Jonathan Cape, 1976.

——, *Image-Music-Text*, ed. and trans. Stephen Heath, London: Fontana, 1977.

——, *A Lover's Discourse: Fragments* [1977], trans. Richard Howard, New York: Hill and Wang, 1978.

——, *The Empire of Signs* [1970], trans. Richard Howard, London: Jonathan Cape, 1983.

——, *Camera Lucida: Reflections on Photography* [1980], trans. Richard Howard, London: Jonathan Cape, 1983.

——, *The Fashion System* [1967], trans. Matthew Ward and Richard Howard, London: Jonathan Cape, 1985.

References and further reading

Althusser, Louis and Étienne Balibar, *Reading Capital* [1968], trans. Ben Brewster, London: NLB, 1970.

Bourriaud, Nicolas, *Relational Aesthetics* [1998], trans. Simon Pleasance and Fronza Woods, Dijon: Les Presses du Reel, 2002.

Bunyan, John, *The Pilgrim's Progress* [1678], ed. James Blanton Wharey, rev. Roger Sharrock, Oxford: Clarendon Press, 1960.

Derrida, Jacques, *Writing and Difference* [1967], trans. Alan Bass, Chicago: University of Chicago Press, 1978.

Joyce, James, *Finnegans Wake* [1939], ed. Robert-Jan Henkes *et al.*, Oxford: Oxford University Press, 2012.

Lévi-Strauss, Claude, 'The Structural Study of Myth', in *Structural Anthropology*, vol. 1, trans. Clair Jacobson and Brooke Grundfest Shoepf, New York: Basic Books, 1963, pp. 206–31.

Saussure, Ferdinand de, *Course in General Linguistics* [1916], ed. Charles Bally, Albert Sechehaye and Albert Reidlinger, trans. Wade Baskin, London: Peter Owen, 1960.

JEAN BAUDRILLARD (1929–2007)

Baudrillard's general reputation is as one of the *enfants terribles* of postmodern thought, a self-consciously maverick figure given to making deliberately provocative announcements such as his infamous suggestion that the First Gulf War (1990–1) had not really taken place, or that television and Disneyland were to be regarded as

America's 'reality' in the later twentieth century, being more 'real' than reality as we traditionally understood the concept (or 'hyperreal' in Baudrillard's formulation). One essay back in the late 1990s even claimed in its title that 'The Year 2000 Will Not Take Place', putting into practice Baudrillard's expressed desire to 'push hypotheses to their limit, remove them from their critical frame of reference, make them go beyond the point of no return' (Baudrillard 1986: 19). He does seem to have an urge to deny the obvious as a way of challenging his audience's assumptions. Baudrillard himself rejected the label of being a postmodernist (a not uncommon reaction amongst figures generally categorised as such, it should be said), although his concepts, such as hyperreality, have been widely adopted by other postmodernist thinkers and creative artists.

Baudrillard's early work is as a sociologist, and it soon takes a distinctly post-Marxist turn, as in his book *The Mirror of Production*, which rails against Marxism's obsession with production as a means of liberating the human race. In common with Jean-François Lyotard's *Libidinal Economy* and Gilles Deleuze and Félix Guattari's *Anti-Oedipus*, *The Mirror of Production* is part of the general turn against Marxism on the part of French intellectuals in the aftermath of the 1968 *événements*, in response to the French Communist Party (PCF) siding with the government against the student- and worker-led revolutionary alliance. As far as Baudrillard is concerned, this obsession with production enslaves rather than liberates us, and in so doing undermines Marxism's claim to be a revolutionary theory leading to the betterment of humankind: 'Can the quantitative development of productive forces lead to a revolution of social relations? Revolutionary hope is based "objectively" and hopelessly on this claim' (Baudrillard 1975: 59). The issue of who owns the means of production, whether capitalists or workers, is to this thinker irrelevant: it is the system itself that is the problem. To take this line is to distance oneself from modernity as a cultural phenomenon, based as it is on the principle that increased production is the critical element in improving the quality of life for humanity as a whole. It was a principle that applied to the communist bloc no less than it did to the Western democracies, as it was believed that would be the way to overcome the West's political dominance.

Essentially, it is still that overriding concern with production that drives mainstream politics in the West: the view that unless the gross domestic product (GDP) is constantly growing year by year, then the nation state in question is not fulfilling its destiny, nor politicians meeting their promises to the electorate. Elections are fought in the main on economic performance. Governments are certainly obsessed with this aspect of the nation's economic life and can soon find themselves under attack from their opposition counterparts if it falls, stagnates or even just slows down in its upward progress on their watch.

Baudrillard's notion of hyperreality captures for many the nature of contemporary existence in a media-dominated and media-saturated world. He describes it as 'the generation by models of a real without origin in reality' (Baudrillard 1983: 2), which is patently what we are confronted with in phenomena such as Disneyland. It is also a remark which could easily be applied to much reality television, which rapidly takes on a life of its own so that it is occurring in its own bubble, but nevertheless is being treated as real by its audience. In fact, Baudrillard considers this simulation of the real to be endemic to the world of media: 'All media and the official news service only exist to maintain the illusion of actuality – of the reality of the stakes, of the objectivity of the facts' (Baudrillard 1983: 71). Simulation has become the norm in our culture; Disneyland simulates a 'history' that never actually took place (a hopelessly romanticised one, at that), offering us the hyperreal instead. The implication of such a radical vision is that our traditional belief systems no longer have any purchase in such a world, which is very much in line with Lyotard's critique of grand narratives' in *The Postmodern Condition*, although Baudrillard derives an altogether more nihilistic message from this state of affairs.

The concept of the simulacrum has resonated in both critical and artistic circles. In the art world, for example, the simulacrum inspired various artists on the New York scene in the later twentieth century, such as the appropriately named simulationists (also known as the neo-geo movement). Simulationism involved artists such as Peter Halley and Jeff Koons, and it was influenced by a range of contemporary French theorists such as Michel Foucault and Guy Debord as well as by Baudrillard. The idea lying behind simulationism was that the system of consumption set the values of the late twentieth-century social order, and that it was therefore the artist's task to reveal how this system was shaping the image culture internationally. Halley used geometrical forms to register criticism of contemporary culture, declaring that '[i]nformed by Foucault, I see in the square a prison; behind the mythologies of contemporary society, a veiled network of cells and conduits' (Halley 2000: 25). Ironically enough, however, Baudrillard was unimpressed with the work of the simulationists.

Baudrillard's later work often has an aphoristic quality, as in *America* and *Cool Memories*, which critics can find quite irritating and lacking in seriousness. The fact that both books were published in 'coffee table' format, with lots of pictures of the American landscape and cityscape in the former, did not help matters; this hardly suggests philosophical seriousness, although it might just be seen as a gesture towards double-coding in an attempt to widen the work's reach. *America* is basically a travelogue, sometimes celebrating America's brashness and lack of tradition, at other times taking a rather wry view of the culture's customs and foibles, such as the penchant for jogging – now more or less a universal phenomenon of course, but not then. The travelogue approach could be seen as a nod towards the postmodernist predilection for blurring the line between popular and high culture, and it is full of Baudrillard's trademark throwaway lines, such as 'it is Disneyland that is authentic here! The cinema and TV are America's reality!' (an example of hyperreality in action) and 'Tomorrow is the first day of the rest of your life' (Baudrillard 1988: 104, 11).

Baudrillard treats America as a mass of sensations which ultimately do not add up to any particular message, and he takes the role of a detached observer who as much as possible will not draw leading conclusions from his experience, as Europeans are traditionally wont to do (such as are found in an earlier French travelogue of America, Alexis de Tocqueville's *Democracy in America* (1835, 1840)). Baudrillard is quite explicit in his refusal to contextualise his trip within some grand narrative: 'The only question in this journey is: how far can we go in the extermination of meaning' (Baudrillard 1988: 10). Another way of reading that phrase might be 'the extermination of interpretation', a characteristically postmodern stance to adopt – much in evidence in the work of Jacques Derrida, for example, with his series of strategies for deferring meaning, seemingly indefinitely. Presumably that is what Baudrillard was signalling when he spoke earlier of the need to 'remove' his hypotheses 'from the critical zone of reference'; that is, to refuse to enter into the game of critical debate. To play that game requires belief in certain foundations of discourse that postmodern thought does not regard as valid. This is the position known as antifoundationalism, since it calls into doubt the foundation of any and all discourses; most dramatically perhaps, the entire discourse of Western philosophy, on which so much of our thought depends. Baudrillard can be considered one of the more extreme examples of this position, insisting that '[s]trictly speaking, nothing remains to us to base anything on. All that remains for us is theoretical violence – speculation to the death, whose only method is the radicalisation of hypotheses' (Baudrillard 1993: 5).

Baudrillard succeeded in making enemies amongst feminists with the arguments in his book *Seduction*, which claimed that techniques of seduction were to be encouraged for their ability to undermine power structures: '*seduction represents mastery over the symbolic universe, while power represents only mastery of the real universe*. The sovereignty of seduction is incommensurable with the possession of political or sexual power' (Baudrillard 1990b: 8). Systems, Baudrillard is arguing, can be brought down by means other than direct confrontation: 'why become stuck undermining foundations, when a *light* manipulation of appearances will do?' (Baudrillard 1990b: 10). It is an approach which draws on the work of the French 'difference feminist' Luce Irigaray (see, for example, Irigaray 1985), and it enables Baudrillard to claim that femininity should be regarded as 'a principle of uncertainty' (Baudrillard 1990b: 12). But that is not a conclusion designed to please the feminist movement in general.

It is easy to mock Baudrillard in his more provocative mode, but he does succeed nevertheless in directing our attention to some very profound changes that have occurred in contemporary consciousness. Mass media have come to play an inordinately large part in our lives, and at times it does seem as if we can hardly envisage the world without them: to be is to text or to tweet; nothing is real until we have seen it on television. Equally, systems can be brought down by methods other than force, as we saw in the late 1980s when the Soviet empire collapsed – even if that is not the kind of message that the more revolutionary would like to hear.

Baudrillard's major writings

Baudrillard, Jean, *The Mirror of Production* [1973], trans. Mark Poster, St Louis, MO: Telos, 1975.

——, *For a Critique of a Political Economy of the Sign* [1972], trans. Charles Levin, St Louis, MO: Telos, 1981.

——, *In the Shadow of the Silent Majorities* [1978], trans. Paul Foss, Paul Patton and John Johnston, New York: Semiotext(e), 1983.

——, *Simulations*, trans. Paul Foss, Paul Patton and Philip Beitchman, New York: Semiotext(e), 1983.

——, 'The Year 2000 Will Not Take Place', in E. A. Grosz *et al.*, *Futur*Fall: Excursions into Post-Modernity*, Sydney: Power Institute, 1986, pp. 18–28.

——, *Forget Foucault* [1977], trans. Nicole Dufresne, New York: Semiotext(e), 1987.

——, *America* [1986], trans. Chris Turner, London and New York: Verso, 1988.

——, *Cool Memories* [1987], trans. Chris Turner, London and New York: Verso, 1990a.

——, *Seduction* [1979], trans. Brian Singer, London and Basingstoke: Macmillan, 1990b.

——, *Symbolic Exchange and Death* [1976], trans. Iain Hamilton Grant, London: Sage, 1993.

References and further reading

Deleuze, Gilles, and Félix Guattari, *Anti-Oedipus: Capitalism and Schizophrenia* [1972], trans. Robert Hurley, Mark Seem and Helen R. Lane, Minneapolis, MN: University of Minnesota Press, 1983.

de Tocqueville, Alexis, *Democracy in America: And Two Essays on America* [1835, 1840], trans. Gerald Bevan, London: Penguin, 2003.

Halley, Peter, *Collected Essays 1981–87* [1988], Zurich and New York: Bruno Bischofberger Gallery and Sonnabend Gallery, 2000.

Irigaray, Luce, *This Sex Which Is Not One* [1977], trans. Catherine Porter, with Carolyn Burke, Ithaca, NY: Cornell University Press, 1985.

Lyotard, Jean-François, *The Postmodern Condition: A Report on Knowledge* [1979], trans. Geoff Bennington and Brian Massumi, Manchester: Manchester University Press, 1984.

——, *Libidinal Economy* [1974], trans. Iain Hamilton Grant, London: Athlone Press, 1993.

ZYGMUNT BAUMAN (B. 1925)

Bauman is one of the most thoughtful commentators on post-modernity, a writer who carefully analyses the socio-political impli-cations of the shift into that condition in the last few decades to bring out both its merits and demerits. One of the primary signals of this shift was the collapse of communism as a political force in Europe in the 1980s, and although he is very critical of the Soviet project in general (Bauman is Polish and left the country during its communist phase to settle in Britain), he suggests that its collapse has removed one of the few checks that the capitalist order was operating under in the post-World War Two world. During the Cold War period, capitalism had to show its best face in order to maintain popular support at home as well as an attractive image abroad; but without the check provided by the existence of a Soviet bloc we soon find ourselves in the undesirable situation of 'living without an alternative' (Bauman 1992: 175) in the political realm. As Francis Fukuyama had put it after the fairly swift collapse of the Soviet empire in the 1980s, the Western system had simply won, seeing off its main competitor, and history was now to be considered at an 'end' (Fukuyama 1992).

With the exception of the rise of religious fundamentalism around the globe, particularly in its Islamic manifestation with its theocratic leanings, 'living without an alternative' is a condition we can still be said to be under in the post-credit crisis era, where liberal democracy with a free-market-based economic system is seen by the ruling classes to be the model form of political organisation for the nation state. The difference in the post-Soviet era is that the system has far less of a welfare safety net to help those who may fall on hard times. Those in power absolve the system from responsibility for any crisis that might arise (such as the recent financial crash), reducing it to the excesses of some corporations and rogue individuals instead. The assumption is made that there is no other way to guarantee economic success than through the free-market model, and that the system is fundamentally sound anyway, it just needs patching up now and again.

In *Postmodernity and Its Discontents* Bauman takes aim at the individualism fostered by a market-based postmodern world, where the primary requirement is that 'one needs to be capable of being seduced by the infinite possibility and constant renewal promoted by the consumer market' (Bauman 1997: 14). Those who for whatever reason (lack of resources etc.) cannot enter into this 'game of consumerism' become 'the new "impure"' (Bauman 1997: 14) of postmodern society, and find themselves in the position of outsiders, the subject of various kinds of punitive action by the state. Bauman rails against the disparity in wealth that the shift to a hyper-individualised society has created, regarding this 'profound division between the haves and the have-nots' (Bauman 1997: 204) as one of the primary sources of social discontent. In the years since he wrote *Postmodernity and Its Discontents* this division has become ever more pronounced, with the credit crisis of 2007–8 exacerbating the problem quite considerably.

As the titles of several of his books indicate, Bauman is very much taken by the idea that we are now living in 'liquid' times; thus we have *Liquid Modernity*, *Liquid Love*, *Liquid Life*, *Liquid Fear*, *Liquid Times* and *Culture in a Liquid Modern World*. This is not a cultural development of which he approves, and he argues that the transition of modernity into a 'liquid' phase has created a sense of disorientation amongst many of us: '"Liquid modern" is a society in which the conditions under which its members act change faster than it takes the ways of acting to consolidate into habits and routines. ... Life in the liquid modern society is a sinister version of the musical chairs game, played for real' (Bauman 2005: 1, 3). One of the main effects of this disorientation, and the uncertainty that comes in its wake, is that we are increasingly beset by 'liquid modern fears' (Bauman 2006: 21) about what could unexpectedly go wrong in our lives. There is no aspect of our lives that has not been profoundly affected by this new condition of liquidity, right down to the level of our personal relationships, where the likelihood is that any romantic attachment that we form will not last for very long. In consequence the bonds between the parties 'need to be only loosely tied, so that they can be untied again, with little delay, when the settings change – as in liquid modernity they surely will, over and over again' (Bauman 2003: vii). Bauman may be overstating the case here, but his ideas on this topic are never less than thought provoking.

In the book to introduce the topic, *Liquid Modernity*, Bauman suggests that the notions of 'fluidity' or 'liquidity' are particularly applicable to the stage we have reached in the development of modernity, where human relationships 'are now malleable to an extent unexperienced by, and unimaginable for, past generations' (Bauman 2000: 8). Modernity for Bauman has been from the beginning concerned with breaking away from the 'solids' of the past (for which we could read 'tradition'), but the difference now is that the process has speeded up very considerably. The fluidity of modern life is all to the benefit of the most powerful forces in our society, who have a vested interest in removing barriers to the exercise of their power and authority, hence the clamour for the deregulation of business and finance that has been such a feature of life in the West for the last few decades. In the name of globalisation, for example, the goal has been for capital and goods to flow unimpeded across national boundaries, regardless of the impact this has on local economies and cultural traditions. The market is to be allowed to dictate how these economies fare, and the market's word is taken to be law. Bauman, however, is scathing of the new world order this has created, warning that technology such as mobile phones has the potential to bring about a dystopia 'fit to replace the fears recorded in Orwellian and Huxleyan-style nightmares' (Bauman 2000: 15).

Although Bauman can make it sound a very bleak condition in which to be caught, postmodernist thinkers have tended to welcome this sense of liquidity, equating it with flexibility in terms of one's beliefs and a release from the constraints of tradition: the 'nomadic' existence celebrated by Gilles Deleuze and Félix Guattari in *A Thousand Plateaus*. Where Bauman laments 'the frailty of human bonds' (Bauman 2003) in contemporary society, regarding it as evidence of a worrying lack of commitment on the part of the majority of the citizenry, postmodernists see instead the freedom to reconstruct one's life when relationships go wrong – as of course they are capable of doing in any society at any time. There can be a misplaced nostalgia about the past on this issue, because much human misery was caused by the pressure exerted by one's peers to adhere to the rigid social bonds that propriety demanded. There was also much hypocrisy involved in the attempt to keep up at least the appearance of propriety if the reality did not quite conform to expectations. Nevertheless, Bauman is right to draw our attention to the less desirable aspect of the nomadic model, that one never knows quite how much trust to put in a nomad's word if they are going to be as 'liquid' in their behaviour as Deleuze and Guattari are urging them to be. Bauman for one does not find this a very satisfactory state of affairs.

Unfortunately for Bauman, the way our culture is developing, especially given the types of new technology that have been coming on stream of late (social networking being the most obvious), is only likely to render our existence progressively more liquid; although admittedly it is modernity rather than postmodernity itself that he considers to be responsible for setting this particular trend in motion. It has to be conceded as well that uncertainty can have its attractions, even if Bauman can only see its downside. While postmodernists may be in favour of liquid life at a personal level, that does not mean, however, that they also agree with all the policies of neoliberalism which urge liquidity throughout all aspects of our economic life – globalisation being a case in point.

Bauman is certainly an outspoken critic of globalisation, which he argues is advantageous only to the elites of the West – that is, the Western corporate sector, the multinationals above all. Those elites can follow their own interests almost with impunity, since in a progressively less regulated free-market system they have been able to gain the power to set the economic agenda worldwide. The developing world is invariably exploited by such practices as Western corporations' outsourcing of production to it for the lowest possible rates, encouraging poor nation states to compete at undercutting each other in order to gain the custom:

> And of course there is the possibility of moving away if things locally get too hot for comfort; the 'globality' of the elite means mobility, and mobility means the ability to escape and evade. There are always places where local guardians of order are glad to look the other way in case a clash does happen.
>
> (Bauman 1998: 125)

Yet there is precious little evidence that outsourcing benefits the life of the workers in those countries, who can find themselves with no option but to accept pay and conditions that would be considered completely unacceptable, and even illegal, in the West if contracts are to be retained (see Naomi Klein's *No Logo* (Klein 2001) for more specific detail on corporate practices in this area). Globalisation represents a logical development of the capitalist order at the heart of the project of modernity, and it could well be argued that it is in need of some viable alternative to make it think again about its exploitative approach.

Overall, Bauman offers an essentially negative view of the way our culture has been developing over the last few decades, and if anything the tone of his writings seems to have grown more pessimistic. *Culture in a Liquid Modern World* goes on to bemoan the effect of a market-led culture on the world of the arts, keeping up the author's reputation as one of the most trenchant critics of the market ethos that we have. The postmodern condition is for Bauman one where the market runs riot, to the detriment of social justice, and the 'postmodern ethics' (see Bauman 1993) that are generated amount to little more than an evasion of moral responsibility

Bauman's major writings

Bauman, Zygmunt, *Intimations of Postmodernity*, London: Routledge, 1992.
——, *Postmodern Ethics*, Oxford and Cambridge, MA: Blackwell, 1993.
——, *Postmodernity and Its Discontents*, Cambridge and Oxford: Polity Press and Blackwell, 1997.
——, *Globalization: The Human Consequences*, Cambridge and Oxford: Polity Press and Blackwell, 1998.
——, *Liquid Modernity*, Cambridge and Oxford: Polity Press and Blackwell, 2000.
——, *Liquid Love: On the Frailty of Human Bonds*, Cambridge and Oxford: Polity Press and Blackwell, 2003.
——, *Liquid Life*, Cambridge and Malden, MA: Polity Press, 2005.
——, *Liquid Fear*, Cambridge and Malden, MA: Polity Press, 2006.
——, *Liquid Times: Living in an Age of Uncertainty*, Cambridge and Malden, MA: Polity Press, 2007.
——, *Culture in a Liquid Modern World*, Cambridge and Malden, MA: Polity Press, 2011.

References and further reading

Deleuze, Gilles and Félix Guattari, *A Thousand Plateaus: Capitalism and Schizophrenia* [1980], trans. Brian Massumi, London: Athlone Press, 1988.

Fukuyama, Francis, *The End of History and the Last Man*, London: Hamish Hamilton, 1992.
Klein, Naomi, *No Logo*, London: HarperCollins, 2001.

DANIEL BELL (1919–2011)

Daniel Bell was one of the most prominent commentators on post-industrialism, which can be subsumed under the heading of the postmodern, marking as it does a dramatic shift away from the heavy industry bias of modernity towards a more service-oriented economy of the kind that most Western nations now espouse in the twenty-first century. In the UK, for example, successive governments from about the 1980s onwards have regarded the financial services provided by the City of London as one of the major sources of national economic growth, and have as a result striven to reduce regulation of that sector to a minimum (the negative side of which has been the credit crisis of 2007–8, largely caused by over-exuberant bank lending). Most major manufacturing corporations in the West have outsourced the bulk of their production to the developing world, largely Asian countries, a move which has dramatically reduced the numbers of those employed in the manufacture of goods throughout the West. While Western politicians often speak of the need to encourage a return to home-based industrial manufacturing, the multinationals rarely pay much attention, knowing that it will always be cheaper for them to continue using the developing world. The West might be largely a post-industrial society, therefore, but only because it has moved the production of the majority of its goods to the non-Western world. Rather interestingly, however, the West is now beginning to outsource some of its service industries, such as call centres, to the developing world – particularly the Indian subcontinent. What the long-term effect of this will be on employment opportunities and consumer demand in the West remains to be seen.

Bell is careful to emphasise that his 'venture in social forecasting' does not assume any 'deterministic trajectory' (Bell 1976: x), and that he is not engaged in the business of prediction, rather in charting the likely implications of certain social tendencies observable in later twentieth-century culture. His concern is with the changes that are taking place in the social frameworks of the world's most advanced industrialised societies, and what agenda can be identified as emerging from these. He specifies five main components to be found in a post-industrial society:

1   Economic sector: the change from a goods-producing to a service economy.
2   Occupational distribution: the pre-eminence of the professional and technical class.
3   Axial principle: the centrality of theoretical knowledge as the source of innovation and of policy formulation for the society.
4   Future orientation: the control of technology and technological assessment.
5   Decision-making: the creation of a new 'intellectual technology'.

(Bell 1976: 14)

All of these components are plainly visible in twenty-first-century Western society, and, as Bell noted, they have led to many serious divisions and tensions between those sections of the population they favour and those they marginalise. Nor can we look for help in resolving these problems from theories, such as Marxism, developed in the industrial age: the social landscape simply has changed too much.

Just to indicate how difficult it is to forecast where changes in social frameworks are likely to lead, however, Bell believed that '[t]he decisive social change taking place in our time … is the subordination of the economic function to the political order' (Bell 1976: 373). Yet a combination of globalisation and systematic deregulation of the market in the interim has enabled neoliberal economic theory to turn that notion on its head: it is the political function that has come to be subordinated to the economic, and the political class of the West has been complicit in what has turned out to be a socially highly divisive phenomenon. Bell also thought that non-profit organisations such as universities and hospitals would grow markedly in importance and power in a post-industrial era, and while this has been true up to a point, it is increasingly at the expense of their non-profit status. The public sector is under considerable pressure throughout the West to embrace the profit motive, as public funding is steadily being withdrawn from it.

The Coming of Post-Industrial Society helped to establish an approach to modern culture which has come to be known as 'endism', also to be found in the work of such thinkers as Francis Fukuyama, as in his highly controversial *The End of History and the Last Man*, where it was argued that the Western system of liberal democracy had now definitively won out over its competitors and was the ideal to which all other systems were inexorably converging. Jean-François Lyotard's proclamation in *The Postmodern Condition* of the end of metanarratives is another example of this viewpoint, and various other thinkers have announced the 'end of philosophy'. There is more than a bit of wishful thinking in such arguments, however, which generally reveal a very Western-centric perspective. Metanarratives plainly did not end with the advent of the postmodern condition, they proceeded to grow ever more powerful in the Islamic world with the rise of Islamic fundamentalism, which is still a major player on the world political scene. Various other religious fundamentalisms have also gained in strength in the last few decades, Christian and Judaic most notably, in America and Israel. Since metanarratives are based on an ideology which regards itself as the received truth, that means that ideology is still alive and well too. Liberal democracy has certainly not conquered the world as yet, and with its economic system, based on the free market, in deep trouble since the crisis of 2007–8, it has lost much of its attractiveness.

Bell's 'endist' tendencies can also be seen in *The End of Ideology*, another work which seems to prefigure the postmodern, given that postmodern thinkers are always so keen to move beyond the old ideological conflicts that have bedevilled modern life. Ideology has only negative connotations for the likes of Lyotard, Michel Foucault, and Gilles Deleuze and Félix Guattari, who see it as an instrument of oppression wielded on behalf of the ruling class. Bell's line is that '[i]n the last decade [the 1950s], we have witnessed an exhaustion of the nineteenth-century ideologies, particularly Marxism, as intellectual systems that could claim *truth* for their views of the world' (Bell 2000: 16). Ideology, he insists, 'has come to be a dead end' (Bell 2000: 393). Few postmodernists would disagree with such conclusions, although it would have to be said that neither Bell nor the major postmodern thinkers foresaw the spirited revival of ideology that has taken place in the last few decades, as expressed through religious fundamentalism (in its various forms) and neoliberal political and economic theory. Bell did suggest that the developing world, mainly Africa and Asia, would generate some new ideologies of its own, based on 'industrialization, modernization, Pan-Arabism, color, and nationalism' (Bell 2000: 403), and this has indeed happened; but these have to a significant degree been subordinated to the increasingly powerful ideologies of religious fundamentalism and neoliberalism.

Scathing though he is of a system where '[o]ne simply turns to the ideological vending machine, and out comes the prepared formulae' (Bell 2000: 405), Bell is also well aware that when ideologies lose their credibility we are left with a political vacuum. Whereas postmodernists are entirely happy with that state of affairs, Bell feels there is still a definite need for utopian political ideas in our society, something for individuals to channel their energies into and give them some hope for a better future for the human race. Sadly, he cannot quite see where these ideas will come from any more, and the book has nothing more positive to recommend than the protection of 'the verities of free speech, free press, the right of opposition and of free inquiry' (Bell 2000: 406). An 'Afterword' written in 1988 defends the book against the charge made by various critics that it was merely upholding the status quo and, as such, was to be regarded as 'an instrument of the Cold War' (Bell 2000: 421). In fact, the political climate of the early twenty-first century, with Marxism gone and neoliberalism tainted by economic failure, is proving to be more congenial to the arguments of works like *The End of Ideology*. Bell is certainly a far subtler thinker than the left made him out to be in the 1960s and 1970s.

In *The Cultural Contradictions of Capitalism*, Bell turns his attention to modernity and 'the problems of managing a complex polity when the values of the society stress unrestrained appetite' (Bell 1976: xi). It is Bell's contention that modern society does not constitute a unified system, but a series of competing, and contradictory, ideas and objectives: 'for the economy, efficiency; for the polity, equality; and for the culture, self-realization (or self-gratification). The resulting disjunctions have framed the tensions and social conflicts of Western society in the past 150 years' (Bell 1976: xi–xii). What had to be faced up to in the later twentieth century was 'the exhaustion of cultural modernism' (Bell 1976: xii), a theme which reverberates throughout postmodern thought, generating such notions as John Barth's 'literature of exhaustion' (Barth 1977) and Lyotard's 'incredulity towards metanarratives' (Lyotard 1984: xxiv). If there ever was such a thing as a holistic, organic society (and Bell is notably sceptical on that score), then it manifestly no longer exists, and neither capitalism nor socialism, Marxian or otherwise, is likely to deliver it to us either.

Bell returns to the debate generated by *The End of Ideology* with a new introductory essay in the book's 2000 reprint, the objective of which is 'to see where we stand today in the post-Cold War world, a situation that I call "the resumption of history"' (Bell 2000: xii). By speaking of 'the resumption of history' as the twenty-first century gets under way, Bell is taking issue with Fukuyama's claim that it has ended in the triumph of liberal democracy. Fukuyama is making the same mistake that Marxism did, of assuming a *telos* to history: history is just never that neat for someone like Bell, who chooses to emphasise the competing and contradictory interests and objectives within society at any given point. The upsurge of nationalism in the aftermath of the collapse of Soviet communism is proof to Bell that history has indeed 'resumed', and that the particular ideological conflict associated with modernity is now over.

Bell's major writings

Bell, Daniel, *Work and Its Discontents: The Cult of Efficiency in America*, Boston, MA: Beacon Books, 1956.

——, *The Reforming of General Education: The Columbia Experience in Its National Setting*, New York: Columbia University Press, 1966.

——, *The Coming of Post-Industrial Society: A Venture in Social Forecasting*, Harmondsworth: Penguin, 1976.

——, *The Cultural Contradictions of Capitalism*, London: Heinemann, 1976.

——, *The Social Sciences Since the Second World War*, Piscataway, NJ: Transaction, 1982.

——, *The Winding Passage: Sociological Essays and Journeys* [1980], Piscataway, NJ: Transaction, 1991.

——, *Communitarianism and Its Critics*, New York: Oxford University Press, 1993.

——, *Marxian Socialism in the United States* [1952], Ithaca, NY and London: Cornell University Press, 2nd edn, 1996.

——, *The End of Ideology: On the Exhaustion of Political Ideas in the Fifties* [1960; 2nd edn 1961], Cambridge, MA and London: Harvard University Press, 2000.

References and further reading

Barth, John, 'The Literature of Exhaustion' [1967], in Malcolm Bradbury (ed.), *The Novel Today: Writers on Modern Fiction*, Manchester: Manchester University Press, 1977, pp. 70–83.

Fukuyama, Francis, *The End of History and the Last Man*, London: Hamish Hamilton, 1992.

Lyotard, Jean-François, *The Postmodern Condition: A Report on Knowledge* [1979], trans. Geoff Bennington and Brian Massumi, Manchester: Manchester University Press, 1984.

HOMI K. BHABHA (B. 1949)

Bhabha is one of the most influential thinkers in postcolonial theory, whose concept of 'hybridity' has been widely adapted by his contemporaries in that area of discourse. His work has been much influenced by Jacques Derrida's deconstruction, and like so many other poststructuralist/postmodernist thinkers Bhabha questions the validity of binary thought. Bhabha encourages us to explore the ways in which apparently binary categories can infiltrate each other, meaning that, for example, coloniser and colonised eventually become hybrid, taking on elements of each other's thought and behaviour rather than being pure in terms of their identity. Each side is altered significantly by the exchange between the two cultures, rather than it simply being a case of the dominant force and its oppressed 'other': a new, more flexible form of cultural identity is created from the encounter. Hybridity breaks down the notion of purity between cultures, and arguments against purity in almost any area of human existence are a primary concern of poststructuralist thought. For postcolonial theorists, such ideas are critical in showing that colonialism is not simply a one-way process, and that colonised peoples are more than just passive in the face of the greater technological power of the colonisers: unless that were so, there would be little hope of them making a success of overcoming the colonial experience and taking some control of their own destiny. For Bhabha, '[w]hat is theoretically innovative, and politically crucial, is the need to think beyond narratives of originary and initial subjectivities and to focus on those moments or processes that are produced in the articulation of cultural differences' (Bhabha 2004: 2).

The Location of Culture puts together a series of Bhabha's essays from various sources, adding some new ones to make up a general exploration of the nature of culture in a world where, in terms of the relations between communities, 'the exchange of values, meanings and priorities may not always be collaborative and dialogical, but may be profoundly antagonistic, conflictual and even incommensurable' (Bhabha 2004: 2). This is the problematic faced by any multicultural society, many of the tensions of which hark back to a colonial past: should multiculturalism mean preserving each culture present in the nation at any one time in its traditional form, or should it lead to a general convergence of lifestyles? *The Location of Culture* very much sees itself as a *fin de siècle* work, a time when '[o]ur existence is marked by a tenebrous sense of survival, living on the borderlines of the "present", for which there seems to be no proper name other than the current and controversial shiftiness of the prefix "post": *postmodernism, postcolonialism, postfeminism*' (Bhabha 2004: 1). 'Posts' are seen to be symptoms rather than solutions to the problems bequeathed by the metanarrative of Western modernity.

Bhabha makes it very clear that he does not want to approach the topic with any preconceptions, nor to be bound by tradition: 'The representation of difference must not be hastily read as the reflection of *pre-given* ethnic or cultural traits set in the fixed tablet of tradition' (Bhabha 2004: 3). Instead, he wants to emphasise the 'complex, on-going negotiation' that has to take place if we are to achieve new 'cultural hybridities' (Bhabha 2004: 3) that escape the restrictions of historical phenomena like colonialism, and the ideologies that lie behind it, as well as the impasse reached by multiculturalism: we should regard culture as a process of becoming rather than a finished state of being. Bhabha's concern is always to go beyond existing prejudices and mind-sets with their tendency towards essentialism. Unless the various 'posts' he mentions help us to make such a breakthrough they will be no more than 'parochial' (Bhabha 2004: 4) in their scope and influence, and Bhabha does suggest a degree of ambivalence to postmodernism in particular over the course of his writings.

Hybridity assumes, not just that the current world order can be challenged, but that there is no prevailing order that can demand adherence to its narrative. The future should never be seen as pre-determined, and it is counter-productive to think that we can return to past modes of existence either. The latter is something that colonised peoples can be prone to, as a way of affirming the validity of their history against that imposed on them by their colonisers. Bhabha sees a prime role for literature in making us aware of the need to develop hybridity: 'Where once, the transmission of national traditions was the major theme of a world literature, perhaps we can now suggest that transnational histories of migrants, the colonized, or political refugees – these border and frontier conditions – may be the terrains of world literature' (Bhabha 2004: 17). Amongst authors who can show us these 'border and frontier conditions' are Nadine Gordimer and Toni Morrison, in works set against the background of apartheid and slavery. It is the achievement of authors like these to 'demonstrate the contemporary compulsion to move beyond; to turn the present into the "post"' (Bhabha 2004: 26) that Bhabha takes to be a socio-political necessity in our time.

In the chapter 'The Postcolonial and the Postmodern: The Question of Agency', Bhabha explores the relationship between these two particular 'posts' and the opportunities they present for developing an ethos of hybridity. He treats postcolonialism as a deliberate departure 'from the traditions of the sociology of underdevelopment or "dependency" theory' (Bhabha 2004: 248), arguing that the colonial system created situations that in many ways anticipated the concerns of contemporary theories such as poststructuralism and postmodernism. It is from this 'hybrid location of cultural value ... that the postcolonial intellectual' (Bhabha 2004: 248) is operating. In that location, Lyotard's phenomenon of the differend keeps arising (see *The Differend*) because of the presence of incommensurable discourses, and finding ways of negotiating these is one of the primary tasks facing the postcolonial intellectual. Bhabha points out that we must remain aware that there is 'always a range of dissonant, even dissident histories and voices' (Bhabha 2004: 6) to be acknowledged – that, for him, is what defines the postmodern condition. The notion of a culturally pure nation is just a fiction, and whenever it gains dominance it almost invariably leads to bloodshed and oppression – the dark side of the differend as Lyotard sees it, and one that we are still having to deal with, Bhabha insists, even in an ostensibly postcolonial era. 'Postcoloniality', for such a thinker, 'is a salutary reminder of the persistent "neo-colonial" relations within the "new" world order and the multinational division of "labour"' (Bhabha 2004: 9). Capitalism has now replaced colonialism as the new 'purist' metanarrative, and for thinkers like Fredric Jameson postmodernism is complicit with this, forming 'the cultural logic of late capitalism' (Jameson 1991).

In his introduction to *Nation and Narration*, Bhabha outlines the book's remit as analysing the narratives that grow to define individual nations, since no matter how 'romantic and excessively metaphorical' these may be, 'it is from those traditions of political thought and literary language that the nation emerges as a powerful historical idea in the west' (Bhabha 1990: 1). He approaches this topic in his own chapter in the collection, 'DissemiNation: Time, Narrative, and the Margins of the Modern Nation' (later reprinted in *The Location of Culture*), by arguing that as far as modern Western nations are concerned their history since around the mid-nineteenth century has been very much tied up with migration; this constituting 'one of the most sustained periods of mass migration within the west, and colonial expansion in the east' (Bhabha 1990: 291). Modern Western nations are thus 'more hybrid in the articulation of cultural differences and identifications' (Bhabha 1990: 292) than they would like to think (particularly the more prejudiced among their populations). Nationalist purity remains largely the romantic myth that Bhabha claims, and we have a legacy of hybridity to build upon. Elsewhere, in *The Location of Culture*, Bhabha speaks of the 'liminality of migrant experience' as an entirely positive element in contemporary society, arguing that its 'in-between' aspect 'moves the question of culture's appropriation beyond the assimilationist's dream, or the racist's nightmare' (Bhabha 2004: 321). Migrant experience provides the basis for hybridity to develop, and the influence of deconstruction reveals itself in Bhabha's emphasis on the critical importance of 'in-between' and marginal states in the process.

Nation and Narration concludes with Bhabha declaring himself to be sceptical about certain aspects of postmodern thought, such as the obsession with continual self-reinvention. Those kinds of notions are to him still rooted in modernity, and have little purchase in a non-Western world: 'what is modernity in those colonial conditions where its imposition is itself the denial of historical freedom, civic autonomy and the "ethical" choice of refashioning?' (Bhabha 2004: 345). It is a point that has been raised more recently by theorists such as Okwui Enwezor, for whom it is more correct to speak of the 'aftermodern' than the postmodern when it comes to ex-colonial areas like Africa (Enwezor 2009: 36), which never really experienced modernity in its fullest sense. Overcoming the faults of modernity's metanarrative cannot have the same resonance in that situation that it does for thinkers like Lyotard. Bhabha's response to this dilemma is to encourage the development of an attitude of 'contra-modernity' (Bhabha 2004: 351).

The Preface to *The Location of Culture*'s 2004 edition takes issue with the spread in influence in the interim of what Bhabha refers to as 'global cosmopolitanism' (Bhabha 2004: xiv), the blend of neoliberalism and globalisation that is still the dominant socio-political/socio-economic paradigm of our time, despite the credit crisis that broke just three years after the new edition's publication. While global cosmopolitanism gives the impression that it is all in favour of cultural pluralism and difference, it is only as long, as Bhabha tartly notes, as those in the developing world, where the greater part of the West's manufacturing has now been outsourced, 'produce healthy profit margins within metropolitan societies' (Bhabha 2004: xiv).

Postcolonialism has had something of a new lease of life of late, being a major stimulus to the development of the altermodern, which aims to move beyond the modern–postmodern debate. In the work of Nicolas Bourriaud, for example, it is suggested that we combine postcolonial theory with a new, more open attitude to modernism, that would be categorised as altermodernism; thereby preserving the political edge that goes along with postcolonialism. Altermodernism has also brought forth Enwezor's interesting notion of the 'after-modern' as a basis for escaping from the binary of modernity and postmodernity, and that clearly owes a debt to thinkers like Bhabha, who has been assiduous in directing our attention to some highly problematical blind-spots within postmodern thought.

Bhabha's major writings

Bhabha, Homi K., 'Representation and the Colonial Text: A Critical Exploration of Some Forms of Mimeticism', in Frank Gloversmith (ed.), *The Theory of Reading*, Brighton: Harvester, 1984, pp. 93–122.

——(ed.), *Nation and Narration*, London and New York: Routledge, 1990, pp. 291–322.

——, *The Location of Culture* [1994], 2nd edn, London and New York: Routledge, 2004.

——, 'Foreword' to Franz Fanon, *The Wretched of the Earth*, trans. Richard Philcox, New York: Grove Press, 2004.

Bhabha, Homi K. and W. J. T. Mitchell (eds), *Edward Said: Continuing the Conversation*, Chicago and London: University of Chicago Press, 2005.

References and further reading

Bourriaud, Nicolas (ed.), *Altermodern: Tate Triennial*, London: Tate Publishing, 2009.

Enwezor, Okwui, 'Modernity and Postcolonial Ambivalence', in Nicolas Bourriaud (ed.), *Altermodern: Tate Triennial*, London: Tate Publishing, 2009, pp. 25–40.

Jameson, Fredric, *Postmodernism, or the Cultural Logic of Late Capitalism*, London: Verso, 1991.

Lyotard, Jean-François, *The Differend: Phrases in Dispute* [1983], trans. Georges Van Den Abbeele, Manchester: Manchester University Press, 1988.

NICOLAS BOURRIAUD (B. 1965)

Bourriaud is an art critic and curator who has developed a theory to explain what it is that differentiates very recent art movements, with their extensive use of installation and conceptual models, from their predecessors. Bourriaud describes such art as 'relational', indicating that it sets up a particular relationship with the individual viewer, an exchange of information as it were, turning the relationship itself into an essential part of the artistic process (the work of Tracey Emin might well fit into this category). Much recent art is therefore dependent upon a 'relational aesthetics', the title of one of Bourriaud's most important works. There are echoes here of Barthes's notion of the 'writerly' text that requires the active participation of the reader, the author being no more than just part of the overall process. Bourriaud sees relational art as similarly inviting such a response, as being incomplete until this has occurred – although of course each particular encounter will complete it in its own particular way (one might see a parallel in the relationship of audience to play in the context of a theatrical performance).

Relational aesthetics calls for a reassessment on our part of the status of the artwork: 'No longer can a work be reduced to the presence of an object in the here and now; rather it consists of a significant network whose interrelationships the artists elaborate' (Bourriaud 2009a: 14). What we have to acknowledge from now on is the *'fragmentation* of the work of art' (Bourriaud 2009a: 14). Unsurprisingly, Bourriaud is attracted to the notion of hypertext, which also builds up complex networks from fragments of textual material, and also, in a possible nod to the thought of Jean-François Lyotard, to the image of the archipelago to describe how the network of interrelationships of artworks is constructed (see, for example, Lyotard 1988: 131).

Much of the art that Bourriaud defines as relational would normally be included under the heading of the postmodern, but interestingly enough Bourriaud sees it as setting up the possibility of transcending the postmodern in a manner that would require a new definition to indicate the shift of perspective that would be involved. As he put it in the catalogue accompanying the Tate Triennial exhibition that he curated at the Tate Britain Gallery in London in 2009, as part of his sojourn there as Gulbenkian Curator of Contemporary Art:

> Numerous contemporary artistic practices indicate … that we are on the verge of a leap, out of the postmodern period and the (essentialist) multicultural model from which it is indivisible, a leap that would give rise to a synthesis between modernism and post-colonialism. Let us then call this synthesis 'altermodernism'.
>
> (Bourriaud 2009a: 12–13)

Postcolonialism is usually identified with the general phenomenon of the postmodern; colonialism being part of the imperialist side of modernity, with its commitment to spreading the gospel of material progress, and the lifestyle that went along with this, everywhere in the world. What Bourriaud is attempting to do, therefore, is to reintroduce certain elements of modernism into postmodern discourse that he feels have been unfairly discredited by postmodern aesthetic theorists. Bourriaud wants to create an aesthetic that escapes the restrictions placed on the artist by both modernism and postmodernism, each of which involves ideological commitments (in the latter's case, very often anti-modernist in tone) that Bourriaud is keen to move beyond. In his view, the altermodern is not in itself an ideological position and does not ask the artist to choose sides in the way that both modernism and postmodernism do.

Bourriaud wants altermodernism to avoid being caught in the struggle between modernism and postmodernism, and for it to open out a new space for artists to operate in beyond these competing, effectively binary, 'isms':

> The term 'altermodern', which serves both as the title of the present exhibition [Tate Triennial 2009] and to delimit the void beyond the postmodern, has its roots in the idea of 'otherness' (Latin *alter* = 'other', with the added English connotation of 'different') and suggests a multitude of possibilities, of alternatives to a single route.
>
> (Bourriaud 2009a: 12)

Bourriaud considers it necessary to develop the concept of the altermodern on the basis that postmodernism has lost its historical context in the wake of the financial crisis that for him marks an equivalent crisis in the project of modernity. The crisis is to be interpreted as 'a definite turning-point in history', which requires new theories and new practices to be instituted in the arts as well as in politics, 'a new modern movement' (Bourriaud 2009a: 16, 20), minus the universalist principles of the previous one.

There are unmistakable political implications to the notion of altermodernism, as Okwui Enwezor goes on to make clear in another essay in Bourriaud's Tate collection. Enwezor argues that modernity as the Western world understood the term ('supermodernity' as it has subsequently been dubbed (Auge 1995)) had barely touched places like Africa, which is more correctly to be described as 'aftermodern' now that colonialism of the old style has largely disappeared. For Enwezor, '[s]uch modernity, more than in other parts of the world, would be based in large part on a project of disinheriting the violence of colonial modernity' (Enwezor 2009: 40). Modernity such as it was in Africa was to be identified with the colonial powers, and therefore a part of the continent's history that it wanted to dissociate itself from in the twenty-first century. There needed to be a new kind of modernity that had no connection with this despised heritage, and, as Enwezor saw it, '[t]his modernity, it is hoped, is one that will emerge at the end of the project of *supermodernity*. It will perhaps mark not only an ideal of the altermodern, but will initiate a new cycle of the *aftermodern*' (Enwezor 2009: 40). Postmodernism from this point of view is still too closely linked to the Western narrative tradition, fighting battles intrinsic to Western rather than developing world culture.

Altermodernism is a very interesting attempt to push on from postmodernism while nevertheless retaining the lessons that it taught us about the many drawbacks of modernity – its authoritarian leanings, the cult it generated of reason and the notion of 'progress', etc. It does in fact share many of the characteristics that we associate with the postmodern: a commitment to pluralism and difference, for example, as well as a desire to escape dogmatism of the type so often found in the modernist aesthetic (the kind that Charles Jencks campaigned so vigorously against in *The Language of Post-Modern Architecture*). In Bourriaud's wish that artists should flit around 'in space, in time, and among the "signs"' (Bourriaud 2009a: 13) of our world, there is what amounts to an invitation to indulge in pastiche in the manner of so many postmodern creative artists from Jencks onwards. The difference in Bourriaud's case is that he does not want to see this being linked to some particular programme, as is so clearly the case in Jencks and the reaction to the modernist school in architecture. Bourriaud's overall view of postmodernism is fairly downbeat, 'the philosophy of mourning' (Bourriaud 2009a: 19) as he defines it.

One might see similarities, however, with Jacques Derrida's vision of the world beyond structuralism, 'a world of signs without fault, without truth, and without origin which is offered to an active interpretation' (Derrida 1978: 292). It is just such an 'active interpretation' that Bourriaud seems to be inviting artists to display in order to project us beyond postmodernism and what for him are its outdated battles. In both writers there is a desire to escape the world of theoretical infighting, where signs come loaded with ideological significance such that the artistic imaginary is severely constrained. The result is that pluralism and difference are yet again suppressed. In a nod towards the work of Gilles Deleuze and Félix Guattari, Bourriaud recommends that to access the altermodern the artist 'turns nomad' (Bourriaud 2009a: 23).

Bourriaud has also explored the aesthetics of the contemporary popular music scene in *Postproduction: Culture as Screenplay*, where he notes how problematic the concept of authorship has become nowadays, given the extensive use of such techniques as sampling and remixing in the industry. Original pieces of music become no more than raw material to work on in such cases, with the original sometimes being altered out of all recognition. (A precedent for this method might be found in the art of arranging in the jazz world, which down the years has performed a not dissimilar function in the way it 'works over' well-known popular tunes so that they become more the product of the arranger and the improvising musicians involved in their performance than the original composer.) The artists involved in such postproduction exercises are engaged in 'the task of selecting cultural objects and inserting them into new contexts' (Bourriaud 2002b: 13), which could be seen as a novel approach to double-coding. It fulfils Jencks's major criterion for double-coding in being a pastiche of styles, although as it is dealing with popular works the original is not necessarily something which has alienated the general public. An existing work is being transformed rather than something entirely new being constructed out of various styles by the artist herself, but it does not seem unreasonable to claim the process as being in the spirit of double-coding.

Bourriaud encourages creative artists to turn themselves into 'radicants', by which he means opposing the notion of radicalism so central to modernism as an aesthetic, the constant search for originality of vision, and becoming immersed instead in the exchange of ideas and in creating networks. This to Bourriaud will constitute a new type of modernity that will break free from the imperialistic quality of the older version. Originality seems a pointless quest to him anyway when 'we are entering the era of universal subtitling, of generalized dubbing' (Bourriaud 2009b: 44); what is wanted in that situation is much more dialogue between artists.

Various commentators, either in jest or in earnest, have wondered what 'post-postmodernism' might look like, and the altermodern might well be considered a candidate for that description. Perhaps Bourriaud's ideas represent not so much a rejection of the postmodern as an extension of the concept, and it will be interesting to observe how the altermodern is developed by other theorists, both inside and outside the realm of aesthetics, since its roots in postcolonialism do, as noted above in the work of Enwezor, give it a definite political edge that is likely to resonate for some time yet. As long as postmodernism is inspiring such responses it cannot be the case, as critical voices have been claiming for at least a decade or so now, that it was a mere passing fancy that has outlived its usefulness. The notion of the 'aftermodern' is certainly worth pursuing too, and offers up an interesting new line of enquiry for the postcolonial critical community to pursue.

Bourriaud's major writings

Bourriaud, Nicolas, *Relational Aesthetics* [1998], trans. Simon Pleasance and Fronza Woods, Dijon: Les Presses du Reel, 2002a.
——, *Postproduction: Culture as Screenplay*, trans. Jeanine Hernan, New York: Lukas and Sternberg, 2002b.
——, *Touch: Relational Art from the 1990s to Now*, San Francisco: San Francisco Art Institute, 2002c.
——, 'Altermodern', in Nicolas Bourriaud (ed.), *Altermodern: Tate Triennial*, London: Tate Publishing, 2009a, pp. 11–24.
——, *The Radicant*, trans. James Gussen and Lil Porten, New York: Lukas and Sternberg, 2009b.

References and further reading

Auge, Marc, *Non-Places: Introduction to an Anthropology of Supermodernity* [1992], trans. John Howe, London and New York: Verso, 1995.
Derrida, Jacques, *Writing and Difference* [1967], trans. Alan Bass, Chicago: University of Chicago Press, 1978.
Enwezor, Okwui, 'Modernity and Postcolonial Ambivalence', in Nicolas Bourriaud (ed.), *Altermodern: Tate Triennial*, London: Tate Publishing, 2009, pp. 25–40.
Jencks, Charles, *The Language of Post-Modern Architecture* [1975], 6th edn, London: Academy Editions, 1991.
Lyotard, Jean-François, *The Differend: Phrases in Dispute* [1983], trans. Georges Van Den Abbeele, Manchester: Manchester University Press, 1988.

JUDITH BUTLER (B. 1956)

Butler is best known for her writings on gender, although she has also published widely on several other topics such as moral philosophy, language use and international politics. Her work challenges some of our most fundamental assumptions about the nature of gender, insisting that it is mostly a performance we engage in rather than a set of natural traits which dictate how we must act socially and sexually. Man/woman, male/female are not such clear-cut binary divisions as they are generally held to be – by feminists as much as anyone else. There is for Butler no such thing as a normative sexuality, let alone a normative heterosexuality of the kind that has prevailed for most of the modern age and is only now beginning to be challenged in any systematic way by the gay and lesbian community. Michel Foucault was of a similar mind, as he made plain in *The History of Sexuality* (which Butler cites throughout her most famous work, *Gender Trouble*), and both thinkers line up against the 'heterosexualisation of desire' (Butler 1990: 17) that is so evident all around us. This state can only be achieved by social coercion, and our culture is very much geared towards that in sexual matters; cultures in the developing world can be even more dramatically so, with homosexuality regarded as a criminal activity in many cases there. In consequence, figures like Butler and Foucault have been subjected to discrimination in their daily lives, leading Butler to suggest that the link between sex and gender ought to be broken:

> When the constructed status of gender is theorized as radically independent of sex, gender itself becomes a free-floating artifice, with the consequence that *man* and *masculine* might just as easily signify a female body as a male one, and *woman* and *feminine* a male body as easily as a female one.
>
> (Butler 1990: 6)

Drag comes to symbolise this free-floating state for Butler, with artifice very much to the fore. Her line is that 'gender is a kind of persistent impersonation that passes as the real', and she is no longer willing to go along with this impersonation just to uphold the system of 'compulsory heterosexuality' (Butler 1990: viii) that demands it. When such impersonation is parodied within gay and lesbian life, as it is in drag, then its constructed nature becomes immediately apparent to viewers. *Gender Trouble* constitutes a Foucault-inspired genealogical enquiry into such supposedly 'natural' cultural systems as compulsory heterosexuality, where Butler's objective is to unmask the various 'gender fables' (Butler 1990: xi) that play such a repressive role in our society for both gays and lesbians. Neither is it in the best interests of heterosexuals, with heterosexual women also being constrained by its rigid notions of what male and female behaviour should be under such a dispensation.

Butler is opposed to the idea that 'the term *women* denotes a common identity' (Butler 1990: 3), suggesting that it is simply not exhaustive enough to cover all eventualities, a line of argument that clashes with much of recent feminist thought. By its insistence on this basic stability of subject identity, Butler claims that feminism does a disservice to the many women around the world who fail to conform to the assumptions upon which it is based. Gender can be constructed otherwise than it is into what are taken to be the stable categories of 'man' and 'woman', and she takes it as her role as a theorist to subvert that mainstream notion as much as she possibly can. *Gender Trouble* constitutes a sustained polemic against universalising thought in general, whether in the service of feminist identity politics or patri- archy. These are both viewed as metanarratives that perpetuate the notion of binary relationships, forcing individuals to define themselves against these – all too often to their personal disadvantage. In a ges- ture towards deconstruction Butler insists that '[g]ender is a com- plexity whose totality is permanently deferred, never fully what it is at any given juncture in time' (Butler 1990: 16). Like Derrida, and poststructuralist and postmodernist thinkers in general, Butler adopts an 'antifoundationalist approach' (Butler 1990: 15) to analysis, which leads her to question some of the most deeply rooted beliefs of our culture.

Butler unleashes a provocative polemic against many of the icons of recent feminist thought, such as Luce Irigaray and Monique Wittig. The former is criticised for assuming the existence of a globally operative 'monolithic as well as monologic masculine economy' (Butler 1990: 13; see, for example, Irigaray 1985); the latter for pro- moting the cause of a lesbian-feminism which 'appears to cut off any kind of solidarity with heterosexual women and implicitly to assume that lesbianism is the logically or politically necessary consequence of feminism' (Butler 1990: 127; see, for example, Wittig 1971). Butler declares herself to be resolutely opposed to any such 'separatist pre- scriptivism' (Butler 1990: 127), which merely repeats the mistakes of identity politics. She also dismisses all attempts to ground present-day feminism in some supposedly utopian matriarchal culture in the dim, distant past, treating all such as instances of misplaced nostalgia that are of no relevance to women's struggles now.

The significance of drag performance for Butler is that, '*in imitating gender, drag implicitly reveals the imitative structure of gender itself* – *as well as its contingency*' (Butler 1990: 137). In other words, the model of 'woman' being performed is itself no more than a performance: there is no 'true', 'real' or 'natural' form lying behind it, no 'foundation' to the set of attributes being ascribed to women. There is no 'original' to a drag act: 'Genders can be neither true nor false, neither real nor apparent, neither original nor derived' (Butler 1990: 141). Ultimately, gender is to Butler merely a discourse, where 'acts, gestures, and desire produce the effect of an internal core of substance, but produce this *on the surface* of the body' (Butler 1990: 136). As Foucault had argued, discourses serve the interests of those in power, which means they can be undermined and changed: so it is with gender, as far as Butler is concerned.

Following these arguments up in a subsequent essay, 'Imitation and Gender Insubordination', Butler declares herself to be uneasy about the realm of theory in general and sub-sets of it such as lesbian or gay theories in particular, posing provocative questions such as: 'What, if anything, can lesbians be said to share?' (Butler 1991: 15). She feels herself to be engaged not in theory but in politics, contesting the homophobia that is so prevalent in the culture around her, arguing that this is about all lesbians may be said to share. Her main point is that she does not want homophobia to determine the character of the resistance to it, any more than she wants compulsory heterosexuality to determine how homosexuality is to be defined – if it is at all to be defined. Hence the attraction of drag, which for Butler should be considered a subordination of gender rather than a mere imitation of it. Gender simply does not define any individual anyway, identity being a much more complex affair than that. Butler therefore queries the validity of trying to devise 'any stable set of typologies that explain or describe something like gay or lesbian identities' (Butler 1991: 27).

Bodies That Matter is structured on two interlinked questions: 'Is there a way to link the question of the materiality of the body to the performativity of gender? And how does the category of "sex" figure within such a relationship?' (Butler 1993: 1). Anything to do with bodies becomes for Butler a matter of the power dynamics in a culture. Heterosexual and homosexual practices may both exist, but it is invariably heterosexuality that sets the standard by which all sexual acts are judged; the prevailing discourse ensuring this through the repetition of 'regulatory norms' (Butler 1993: 2) based on heterosexuality. Once again, Butler takes it as her role to disrupt this discourse. There is a clear desire expressed throughout her work on gender to be set free from such a constraining influence, for the 'release of alternative imaginary schemas for constituting sites of erotogenic pleasure' (Butler 1993: 91) so that heterosexuality no longer sets the agenda for how sex, bodies and relationships are perceived.

Of late, Butler has courted yet more controversy by her contributions to the debate over Israeli government policy with regard to Palestine, which she outright condemns. This is by no means a popular line to argue in America, with its substantial Jewish population and official government support for the state of Israel since its establishment in 1948. Butler is highly critical of the tendency to dub anyone who attacks Israeli politics anti-Semitic, insisting that she is defending traditional Jewish values of social justice against their distortion by Zionism. It is a topic she has pursued in several books, as in *Parting of the Ways: Jewishness and the Critique of Zionism*, where she describes her task as consisting of 'showing that there are Jewish resources for the criticism of state violence' (Butler 2012: 1), such as that deployed against the Palestinian population by Israel.

Whether gender really is as malleable a concept as Butler chooses to picture it has to remain questionable – although she does qualify that notion to some extent by defining it as 'a practice of improvisation within a field of constraint' (Butler 2004: 1). She is right, nevertheless, to draw attention to the fact that the character traits traditionally associated with men and women are nothing like as fixed and predictable as conventional wisdom would have it. Rationality is certainly not an exclusive male prerogative nor emotional intelligence exclusively a female one, as is so commonly believed: men can be homemakers and carers, women business leaders and politicians, and there is no lack of examples to choose from to make such a point nowadays. But it is a considerable leap from there to saying that gender identity is merely the repeated performance of certain closely monitored norms. Problematical though Butler's overall thesis may be, she has stirred up considerable debate about the assumptions we tend to make over gender behaviour (male rational, female emotional, etc.), and that has opened up new lines of enquiry in feminist theory, queer theory and the area of sexuality in general. If we were to claim Butler for postmodernism, it would be for her persistent concern to subvert the notion that there is any metanarrative of gender or sexuality to which we must all be expected to adhere. In characteristic postmodern fashion, Butler is an anti-universalising thinker.

Butler's major writings

Butler, Judith, *Gender Trouble: Feminism and the Subversion of Identity*, London and New York: Routledge, 1990.

——, 'Imitation and Gender Insubordination', in D. Fuss (ed.), *Inside/Out: Lesbian Theories, Gay Theories*, London and New York: Routledge, 1991, pp. 13–31.

——, *Bodies That Matter: On the Discursive Limits of 'Sex'*, London and New York: Routledge, 1993.

——, *Excitable Speech: A Politics of the Performative*, London and New York: Routledge, 1997.

——, *The Psychic Life of Power: Theories in Subjection*, Stanford, CA: Stanford University Press, 1997.

——, *Subjects of Desire: Hegelian Reflections in Twentieth-Century France*, New York: Columbia University Press, 1999.

——, *Precarious Life: The Power of Mourning and Violence*, London and New York: Verso, 2004.

——, *Undoing Gender*, London and New York: Routledge, 2004.

——, *Giving an Account of Oneself*, New York: Fordham University Press, 2005.

——, *Parting of the Ways: Jewishness and the Critique of Zionism*, New York and Chichester: Columbia University Press, 2012.

References and further reading

Foucault, Michel, *The History of Sexuality: Volume I. An Introduction* [1976], trans. Robert Hurley, Harmondsworth: Penguin, 1981.

Irigaray, Luce, *This Sex Which Is Not One* [1977], trans. Catherine Porter, with Carolyn Burke, Ithaca, NY: Cornell University Press, 1985.

Wittig, Monique, *Les Guérillères* [1969], trans. David Le Vay, London: Peter Owen, 1971.

JOHN D. CAPUTO (B. 1940)

Religious studies has taken a distinctive turn to the postmodern in recent years, finding the latter's anti-rational bias to be quite congenial to its subject. Religion has traditionally placed faith above mere reason, and for the faculty of reason to be called into question is to make it easier to argue the case of faith – even if that is not necessarily the point intended by most postmodern theorists, for whom religion in the main constitutes a grand narrative of the kind to which they are opposed. Religions, after all, usually come complete with a code of principles by which to live your life (they often have a bias towards theocracy in this respect), and do not in the main allow any serious questioning of those principles. Yet postmodernism's critique of reason, and return of interest in the sublime as a critical factor in human existence, particularly in the work of Jean-François Lyotard, at the very least opens up the possibility of dialogue between it and religious studies. One of the most important voices in this change of direction has been John D. Caputo, who has adapted certain elements of deconstruction for use in his work, and it has to be conceded that deconstruction does lend itself well to such an exercise. One of Caputo's most recent books is the splendidly named *What Would Jesus Deconstruct?*, which sets itself the task, alarming as this undoubtedly will sound to the religious establishment, of 'giving the spiritual journey some postmodern teeth' (Caputo 2007: 39).

Caputo uses Jacques Derrida to interesting effect in his essay 'Temporal Transcendence: The Very Idea of *à venir* in Derrida', in the edited collection *Transcendence and Beyond: A Postmodern Inquiry* (Caputo and Scanlon 2007), where he relates the concept of *à venir* ('to-come') both to democracy and to Christian belief – particularly the belief in the second coming of Christ. What we have to face in both instances, Caputo argues, is that '[t]he very idea of the to come is the idea of what does *not* come – of what is coming but never comes. It never actually and indeed shows up' (Caputo and Scanlon 2007: 196). This constitutes an intriguing application of Derrida's concept of *différance* to Christian belief, in this case representing our hope of the second coming and the unlikelihood of its ever being experienced, since it would spell the end of the future and time itself. The second coming must always be in a state of being deferred, with Caputo insisting that '[t]he very idea of the messianic is to keep the future open, which is possible only with the deferral of his appearance' (Caputo and Scanlon 2007: 196). (Democracy undergoes the same treatment, turning into 'just a way of keeping the future open' (Caputo and Scanlon 2007: 195).)

It is an ingenious argument, recalling Derrida's rejection of the notion of logocentricity on the grounds that the sign could never attain the totality this would require – 'half of it always "not there", and the other half always "not that"', as Gayatri Chakravorty Spivak neatly put it in her Introduction to Derrida's *Of Grammatology* (Derrida 1976: xvii). Whether it would ever convince religious sceptics is another issue: another way of putting Caputo's argument would be to say that it lacks proof for what it believes in, and that in fact such proof could never be forthcoming. From a postmodernist perspective, however, the second coming takes on the characteristics of the sublime, which similarly lies beyond all notions of proof. Postmodernist thinkers like Lyotard insist that we acknowledge the presence of the sublime in our lives, and it forms a key role in their critique of what might be called the imperialism of rationality (see Lyotard, *Lessons on the Analytic of the Sublime*, for example).

Caputo claims there is a 'religious side' to Derrida's work which comes to the fore in notions like *à venir*, although he does not interpret it in any conventional sense: 'this religion has nothing to do with going to heaven. The very idea of the to-come is the very idea of life in time, of hope and expectation, of prayers and tears, of being toward a future that does not and will not arrive' (Caputo and Scanlon 2007: 198). Somehow one can't see this much pleasing traditionalists either, never mind religious sceptics. In many ways, Caputo's vision of divinity and its role in human affairs seems closer to Samuel Beckett's *Waiting for Godot* than it does to the Bible, with Jesus cast in the unlikely role of Godot, which is hardly how the religious establishment perceives the concept of belief or the message it wants to pass on to humankind.

Caputo has developed a very distinctive approach to religious belief entitled 'weak theology', which he describes as follows:

> On the classical account of strong theology, Jesus was just holding back his divine power in order to let his human nature suffer. He freely chose to check his power because the Father had a plan to redeem the world with his blood. ... That is not the weakness of God that I am here defending. God, the event harbored by the name of God, is present at the crucifixion, as the power of the powerlessness of Jesus, in and as the protest against the injustice that rises up from the cross, in and as the words of forgiveness, not a deferred power that will be visited upon one's enemies at a later time. God is in attendance as the weak force of the call that cries out from Calvary and calls across the epochs, that cries out from every corpse created by every cruel and unjust power.
>
> (Caputo 2006a: 44)

This is very firmly a New Testament rather than Old Testament vision of God, with the emphasis on salvation rather than vengeance, on divine forgiveness rather than anger; but it is fair to say that for the fundamentalist wing of Christianity the latter is the one most preferred nowadays. Caputo's line, however, is that the advent of postmodernity has made it possible to rejuvenate religious studies, offering it the chance to connect with the major socio-political debates of the day and take on a new relevance.

As to what Jesus *would* deconstruct, Caputo suggests that he would start with organised religion itself, particularly as practised by the Christian Right in America, with its simplistic assumption that if we keep asking ourselves, 'What would Jesus do?' we are paving the way to a better society. Caputo will have none of this, remarking tartly:

> What would Jesus do [WWJD]? He would deconstruct a very great deal of what people do in the name of Jesus, starting with the people who wield this question like a hammer to beat their enemies. My hypothesis is that the first thing that Jesus would deconstruct is WWJD itself, the whole 'industry', the whole commercial operation of spiritual and very real money-making Christian capitalists.
>
> (Caputo 2007: 31)

For Caputo, the arrival of Jesus on the scene would constitute an 'event' in the deconstructive sense of the term, something that would disrupt the order of what was taking place in the world of belief, that would challenge its assumptions. The gap between what Jesus preached and what the church actually practises is to be regarded as a deconstructive aporia that can never be breached, an aporia which ought to make us aware of the church's failings. So great is that gap that exists that Caputo feels compelled to conclude that Jesus would have no option but to deconstruct the church itself, provocatively claiming that this would be very much to the church's benefit, since it was only ever designed to be a provisional entity anyway until the second coming. The church 'occupies the space of the "deferral," of the distance or "difference," between two comings' (Caputo 2007a: 35).

Whether it makes sense to speak of the second coming if it has to remain in a state of constant deferral, as Caputo is arguing elsewhere, is, however, a question that Enlightenment 'realists' can hardly avoid asking. Neither will Caputo's arguments on this issue endear him much to America's evangelicals, for whom the 'rapture' is an imminent event, eagerly awaited, when the faithful will be conveyed instantly up to heaven and God's vengeance will be exacted on all others left on Earth. For such a community, postmodernity is patently *not* good news, and Caputo's jaunty tone in delivering such heresy – as hardline evangelicals will receive it, anyway – will grate considerably. Caputo's iconoclastic approach to Christian doctrine does leave him dangerously exposed to attack from both believers and non-believers alike, but it is not uncommon for postmodernism to generate such a wide diversity of opponents.

While there is no denying the ingenuity of Caputo's application of deconstruction to religious studies, one can come away from his work wondering why we need a God at all. Rather as Foucault reduces the author to 'a function of discourse' (Foucault 1977: 124), God in Caputo comes across as little more than a God-function in a religious discourse. From an atheistic perspective, Caputo raises more questions than he answers, and to speak of God's 'weakness' is effectively to play right into an atheist's hands: God, after all, is supposed to be omnipotent, not a 'weak force' echoing over human history – never mind a human history scarred by countless acts of cruelty and injustice against the most vulnerable of humanity. To appropriate another contemporary frame of reference, this is God as something like dark matter; necessary to underpin a certain vision of the universe, but so far unlocatable and undetectable, existing in a theoretical world only and in danger of being overtaken by another theory if some evidence of its existence is not soon forthcoming.

What one has to concede, however, is the sheer fascination that the realm of the religious has been able to exert on humanity throughout human history, and its ability to engage with new critical theories and philosophies no matter how apparently secular they might appear to be. A deconstructive God is just as plausible as an existentialist one, and Caputo makes as persuasive a case for his choice as circumstances allow.

Caputo's major writings

Caputo, John D., *The Mystical Element in Heidegger's Thought*, Athens, OH: Ohio University Press, 1978.

——, *Against Ethics – Contributions to a Poetics of Obligation with Constant Reference to Deconstruction*, Bloomington, IN: Indiana University Press, 1993.

——, *Radical Hermeneutics: Repetition, Deconstruction and the Hermeneutic Project*, Bloomington, IN: Indiana University Press, 1993.

——, *The Prayers and Tears of Jacques Derrida*, Bloomington, IN: Indiana University Press, 1997.

——, *The Weakness of God: A Theology of the Event*, Bloomington, IN: Indiana University Press, 2006a.

——, *Philosophy and Religion*, Nashville, TN: Abingdon Press, 2006b.

——, *What Would Jesus Deconstruct?: The Good News of Postmodernity for the Church*, Grand Rapids, MI: Baker Academic, 2007.

Caputo, John D. and Gianni Vattimo, *After the Death of God*, ed. Jeffrey W. Robbins, New York and Chichester: Columbia University Press, 2007.

Caputo, John D. and Michael J. Scanlon (eds), *God, The Gift and Postmodernism*, Bloomington, IN: Indiana University Press, 1999.

——(eds), *Transcendence and Beyond: A Postmodern Inquiry*, Bloomington, IN: Indiana University Press, 2007.

References and further reading

Beckett, Samuel, *Waiting for Godot*, in *The Complete Dramatic Works*, London and Boston: Faber and Faber, 1986.

Derrida, Jacques, *Of Grammatology* [1967], trans. Gayatri Chakravorty Spivak, Baltimore, MD and London: Johns Hopkins University Press, 1976.

Foucault, Michel, 'What Is an Author?', in *Language, Counter-Memory, Practice*, ed. Donald F. Bouchard, trans. Donald F. Bouchard and Sherry Simon, Ithaca, NY: Cornell University Press, 1977, pp. 113–38.

Lyotard, Jean-François, *Lessons on the Analytic of the Sublime* [1991], trans. Elizabeth Rottenberg, Stanford, CA: Stanford University Press, 1994.

HÉLÈNE CIXOUS (B. 1937)

Cultural theorist, critic, novelist and playwright, Cixous's work is unmistakably interdisciplinary, Verena Andermatt Conley describing her as 'a *writer* who blurs the accepted lines between styles, modes and genres' (Conley 1992: xiii). Her main theme is how writing can be deployed to overcome patriarchal oppression. She is a key player in the development of difference feminism, itself a key part of second-wave feminism, which has taken a notably more assertive stance to the issue of gender relations than its first-wave counterparts, such as Simone de Beauvoir. Difference feminism involves the application of deconstructionist and other poststructuralist techniques to feminism, and, as the term suggests, emphasises the factor of difference between the sexes. Deconstruction feels that we live in a society which chooses to suppress difference, and takes it as a major part of its brief to make us aware of the pervasiveness of difference in our lives. In that respect, difference feminism is a logical extension of the deconstruction exercise, which in turn can be subsumed under postmodernism in general, where the defence and promotion of difference are a central concern of all the major theorists.

As a playwright, Cixous worked particularly closely with the Théâtre du Soleil company in France in the 1980s. She has also written extensively about various literary figures, including the Brazilian Clarice Lispector, with whom she feels a special affinity (see *Reading with Clarice Lispector*), and a recent study of Samuel Beckett, *Zero's Neighbour*. Postcolonial issues are addressed in her plays, although she can be critical of postmodernism.

Cixous makes a point of the need for a gender-specific quality to writing, advocating the development of a specifically female form of writing, an *écriture féminine* that will break with the male-oriented tradition:

> I shall speak about women's writing: about *what it will do*. Woman must write her self: must write about women and bring women to writing, from which they have been driven away as violently as from their bodies – for the same reasons, by the same law, with the same fatal goal. Woman must put herself into the text – as into the world and into history – by her own movement. ... I write woman: woman must write woman. And man, man.
>
> (Cixous 1981: 245, 247)

As in the work of Luce Irigaray, this raises the spectre of biological essentialism, which not all feminists are happy to be identified with (Judith Butler, amongst others, complains of just this in *Gender*

Trouble), feeling that it undermines their attempts to achieve equality with men in the public domain. Separate development would seem to render such campaigns largely redundant, and the male powers-that-be could well take advantage of that to deflect attempts to change the existing system. However, at least one commentator on Cixous's work, Sandra M. Gilbert, has repudiated that interpretation, inviting us instead to view *écriture féminine* as 'a fundamentally political strategy' on Cixous's part, that is 'designed to redress the wrongs of a culture through a revalidation of the rights of nature' (Introduction to Cixous and Clément 1987: xv). Put that way, Cixous's aim is to encourage women to make their voice known and not to allow men to dominate the field of public discourse, as they invariably have done historically. To campaign for an *écriture féminine*, therefore, is to seek to subvert the assumption of superiority built into patriarchal culture.

'The Laugh of the Medusa' puts the case for a new kind of writing by women that will help to undermine the alliance that for Cixous exists between logocentrism and phallocentrism. The accusation is that throughout Western history 'writing has been run by a libidinal and cultural – hence political, typically masculine – economy' (Cixous 1981: 249). Furthermore, writing has traditionally been associated with 'reason', which is castigated as an essentially phallo-centric discourse. Unless women are writing specifically for women, and rewriting the history of women, this repression will continue, putting writing in the frontline of the struggle against patriarchy: 'A feminine text cannot fail to be more than subversive. It is volcanic; as it is written it brings about an upheaval of the old property crust, carrier of masculine investments' (Cixous 1981: 258).

It is in *The Newly Born Woman*, co-authored with Catherine Clément, that *écriture féminine* is outlined in most detail. Part 1 of the book is by Clément, Part 2 by Cixous, and Part 3 consists of a dialogue between the two. Part 1, 'The Guilty One', firmly sets the polemical tone for the book by emphasising how our picture of women in history, including the stories and myths of women that have been handed down through the generations, has, until very recently, been filtered almost entirely through men: 'One must go through the audience of writers, psychiatrists and judges to recon-stitute the mythical stage on which women played their ambiguous role' (Cixous and Clément 1987: 5). Women have to start recounting this history from their own point of view, to deliver 'a history read differently' (Cixous and Clément 1987: 6) than the received one.

In Part 2, 'Sorties', Cixous explores the implications for feminism of the ubiquity of binary concepts, and the oppositions they set up, in

Western culture. Philosophy, she suggests, 'is marked by an absolute *constant* which orders values and which is precisely this opposition, activity/passivity' (Cixous and Clément 1987: 64). Women are always classified under passivity, signalling a male–dominated world where women have no real authority. Identifying a 'solidarity between logocentrism and phallocentrism' (Cixous and Clément 1987: 65), Cixous ponders on what would happen if this became widely acknowledged, echoing the point made earlier by Clément that 'all the history, all the stories would be there to retell differently; the future would be incalculable; the historic forces would and will change hands and change body' (Cixous and Clément 1987: 65). The binary of activity/passivity has systematically erased the difference of women from history to entrench masculine domination, where women are reduced to being 'the non-social, non-political, nonhuman half of the living structure' (Cixous and Clément 1987: 66). Within that culture female desire has always been suppressed, and women's bodies 'have been colonized' (Cixous and Clément 1987: 68). *Écriture féminine* is designed to alter that state of affairs, bringing women into history on their own terms, and bisexuality is put forward by both writers as a method of breaking away from the power of the repressive binaries on which so much of our culture is structured.

Taking issue with Sigmund Freud, Cixous insists that sexual difference is not just a matter of anatomy, rather it 'becomes most clearly perceived on the level of *jouissance*, inasmuch as a woman's instinctual economy cannot be identified by a man or referred to the masculine economy' (Cixous and Clément 1987: 82). This is a point also firmly made by Luce Irigaray in *This Sex Which Is Not One*. Cixous rejects the notions of destiny, nature and essence, seeing these as the product of particular cultural formations in history, insisting that we can change and reinvent history to overcome these beliefs, which she regards as part of our legacy of phallocentrism. Looking into the future, she sees the possibility of a significant cultural shift occurring, with difference coming into its own and even generating many new differences in its wake. However, on a more pessimistic note, she remarks that 'we are still floundering – with few exceptions – in Ancient History' (Cixous and Clément 1987: 83). Hence the emphasis she lays on the need to make woman's voice more widely heard through writing.

Cixous's prose style is highly poetic, and all her descriptions of *écriture féminine* are phrased in that register. In *Coming to Writing*, for example, she pictures the state of expressing herself as follows: 'Let yourself go, let the writing flow, let yourself steep; bathe, relax, become the river, let everything go, open up, unwind, open the floodgates, let yourself roll' (Cixous 1991: 56–7). She also speaks of 'the uncalculated writing of our wild and populous texts' (Cixous 1991: 58), which suggests that *écriture féminine* should be more emotionally, perhaps even subconsciously, based than male writing, less concerned to fit into rational norms. This can be challenging to her readers, with Eric Prenowitz referring in his Foreword to an English edition of Cixous's plays to 'the resistance to translation for which her texts are known' (Cixous 2004: viii). In her Introduction to *Coming to Writing*, Susan Rubin Suleiman sees similarities between Cixous's remarks here and the Surrealist Manifesto's defence of automatic writing, wondering whether this might be an attempt on the author's part 'to rewrite the avant-garde by feminizing it!' (Cixous 1991: x). Cixous ponders on the qualities required for *écriture féminine*: 'Continuity, abundance, drift – are these specifically feminine? I think so' (Cixous 1991: 57). Although interestingly she does not rule out male writers exhibiting these features in their work; it would mean that in at least some of them 'femininity is not forbidden' (Cixous 1991: 57).

Cixous's *Portrait of Jacques Derrida as a Young Jewish Saint* explores the Algerian Jewish heritage that they both share. Like Derrida (see his *Monolingualism of the Other*) she is very aware of being an outsider in French cultural life, with a background that is not consistent with the metanarrative of French history. Neither do they really 'belong' in Algeria any more, now that it is an independent Islamic state and no longer a constituent part of the French nation. Identity is a very fluid notion under such circumstances, something always in a process of becoming; a point that comes through forcefully in the work of each writer.

Despite a critical attitude towards postmodernism, Cixous's work does seem to have very similar concerns overall, particularly the emphasis on difference and the opposition to the West's prevailing cultural metanarrative. The dominant characteristic of that metanarrative for her is that it is phallocentric, and unless that issue is addressed she does not feel that a truly significant alteration will take place in the way that our society is organised.

Cixous's major writings

Cixous, Hélène, 'The Laugh of the Medusa' [1975], in Elaine Marks and Isabelle de Courtivron (eds), *New French Feminisms*, Brighton: Harvester, 1981, pp. 245–64.
——, *Angst* [1977], trans. Jo Levy, New York: Riverrun, 1985.

——, *Reading with Clarice Lispector*, trans. and ed. Verena Andermatt Conley, Minneapolis, MN: University of Minnesota Press, 1990.

——, *'Coming to Writing,' and Other Essays*, trans. Deborah Jenson, Cambridge, MA and London: Harvard University Press, 1991.

——, *Portrait of Jacques Derrida as a Young Jewish Saint* [2001], trans. Beverley Bie Brabic, New York and Chichester: Columbia University Press, 2004a.

——, *The Selected Plays Of Hélène Cixous*, ed. Eric Prenowitz, London and New York: Routledge, 2004b.

——, *Stigmata: Escaping Texts*, London and New York: Routledge, 2005.

——, *White Ink: Interviews on Sex, Text and Politics*, ed. Susan Sellers, Durham: Acumen, 2008.

——, *Zero's Neighbour: Sam Beckett* [2007], trans. Laurent Milesi, Cambridge and Malden, MA: Polity Press, 2010.

——, *Volleys of Humanity: Essays 1972–2009*, ed. Eric Prenowitz, Edinburgh: Edinburgh University Press, 2011.

Cixous, Hélène and Catherine Clément, *The Newly Born Woman* [1975], trans. Betsy Wing, Manchester: Manchester University Press, 1987.

References and further reading

Butler, Judith, *Gender Trouble: Feminism and the Subversion of Identity*, London and New York: Routledge, 1990.

Conley, Verena Andermatt, *Hélène Cixous*, Hemel Hempstead: Harvester Wheatsheaf, 1992.

Derrida, Jacques, *Monolingualism of the Other; or, The Prosthesis of Origin* [1996], trans. Patrick Mensah, Stanford, CA: Stanford University Press, 1998.

Irigaray, Luce, *This Sex Which Is Not One* [1977], trans. Catherine Porter, with Carolyn Burke, Ithaca, NY: Cornell University Press, 1985.

GUY DEBORD (1931–94)

A writer, theorist and filmmaker, Debord was one of the major figures in the Situationist movement, which came to be a major source of the inspiration behind the 1968 Paris *événements*, a phenomenon which resonated very strongly amongst the French intellectual community, helping to shape the character of much poststructuralist and postmodern thought. The movement itself disbanded in 1972, closing down its house journal at the same time. Debord's main work, *The Society of the Spectacle* (later to form the basis for a film of the same name by Debord), was a highly influential text during this period, and as he commented a quarter of a century later in his preface to the third French edition: 'This book should be read bearing in mind that it was written with the deliberate intention of doing harm to spectacular society. There was never anything outrageous, however, about what it had to say' (Debord 1995: 10). The spontaneity of the *événements* represented a definite departure from traditional left-wing methods of challenging the establishment, catching them very much by surprise. It was no less a surprise to the French Communist Party (PCF), which advocated careful planning for any revolutionary activity rather than the unruly outburst which marked the *événements*. Marxists have traditionally been very suspicious of all forms of spontaneity in the political arena, putting their faith instead in centralised power.

In its publications Situationism made extensive use of advertising images, which were often altered or painted over by artists like Asger Jorn, a technique known as *détournement* which subsequently had a considerable influence on the underground press of the 1960s and 1970s. The idea was that this process distorted the message contained in the original image by diverting it from its intended objective. Another concept the Situationists employed was that of the *dérive*, the act of drifting through an urban landscape led by one's feelings, which had an affinity with Charles Baudelaire's notion of the *flâneur* (see Baudelaire 1995: 4). The *dérive* was designed to map out the 'psychogeography' of the cityscape; that is, what the particular surroundings we found ourselves in evoked in us.

With its short, numbered, theses and many eminently quotable lines, *The Society of the Spectacle* is a very effective piece of polemic, as its role in the *événements* amply proved. Consider, for example, theses 34 and 124: 'The spectacle is *capital* accumulated to the point where it becomes image'; 'Revolutionary theory is now the sworn enemy of all revolutionary ideology – *and it knows it*' (Debord 1995: 24, 90). Debord's claim in the work was that the impact of consumer culture and its signs and images had become so powerful that we no longer had any effective control over our own lives: 'The whole life of those societies in which modern conditions of production prevail presents itself as an immense accumulation of *spectacles*. All that once was directly lived has become mere representation' (Debord 1995: 12). This development could be thought of as something of a modern version of 'bread and circuses' perhaps, by which the population was being deflected away from challenging the socio-political status quo. With the spread of modern media, that tendency has become ever more pronounced. That notion of reality being replaced by 'mere representation' will resurface in the work of many postmodernist thinkers, as in Jean Baudrillard's concept of 'simulation' (see Baudrillard 1983).

Debord is in no doubt as to the dangers posed by the spectacle, referring to it as the sector of society that 'is the locus of illusion and false consciousness' (Debord 1995: 12). Even communism falls victim to this process, presenting us with 'an *image of the working class*' (Debord 1995: 69) rather than that class as it actually is (Debord finds little of value in the communist project as a whole). The spectacle's role is to keep us ideologically enslaved, and unless we are on our guard against its effect, it becomes the basis for all our social relationships. The spectacle is to be understood as 'a world view transformed into an objective force. ... [T]he total practice of one particular economic and social formation' (Debord 1995: 13, 15) that manipulates us at will. Lyotard is later to conceive of 'grand narrative' (Lyotard 1984: xxiii) in much the same way, although he considers it to be in a much weaker state than Debord does, indeed as no longer communicating any sign of credibility and thus losing the hold it formerly had over much of the population.

The spectacle operates now largely through the economic realm: Debord seems to have foreseen the meteoric rise of neoliberalism and globalisation in this respect, referring to how the spectacle is 'turning the whole planet into a single world market' (Debord 1995: 27). There is no way any of us can escape the realm of the economic, and we are drawn into the consumer culture that it promotes so aggressively – a factor of even greater significance in twenty-first-century life than when *The Society of the Spectacle* was first being published. Debord wants us to recognise the extent to which we are now living under the sway of 'commodity fetishism' (Debord 1995: 26). What this means is that we are never really free of the spectacle, since it is now controlling our leisure time as well through our purchase of consumer goods. The resultant situation is one where 'the individual's own gestures are no longer his own, but rather those of someone else who represents them to him' (Debord 1995: 23). Presciently enough, Debord regards consumerism as essentially an isolating activity, especially when it involves advanced technological products such as cars and television. The new technology of the last couple of decades, with its increasingly personalised products like mobile phones, personal stereos and iPads, is even more isolating than that, as many social commentators have been noting with a certain amount of dismay.

Comments on the Society of the Spectacle went on to complain that the spectacle was even more in charge twenty years later. Noting that the various uprisings of 1968 had failed to effect significant change in any country, Debord has to admit that 'the spectacle has thus continued to gather strength; that is, to spread to the furthest limits on all sides, while increasing its density in the centre' (Debord 1998: 2–3). Then in the 1992 Preface to *The Society of the Spectacle* he cites the fall of the Soviet Empire as yet further proof of the spectacle's growing power over our lives, enabling 'the current *ideology* of democracy' (Debord 1995: 9), as he describes it, to present a unified face to the world.

Considerations on the Assassination of Gérard Lebovici provides an intriguing insight into Debord's relationship with, and place within, French society, as well as the lingering suspicions that remained attached to his reputation well after the *événements* and the disbandment of the Situationist International (a topic dealt with by Debord in *The Real Split in the International*). Lebovici was a well-known film producer and publisher, particularly of left-wing authors like Debord, who was murdered in mysterious circumstances in Paris in 1984. The press ran a series of sensationalist stories about possible motives for the crime that eventually led to Debord, a friend of Lebovici, being questioned by the police as a likely suspect. Debord's response to what rapidly turned into a media circus, with accusations flying back and forth between left and right, was to launch a savage attack on the press in *Considerations*:

> Nothing, however, in more than 30 years of false ignorance and blatant lies, was so concentrated and so inept in its spectacular falseness as the reports that the French press on all sides resorted to in the aftermath of March 5, 1984, the day that Gérard Lebovici, my publisher and friend, was drawn into an ambush and assassinated in Paris.
>
> (Debord 2001: 2)

Delivered in a tone of biting sarcasm, the book is a sustained exercise in reputation-clearing, on behalf of both Debord and Lebovici, with Debord dismissing out of hand a series of falsehoods, such as that Lebovici 'was one of the masterminds behind the Situationist International' (Debord 2001: 4) at the time of the *événements*, pointing out that they did not even meet until three years after that. Not surprisingly, Debord treats the whole episode as a glaring example of 'the society of the spectacle's specious reasonings' (Debord 2001: 14). Lebovici's murder was never solved.

Debord's work raises the same problem that so often comes to the fore in poststructuralist/postmodernist thought: that the enemy it describes is presented as so powerful a force, with such an iron grip on the mode of production and the mass media, that it is difficult to see how it can be overcome. Power, as he notes, 'has always had a spectacular aspect' (Debord 1992: 20) when we look back in history. But we are now confronted by something far more sophisticated than earlier generations had to face, with Debord's writing reporting a steady increase in the spectacle's reach over the last few decades of the twentieth century. It is all too easy to be overwhelmed by this state of affairs and to take refuge in pessimism or cynicism – as many post-structuralist/postmodernist thinkers have been accused of doing. We seem to be only too effectively enslaved and rendered unable to prevent the continued growth of the spectacle's power. As Debord sees it, '[t]he spectacle manifests itself as ... out of reach and beyond dispute' (Debord 1992: 15). To be told that '[t]he spectacle is by definition immune from human activity' (Debord 1992: 17) is hardly to offer much in the way of hope or encouragement to those who may be desperate to escape from the spectacle's control. Debord puts his faith in workers' councils, but there is little sign of this idea taking off – unless one considers this to be what happened, briefly and unsuccessfully, in the *événements*.

The spectacle comes across in Debord as a gigantic, and hugely successful, conspiracy, always able to adapt itself to absorb new technological developments and turn these to its own ends: as Debord more than somewhat ominously informs us, 'the spectacle is everywhere' (Debord 1992: 23). That is certainly the picture we are left with after *Considerations*, where a beleaguered Debord, his revolutionary days well behind him, nevertheless finds himself pursued by a ruthless state-spectacle that appears able to act with impunity, mobilising the media to carry out its agenda. So the spectacle is not only everywhere, but it never forgets either, and that holds a sobering lesson for radicals everywhere.

Debord's major writings

Debord, Guy, *Panegyric* [1989], trans. James Brook, London: Verso, 1992.
——, *The Society of the Spectacle* [1967], trans. Donald Nicholson-Smith, New York: Zone Books, 1995.
——, *Comments on the Society of the Spectacle* [1988], trans. Malcolm Imrie, London: Verso, 1998.
——, *Considerations on the Assassination of Gérard Lebovici* [1985], trans. Robert Greene, Los Angeles: TamTam Books, 2001.
——, *Complete Cinematic Works: Scripts, Stills, Documents* [1978], trans. and ed. Ken Knabb, Edinburgh: AK Press, 2003.

——, *The Real Split in the International: Situationist International* [1972], trans. John McHale, London: Pluto Press, 2003.

——, *A Sick Planet* [2004], trans. Donald Nicholson-Smith, London: Seagull, 2008.

——, *Correspondence: The Foundation of the Situationist International (June 1957–August 1960)* [1999], Los Angeles: Semiotext(e), 2009.

——, *Report on the Construction of Situations* [June 1957], trans. Ken Knabb, *Situationist International Online*, http:// www.cddc.vt.edu/sionline/si/report.html (accessed 24 October 2012).

References and further reading

Baudelaire, Charles, *The Painter of Modern Life and Other Essays*, trans. Jonathan Mayne, London and New York: Phaidon Press, 1995.

Baudrillard, Jean, *Simulations*, trans. Paul Foss, Paul Patton and Philip Beitchman, New York: Semiotext(e), 1983.

Lyotard, Jean-François, *The Postmodern Condition: A Report on Knowledge* [1979], trans. Geoff Bennington and Brian Massumi, Manchester: Manchester University Press, 1984.

GILLES DELEUZE (1925–95) AND FÉLIX GUATTARI (1930–92)

Although they also published separately in their own specialist fields of philosophy and psychiatry, Deleuze and Guattari are probably best known in critical and cultural theory circles for their two jointly authored books, *Anti-Oedipus* and *A Thousand Plateaus*. The two works marked a distinctive break with political traditions such as Marxism, offering instead an anarchic programme to combat the forces of repression operating within late twentieth-century society. Collectively, those forces were dubbed 'Oedipus', and the authors' objective was to indicate ways in which 'Oedipus' could be subverted – as, for example, by the adoption of schizophrenic behaviour on the part of the individual. The suggestion was that the socio-political system would not cope with this, since it preferred us to have similar, compliant, personalities that it could monitor and control more easily in terms of a norm of behaviour which it could set. The two works are full of such maverick ideas, which, in the spirit of the aftermath of the 1968 *événements* in Paris, signal a turn away from the traditional left-wing notions of how to counter socio-political oppression, a move from the collective to the local and individual. It is an orientation that marks out postmodern thought in general, which can only regard the collective as at least potentially a source of authoritarian policies, preferring to put its faith in individual actions or small-scale political groupings (Jean-François Lyotard's 'little narratives' (Lyotard 1984: 60), for example).

Oedipus is an avowed enemy of desire, which for Deleuze and Guattari is a force that must be allowed expression: collectively, we constitute 'desiring machines' (Deleuze and Guattari 1983: 2). Yet Oedipus cannot allow this expression to occur because it would be unable to control it (desire being unpredictable), and above all it seeks to exert control and maintain its position of power over the population at large. Any behaviour threatening this will be prohibited: desire thus finds itself constantly being restricted and repressed. Psychiatry is for Deleuze and Guattari a key component in an Oedipal culture, based as the practice is on a model of what a normal, well-adjusted person should be, and its subsequent methods of constraining the individual into that pattern of behaviour. The end-result of psychiatric treatment, when successful according to its socially and politically determined objectives, is that desire is curbed and, as far as possible, tamed such that it presents no threat to the ruling order. Against this process Deleuze and Guattari recommend the adoption of 'schizoanalysis' (Deleuze and Guattari 1983: 296), which is designed to confound both psychiatry and the authorities lying behind it. The authors make a big point in their work of identity actually being a very fluid and flexible concept, rather than the fixed entity we are culturally conditioned to believe it is by 'Oedipus'.

They also draw attention to the problems posed by what they call the 'body without organs', this being described as 'the unproductive, the sterile, the unengendered, the unconsumable' (Deleuze and Guattari 1983: 8). Capitalism can be considered the body without organs of contemporary culture, existing parasitically on the productive efforts of everyone in that culture, 'thereby appropriating for itself all surplus production and arrogating to itself both the whole and the parts of the process, which now seem to emanate from it as a quasi cause' (Deleuze and Guattari 1983: 10). Desiring machines find themselves under the power of this insatiable system, as if serving it constituted their destiny in life.

A Thousand Plateaus recommends nomadism as a method of subverting authoritarian- and totalitarian-minded socio-political systems such as Oedipus confronts us with. Nomads are described as being 'deterritorialized' (Deleuze and Guattari 1988: 9), that is, as having no allegiance to particular tracts of land and therefore as not feeling any need to defend these as home territory against outsiders. If their group is in any way placed under threat, nomads can move away to avoid this. Adopted more widely, nomadism would lead to the withering away of the nation state, and with that most of the oppressive mechanisms we find ourselves plagued by at present. Just as Oedipus demanded normative behaviour, so its agents demanded the conditions by which this could be constantly policed, and nomadic behaviour did not fit its template. Modern cultures prefer to 'fix' the population in monitored areas such that they can be recorded and tracked for taxation purposes, or mobilised against any outside threat in a hurry, etc. Even minor disruptions of this routine, as with local Roma groups which do move around the country, can create unease amongst the authorities, who are continually pressing them to adopt a more settled lifestyle; that is, to conform to a particular model of social existence. The Roma never form any very large percentage of a national population now, and the reaction to them by the relevant authorities is very often out of proportion to any difficulty they have in dealing with their itinerant lifestyle, being more a product of the Oedipal consciousness and its desire for complete conformity at all times and in all places.

For Deleuze and Guattari, being nomadic is as much a metaphysical as a physical condition, involving a refusal to take up fixed positions on social or political matters that then trap us into predetermined courses of action – as the system actively encourages us to do. Instead, nomads are expected to keep any intellectual allegiances they may have as light as possible and to be willing to change these when circumstances alter; in effect, to migrate to another location. In the authors' view this would preclude any drift into authoritarian or totalitarian government, where political principles are defended in the face of all opposition – the tactic adopted by movements such as communism, which notoriously refuses to countenance any dissent from the party line and punishes harshly any of its adherents who offer a challenge to this. Both volumes are implicitly post-Marxist in tone, rejecting mass movements in favour of more local, even anarchic, responses to political problems, and they helped to set the tone for post-*événements* theory in French intellectual life, where the Marxist approach very rapidly became discredited.

Deleuze and Guattari present a strong argument against totality through their concept of the rhizome, which is capable of forming connections between any two points on its surface, and can be taken as a more creative method of organising systems. They differentiate this from the more traditional way of conceiving of systems, such as knowledge, in the form of a tree, with its rational and linear way of representing growth through branches stemming from the main body such that a clear line of influence can be seen. The development of the internet might be seen to bear out their views, given that it works in an essentially rhizomatic fashion, offering up endless possibilities for connecting disparate bodies of knowledge and information according to the individual's wishes. Hypertext, for example, can take whatever form the user chooses, and its trajectory cannot be determined in advance; it will differ with each user. As so often is the case in post-modern thought, the concern is to find a model for thought that is not linear but digressive, thus creating unpredictable states of affairs as it goes: Lyotard's image of thought as being like clouds (see *Peregrinations*) is similarly motivated.

What Is Philosophy? asserts that the subject should concern itself with 'forming, inventing, and fabricating concepts' (Deleuze and Guattari 1994: 2), and, crucially, 'concepts that are always new' (Deleuze and Guattari 1994: 5). Philosophy should have nothing to do with the commercial world and the market, the 'society of infor-mation services and engineering' (Deleuze and Guattari 1994: 11) as they dismissively refer to it; although, sadly enough, that is what humanities subjects are being pushed into doing these days by the powers-that-be of neoliberal capitalism, who seem bent on turning higher education into a 'factory' producing 'products' of proven economic worth, to be offered for sale to student 'consumers'. Deleuze and Guattari see philosophy as something far less predictable, a subject which, like art and science too, is 'always confronting chaos' (Deleuze and Guattari 1994: 197). It is a rather romantic view, but one that nevertheless deserves support in a culture that is increasingly being brought under the rule of the profit motive and cannot see value in anything which cannot be bought and sold on the market. Going back to the defence of nomadism in *A Thousand Plateaus*, the argument is that philosophers should resist any attempt to 'territorialise', or in other words tame, their subject.

Deleuze and Guattari's other collaboration, *Kafka: Towards a Minor Literature*, claims that we should regard Kafka's work as 'a rhizome, a burrow' (Deleuze and Guattari 1986: 3) that can be interpreted in any number of ways; the way they choose is to emphasise its political and culturally subversive aspect. As a Jew writing in German in Prague, for most of his life a part of the Austro-Hungarian empire, where German was the dominant language, but with a majority Czech-speaking population, Kafka finds himself working in 'a deterritor-ialized language, appropriate for strange and minor uses' (Deleuze and Guattari 1986: 17). This makes him an exponent of a 'minor literature', one of the main characteristics of which is that it cannot help but be political, whatever its subject may be. As a writer in 'the margins' Kafka is granted the opportunity 'to express another possible community and to forge the means for another consciousness and another sensibility' (Deleuze and Guattari 1986: 17), giving his work revolutionary potential.

Deleuze's writings have proved to be very influential since his death, and his ideas are now being widely applied across a broad range of disciplines, such as film studies, literary studies, and even religious studies. As well as a series of monographs on key figures in the history of philosophy (from Gottfried Leibniz, Immanuel Kant, and Friedrich Nietzsche, through to his contemporary Michel Foucault), he was the author of a two-volume work on cinema.

Deleuze's ideas on difference are outlined in detail in *Difference and Repetition*, often regarded as his most important work, where he takes issue with the notion of identity and how it always seems to take precedence over difference in Western thought:

> We tend to subordinate difference to identity in order to think it (from the point of view of the concept of the subject: for example, specific difference presupposes an identical concept in the form of a genus). We also have a tendency to subordinate it to resemblance (from the point of view of perception), to opposition (from the point of view of predicates), and to analogy (from the point of view of judgment). In other words, we do not think difference in itself.
>
> (Deleuze 1994: xv)

The defence and promotion of difference is one of the defining themes of postmodernism, which sees its suppression as one of the key aims of a modern society, where homogenisation is to the benefit of the ruling class. Foucault is making a similar point in his 'archae-ologies' tracing the rise of the asylum, prison and hospital systems in the West since the seventeenth century; Jacques Derrida too in his deconstruction of the structuralist enterprise; then Lyotard in his insistence that we respect the 'differend'. To seek 'difference in itself' as Deleuze does, therefore, is to go against the grain of modernity, as well as of those philosophies which have emerged from the Enlight-enment project, such as Marxism, with its belief in universalisation.

From universalising tendencies emerge figures such as 'the politi-cian, who is above all concerned to deny that which "differs", so as to conserve or prolong an established political order, or to establish a historical order which already calls forth in the world the forms of its representations' (Deleuze 1994: 53). Deleuze is a keen champion of those creative artists whose work breaks free from what that established order wants; in particular those who break with the tradition of realistic representation. Representation for Deleuze equals an affirmation of the world as it is seen by the mass, and thus by its ruling order; what Deleuze looks for in creative activity is the disturbance of that order. His own philosophical writing and collaborative efforts with Guattari seem designed to achieve the same kind of end, since the product in both cases so rarely conforms to the norms expected of academic philosophical discourse. In fact, he argues that philosophy as we have traditionally understood it is fast becoming outmoded: 'The time is coming when it will hardly be possible to write a book of philosophy as it has been done for so long: ... The search for a new means of philosophical expression was begun by Nietzsche, and must be pursued today in relation to the renewal of certain other arts, such as the theatre or the cinema' (Deleuze 1994: xxi).

Cinema goes on to become a major interest of Deleuze, and his two-volume work *Cinema I* and *Cinema II* has had a considerable impact in the field of film studies. The translators of *Cinema I* describe the project as 'a kind of intercutting of cinema and philosophy' (Deleuze 1986: xii). Deleuze himself announces that the study is to be regarded as 'a taxonomy, an attempt at the classification of images and signs' (Deleuze 1986: xiv), and declares a debt to the work of the American philosopher Charles Peirce on semiotics. The concern of volume I is with the movement-image, and here, as in volume II, Deleuze moves freely around cinematic history for examples to illustrate his theses, choosing 'great directors', who deserve to be treated as, above all, 'thinkers' (Deleuze 1986: xiv). What is striking here is not so much that idea itself, but that Deleuze is suggesting that such thought can claim the same status as philosophical thought. It is as if he is dismissing the notion, so generally held in traditional philosophical circles, that philosophy should be considered the metanarrative of thinking, the discipline that sets the criteria for all analytical thought. That is an activity Deleuze believes is no longer necessary, or particularly helpful for us in understanding the world; we are now in the world of post-philosophy, which requires a different approach.

Deleuze differentiates between pre- and post-World War Two cinema, arguing that this involves a shift from a cinema based on the movement-image to one based on the time-image. The latter marks a world that has become much less secure and understandable than the one that went before, hence Deleuze's decision to start the volume with neo-realist cinema, which grew out of the disorientation produced by the end of the war in Italy, and in so doing represented a clear break with the classic period. Neo-realism is for Deleuze defined by a 'build-up of purely optical situations (and sound ones, although there was no synchronized sound at the start of neo-realism), which are fundamentally distinct from the sensory-motor situations of the action-image in the old realism. It is perhaps as important as the conquering of a purely optical space in painting, with impressionism' (Deleuze 1989: 2). What we are faced with in neo-realism is a style that homes in on the 'fragmentary' and 'ephemeral' (Deleuze 1989: 1) aspects of the immediately postwar situation in Italy.

Throughout both volumes Deleuze insists that we have to form our concepts and theories about cinema from the cinematic experience itself, rather than just applying a theory developed outside that context to explain it. Cinema sets its own rules in this respect, 'there is something specific to it which has nothing to do with theatre' (Deleuze 1989: 263), and, unlike cinema, television is locked in the present. (Deleuze was writing before filmmakers like David Lynch had started to experiment with the television medium, as in *Twin Peaks*; Lynch's style seems to bear out many of the points that Deleuze is making about the nature of the time-image.) In postwar cinema, Deleuze contends, '[t]ime ceases to be derived from the movement, it appears in itself and itself gives rise to *false movements*' (Deleuze 1989: xi). Hence the extensive use of what Deleuze dubs 'irrational cuts' (Deleuze 1989: xi) in the editing process. The linear narratives of the classic period give way to something more disjointed.

An obvious objection to Deleuze's division of cinema into two main periods is that such things are rarely that clear cut (periodisation is almost always problematical). Not every director will fit into such a schema, although, as noted earlier, Deleuze himself is aware of this and concedes that he will be dealing with what he considers to be the medium's 'great directors'. Whether there would be general agreement as to who should count as 'great' is another issue; but there is no doubt that Deleuze has opened up a new perspective on film's history that invites response from and development by others working in the field.

Guattari was a key figure in the development of ecosophy, a term first put forward by the Norwegian 'deep ecology' theorist Arne Naess (see, for example, Naess 1989), which argued that we should strive to achieve a greater sense of harmony with our environment rather than ruthlessly exploiting it in the way that capitalism has urged us to. In similar vein, in his book *The Three Ecologies* Guattari argued that '[w]ithout modifications to the social and material environment, there can be no change in mentalities. Here, we are in the presence of a circle that leads me to postulate the necessity of founding an "ecosophy" that would link environmental ecology to social ecology and to mental ecology' (Guattari 2000: 27).

Guattari's last written work, *Chaosmosis*, sets out 'to forge a more transversalist conception of subjectivity' (Guattari 1995a: 4) in opposition to the kinds of subjectivity fostered by contemporary capitalism (including reactions to it such as religious fundamentalism). He sees himself as engaged in 'shifting the human and social sciences from scientific paradigms towards ethico-aesthetic paradigms' (Guattari 1995a: 10), on the grounds that science has far too powerful a hold on the contemporary imagination. Yet again there is a defence of 'desiring machines', and a critique of the world of 'Oedipus': 'Psychoanalysis is in crisis; it is bogged down in routine practices and ossified conceptions' (Guattari 1995a: 58). What we ought to be aiming for instead is a 'subjective resingularisation' (Guattari 1995a: 97) that will be immune to the dictates of 'Oedipus'.

Guattari was to express some serious doubts about the postmodern approach to politics in his later life (perhaps recalling his youthful Trotskyist sympathies), arguing that it lacked proper revolutionary intent and so posed little threat to the established order. In an interview he decries what he regards as 'the virtual ethical and aesthetic abdication of postmodern thought' (Guattari 1996: 116). Oedipus was still in overall control; although that could be put down to the lack of practical political advice being offered by thinkers such as Guattari and Deleuze, which leans towards advocating withdrawal from the system (by means of schizophrenia and nomadism, for example) rather than active confrontation with it. Much the same objection could be made, however, to others of Deleuze and Guattari's contemporaries, such as Lyotard and Derrida, and, come to that, of the postmodern movement generally. Even theories which directly address the issue of political agency and recasting the existing method of politics in our society, such as Ernesto Laclau and Chantal Mouffe's 'radical democracy' (see Laclau and Mouffe 1985), have been found wanting when it comes to specifics on this score. Guattari's ultimate solution was, as he described it in a book jointly written with Toni Negri, 'to rescue "communism" from its own disrepute' (Guattari and Negri 1990: 7), but events since 1985, when *Communists Like Us* was first published, hardly suggest there is much support for such a project.

Deleuze and Guattari's major writings

Deleuze, Gilles and Félix Guattari, *Anti-Oedipus: Capitalism and Schizophrenia* [1972], trans. Robert Hurley, Mark Seem and Helen R. Lane, Minneapolis, MN: University of Minnesota Press, 1983.

——, *Kafka: Towards a Minor Literature* [1975], trans. Dana Polan, Minneapolis, MN and London: University of Minnesota Press, 1986.

——, *A Thousand Plateaus: Capitalism and Schizophrenia* [1980], trans. Brian Massumi, London: Athlone Press, 1988.

——, *What Is Philosophy?*, trans. Hugh Tomlinson and Graham Burchell, London and New York: Verso, 1994.

Deleuze's major writings

Deleuze, Gilles, *Nietzsche and Philosophy* [1962], trans. Hugh Tomlinson, London: Athlone Press, 1983.

——, *Kant's Critical Philosophy: The Doctrine of the Faculties* [1963], trans. Hugh Tomlinson and Barbara Habberjam, Minneapolis, MN: University of Minnesota Press, 1985.

——, *Cinema I: The Movement-Image* [1983], trans. Hugh Tomlinson and Barbara Habberjam, Minneapolis, MN: University of Minnesota Press, 1986.

——, *Foucault* [1986], trans. Sean Hand, Minneapolis, MN: University of Minnesota Press, 1988.

——, *Cinema II: The Time-Image* [1985], trans. Hugh Tomlinson and Barbara Habberjam, Minneapolis, MN: University of Minnesota Press, 1989.

——, *The Fold: Leibniz and the Baroque* [1988], trans. Tom Conley, Minneapolis, MN: University of Minnesota Press, 1993.

——, *Difference and Repetition* [1968], trans. Paul Patton, London: Athlone Press, 1994.

——, *Essays Critical and Clinical* [1993], trans. Daniel W. Smith and Michael A. Greco, London and New York: Verso, 1998.

Guattari's major writings

Guattari, Félix, *Chaosmosis: An Ethicoaesthetic Paradigm* [1992], trans. Paul Bains and Julian Pefanis, Sydney: Power Publications, 1995a.

——, *Chaosophy: Texts and Interviews 1972–1977*, ed. Sylvère Lotringer, New York: Semiotext(e), 1995b.

——, *The Guattari Reader*, ed. Gary Genosko, Oxford and Cambridge, MA: Blackwell, 1996.

——, *The Three Ecologies* [1989], trans. Ian Pindar and Paul Sutton, London and New York: Continuum, 2000.

——, *The Anti-Oedipus Papers*, ed. Stephane Nadaud, trans. Kélina Gotman, New York: Semiotext(e), 2006.

——, *The Machinic Unconscious: Essays in Schizoanalysis* [1979], trans. Taylor Adkins, Los Angeles: Semiotext(e), 2011.

Guattari, Félix and Antonio Negri, *Communists Like Us: New Spaces of Liberty, New Lines of Alliance* [1985], trans. M. Ryan, New York: Semiotext(e), 1990.

References and further reading

Laclau, Ernesto and Chantal Mouffe, *Hegemony and Socialist Strategy: Towards a Radical Democratic Politics*, London and New York: Verso, 1985.
Lynch, David (dir.), *Twin Peaks*, 1990.
Lyotard, Jean-François, *The Postmodern Condition: A Report on Knowledge* [1979], trans. Geoff Bennington and Brian Massumi, Manchester: Manchester University Press, 1984.
——, *Peregrinations: Law, Form, Event*, New York: Columbia University Press, 1988.
Naess, Arne, *Ecology, Community and Lifestyle*, trans. David Rothenberg, Cambridge: Cambridge University Press, 1989.

JACQUES DERRIDA (1930–2004)

With his development of the technique of deconstruction, Derrida looms large over cultural theory and philosophical thought of the closing decades of the twentieth century. An academic in Paris, Derrida also maintained close links with American academic life, particularly at Yale University. Deconstruction emphasised the ambiguity of language and discourse, taking issue with structuralism's system-bound nature, and also positioning itself at the opposite end of the spectrum from analytical philosophy's search for linguistic precision in discourse. For deconstructionists such precision was an illusion; ambiguity was intimately bound up with both the use and the reception of language, which could never achieve full 'presence' of meaning in any communication, whether in spoken or written form. Words invariably hinted at other meanings, other contexts than the one of utterance – the process Derrida dubbed *différance*, playing on the fact that the verb *différer* could mean either 'differ' or 'defer'. The very notion of presence was to be called into question by Derrida, who developed a writing style making extensive use of puns and word-play in order to demonstrate its impossibility. It was a style which polarised critical opinion of the deconstructionist exercise, infuriating some while galvanising others into enthusiastic imitation (see Geoffrey H. Hartman's work, such as *Saving the Text*, for example).

Derrida did not see himself as founding yet another school of thought, but as pointing out the defects in other schools such as structuralism. His is an essentially tactical approach, which denies that deconstruction is a theory in any traditional sense, more a way of reading texts that reveals how they consistently undermine the assumptions on which their writing is based: 'deconstruction', as he puts it, 'interferes with solid structures' (Derrida 1987: 19). Among the 'solid structures' that it 'interfered' with was that of Western philosophy, the foundations of which were cast into doubt by language's persistent failure to achieve precision. If meaning could not be guaranteed, then no discourse could ever lay claim, never mind exclusive claim, to possession of the truth.

Derrida's early work opens a dialogue with Husserl and Heidegger that generates a different conception of phenomenology than was current at the time in the French philosophical tradition, a conception steering away from the existentialist insistence on anguish as an inescapable part of human experience. Structuralism is also an early target of Derrida's, particularly its totalising bias, which he is very critical of in *Writing and Difference*, one of the first works of his to create an impression in the English-speaking world. His attack on structuralist method in the collection's opening essay, 'Force and Signification', and then later on in the book, in 'Structure, Sign, and Play in the Discourse of the Human Sciences', lays down markers for the development of the poststructuralist ethos, with its dislike of systems claiming universal application and, with that, authority. The main criticism that Derrida has of structuralism is that its method predetermines the findings its analysis then goes on to make, and he views criticism in general as a deterministic activity that imposes its own principles on the works that it studies. As a case in point, the critic Jean Rousset analyses the work of the classic French playwright Corneille in terms of an assumed teleology, in which the author is edging ever closer to the full realisation of his artistic vision in the play *Polyeucte*:

> Everything transpires as if everything within the dynamics of Corneillean meaning, and within each of Corneille's plays, came to life with the aim of final peace, the peace of the structural *energeia*: *Polyeucte*. Outside this peace, before and after it, movement, in its pure duration, in the labor of its organization, can itself be only sketch or debris.
>
> (Derrida 1978: 21)

There is for Derrida an unmistakable sense of 'preformationism' (Derrida 1978: 21) in such an approach that is an unavoidable consequence of the belief in the existence of a 'deep structure' in an author's work. Structuralist criticism becomes a search for that deep structure, which will then explain the artist's entire oeuvre. Criticism in any era is, in fact, a quintessentially structuralist activity for this thinker, and deconstruction is designed to undermine its claims, to demonstrate that writing cannot be reduced to a teleology, that it consistently escapes such patterning.

A key element of Derrida's thought is his attack on what he calls the belief in the 'metaphysics of presence' in Western thought. This is the belief that discourse, spoken discourse in particular, succeeds in communicating words, and thus ideas, without any slippage of meaning occurring. The meanings of words and ideas are assumed to be fully present in the mind of both the speaker and the listener at the time of utterance. In terms of structuralist linguistics, derived from the theories of Ferdinand de Saussure in his posthumously published *Course in General Linguistics*, signifier (word) and signified (concept) combine in the speaker's and listener's mind to form a sign, where meaning is unambiguous. Derrida's interpretation of Saussurean linguistics, however, is that the sign can never attain this state of purity, that it is perpetually contaminated by other meanings and usages ('traces', as he puts it): under those circumstances, slippage of meaning cannot be avoided. Meaning is to be considered as inescapably plural and always in a state of becoming: never fully present, and incapable of ever being so. The sign, according to Gayatri Chakravorty Spivak, is a split entity: 'half of it always "not there" and the other half always "not-that"' (Introduction to Derrida 1976: xvii). To Derrida, this problematises the claims to authority of such discourses as Western philosophy, which depend very heavily on exactly that principle of full presence. Interpretation in that tradition is a matter of 'deciphering a truth or an origin which escapes play and the order of the sign', whereas for the deconstructionist interpretation 'affirms play and tries to pass beyond man and humanism' (Derrida 1978: 292).

The upshot of Derrida's questioning of the validity of presence and traditional styles of interpretation is to render the art of criticism all but impossible, and he attempts to demonstrate this through his writing on artworks, which continually defers the critical act as we normally understand it. Thus in *The Truth in Painting* an apparent analysis of what the phrase 'I owe you the truth in painting and I will tell it to you' (in a letter from Paul Cézanne to an acquaintance) might mean and how it might help us to understand Cézanne's work turns into series of digressive reflections that keep actual criticism at bay:

what must truth be in order to be *owed* [*due*], even be *rendered* [*rendue*]? In painting? And if it consisted, in painting, of *rendering*, what would one mean when one promised to render it itself as a due or a sum rendered [*un rendu*]? What does it mean, to render? What about restriction? And in painting?

(Derrida 1987a: 4)

The book continues in similar vein, writing '*around* painting' as Derrida describes it (Derrida 1987; 9), even when engaging with actual artworks such as Vincent Van Gogh's *Old Shoes with Laces*: 'What of shoes? What, shoes? Whose are the shoes? What are they made of? And even, who are they? Here they are, the questions, that's all' (Derrida 1987: 257). These are hardly the kind of considerations that would worry art critics, being at best a preliminary to interpretation of the painting and the artist's oeuvre and social context; but Derrida spins them out interminably, enacting deconstruction in his writing style, which deliberately flits from subject to subject in an association-of-ideas manner that his detractors find extremely irritating (not to mention highly unprofessional in an academic).

Derrida's style is often deliberately playful in this manner, the objective being to focus attention on what for him is language's inbuilt tendency to generate almost endless associations of ideas in listeners and readers; hence his extensive use of literary devices like puns, plus even more esoteric methods such as footnotes running the whole length of a text and thereby taking on lives of their own. The associations would of course differ markedly from listener to listener, reader to reader, and even in the same reader or listener at different times in their lives, which reinforces Derrida's point about the inevitability of linguistic slippage in any communication. To his detractors, however, this style of writing is game-playing for game-playing's sake, cavalier to the point of being insulting to his readers, particularly his academic peers. To his defenders, on the other hand, it is a demonstration of how language will always undermine criticism's pretensions to authority and linguistic precision.

Not surprisingly, such works as *The Truth in Painting*, and the style of commentary they embody, have generated huge controversy within the academic world, being dismissed as non-philosophical by many philosophy departments, and critically superficial by other humanities subjects such as literary studies. Yet they have also inspired many followers to offer imitations, as in the work of the high-profile 'Yale School' of literary critics: Harold Bloom, Geoffrey Hartman,

J. Hillis Miller and Paul de Man (see their collective effort with Derrida entitled *Deconstruction and Criticism*, for example).

Specters of Marx brings Derrida into the frame of post-Marxism, although with his characteristically iconoclastic approach to the topic very much in evidence. While conceding that Marx is a critical part of our cultural background, one which cannot be ignored by any serious cultural theorist, he also insists that he has left us with no unified message, and that he should instead be viewed as 'plural' – a typically poststructuralist demand, steering us away from any sense of purity of meaning. Marx, like any other thinker of note, can be interpreted in any number of ways, a point Derrida had made earlier about Martin Heidegger to challenge the notion of him as an essentially Nazi thinker (other major figures of French intellectual life such as Jean-François Lyotard strongly disagreeing with him on this particular issue). For Derrida, Heidegger too was to be considered plural; capable of being appropriated by either the right or the left. Yet again, any particular interpretation of Marx's works, and what they might mean to us in the later twentieth century, is studiously avoided by the author, who writes 'around Marx' in much the same manner that he did 'around painting'. Marx becomes the pretext for another of Derrida's linguistic *tours de force*. It is that persistent refusal to acknowledge the validity of authority, the desire to reveal just how shaky its foundations are, that positions Derrida firmly within the ambit of postmodernism.

Derrida's major writings

Derrida, Jacques, *'Speech and Phenomena' and Other Essays on Husserl's Theory of Signs* [1967], trans. David B. Allinson, Evanston, IL: Northwestern University Press, 1973.

——, *Of Grammatology* [1967], trans. Gayatri Chakravorty Spivak, Baltimore, MD and London: Johns Hopkins University Press, 1976.

——, *Writing and Difference* [1967], trans. Alan Bass, Chicago: University of Chicago Press, 1978.

——, *Spurs: Nietzsche's Styles* [1978], trans. Barbara Harlow, Chicago and London: University of Chicago Press, 1979.

——, *The Truth in Painting* [1978], trans. Geoff Bennington and Ian McLeod, Chicago and London: University of Chicago Press, 1981.

——, *Margins of Philosophy* [1972], trans. Alan Bass, Chicago: University of Chicago Press, 1982.

——, *Glas* [1974], trans. J. P. Leavey and R. Rand, Lincoln, NE and London: University of Nebraska Press, 1986.

——, *Dissemination* [1972], trans. Barbara Johnson, Chicago: University of Chicago Press, 1987a.

——, *The Post Card: From Socrates to Freud and Beyond* [1980], trans. Alan Bass, Chicago and London: University of Chicago Press, 1987b.
——, *Specters of Marx: The State of the Debt, the Work of Mourning, and the New International* [1993], trans. Peggy Kamuf, London: Routledge, 1994.

References and further reading

Bloom, Harold *et al.*, *Deconstruction and Criticism*, London and Henley: Routledge and Kegan Paul, 1979.
Hartman, Geoffrey H., *Saving the Text: Literature/Derrida/Philosophy*, Baltimore, MD and London: Johns Hopkins University Press, 1981.
Saussure, Ferdinand de, *Course in General Linguistics* [1916], ed. Charles Bally, Albert Sechehaye and Albert Reidlinger, trans. Wade Baskin, London: Peter Owen, 1960.

UMBERTO ECO (B. 1932)

Eco's work spans semiotic theory, cultural studies and creative literature, with his novel *The Name of the Rose* constituting an all but textbook example of the postmodern literary aesthetic in action, particularly as regards its use of the concept of double-coding as well as its playful and cleverly deployed intertextuality. For Brian McHale *The Name of the Rose* may be a 'text, queasily poised between modernism and postmodernism' (McHale 1992: 11), but that is a conclusion dependent on acceptance of McHale's classification system for the postmodern, as outlined initially in his study *Postmodernist Fiction*. That system aside, *The Name of the Rose* contains most of the narrative features we have come to expect in postmodern art, and in that sense can be taken as representative of the literary postmodern. The narrative mixes together medieval theology, Aristotelian and Platonic aesthetic theory, semiotic theory and crime fiction in such a way as to attract both popular and intellectual readers, and it was notably successful in doing so.

Eco's work is initially in the field of semiotics, which he taught for many years at the University of Bologna. His semiotic theories are outlined in a series of works, such as *A Theory of Semiotics*, *Semiotics and the Philosophy of Language* and *The Role of the Reader*. *A Theory of Semiotics* boldly proclaims: 'The aim of this book is to explore the theoretical possibility and the social function of a unified approach to every phenomenon of signification and/or communication' (Eco 1977: 3). For Eco this means formulating a theory of both codes and sign production, in what he intends to be a 'general semiotic theory'

(Eco 1977: 5) that will go beyond the model left to us by Ferdinand de Saussure in his *Course in General Linguistics* in its sophistication and scope. Eco outlines an ambitiously wide range of areas where he feels that semiotics can be studied, from 'zoosemiotics' (animal behaviour), at the lowest level, up through olfactory signs (scents), tactile communication and systems of objects, to more obvious areas such as mass communication and rhetoric. Since 'every aspect of culture becomes a semantic unit' (Eco 1977: 27), Eco puts forward the hypothesis that '[c]ulture can be studied completely under a semiotic profile' (Eco 1977: 28).

In *Semiotics and the Philosophy of Language* Eco positions himself in terms of the history of semiotic theory in order to develop his own particular, more open-ended, approach to the subject. He comes up with the image of the net and the labyrinth to describe semiotics' field of operation, the net being an object which admits of an infinite variety of routes by which to journey between any two points on its surface (akin, as Eco emphasises, to Gilles Deleuze and Félix Guattari's rhizome), whereas the traditional notion of the labyrinth offers only one true route from beginning to end: 'A net is an unlimited territory. ... The territory of the United States does not oblige anybody to reach Dallas from New York by passing through St. Louis; one can also pass through New Orleans. ... [T]he abstract model of a net has neither a center nor an outside' (Eco 1984b: 81). Narratives are to be regarded as open to multiple interpretations (as Roland Barthes had also insisted in *S/Z*), rather than as susceptible to being tied down to specific grammatical moves in the manner of high structuralist theory. For Eco, therefore, the 'universe of semiosis' has characteristics like the following:

> (a) It is structured according to a *network of interpretants*. (b) It is virtually *infinite* because it takes into account multiple interpretations realized by different cultures: a given expression can be interpreted as many times, and in as many ways, as it has been actually interpreted in a given cultural framework.
>
> (Eco 1984b: 83)

In *The Role of the Reader*, Eco explores the relationship between reader and text, insisting that the text can never be considered in isolation – as to some extent high structuralist critics believed (Eco takes issue with Claude Lévi-Strauss on this), and before them in the Anglo-Saxon tradition the New Critics, such as F. R. Leavis: 'To postulate the cooperation of the reader does not mean to pollute the structural analysis with extratextual elements. The reader as an active participant of interpretation is a part of the picture of the generative process of the text' (Eco 1981: 4). Eco is careful to make clear, however, that the reader is being steered towards certain interpretations by the text, although that still allows the reader considerable scope as to how s/he responds to the text's codes (how that relationship works in practice will be seen below when we explore Eco's most famous piece of fiction, *The Name of the Rose*). Distinguishing between 'closed' and 'open' texts, Eco rather counter-intuitively calls a text 'closed' when it admits of any number of readings. This occurs when an author assumes an 'average' reader who will follow a pre-determined path laid down by that author, but when the reader does not conform to that assumed average almost any reading at all, no matter how aberrant to the text, becomes possible. In trying to close off the reader's interpretative skills, the author paradoxically renders the text 'immoderately "open"' (Eco 1981: 8). Eco's version of an 'open' text is one that requires the reader to engage with the various interpretations it offers, while realising that s/he has to stay within those bounds laid down by the text: 'You cannot use the text as you want, but only as the text wants you to use it' (Eco 1981: 9). It is Eco's take on Roland Barthes's readerly/writerly distinction (see Barthes, *S/Z*).

The Name of the Rose is one of the most striking examples of double-coding in recent literature, being simultaneously a murder mystery/detective thriller, with a popular audience (the book has sold several million copies, been widely translated and adapted into a Hollywood film), as well as a disquisition on the opposing values of Platonic and Aristotelian aesthetics and the values of the medieval Christian church. Eco cleverly adapts semiotic theory to the murder mystery side of the narrative, with his detective figure, the monk William of Baskerville (a clear nod towards the Sherlock Holmes series here), trying to piece together the disparate collection of signs left behind after the murders in order to construct a trail leading back to the murderer. In line with Eco's theory of the net and the labyrinth the signs offer a multiplicity of ways of interpretation, all of them making sense within the parameters of the particular belief-system that is being used. Thus for the monastic establishment they constitute infallible proof of the work of the devil, whereas for the more rationalist-minded William of Baskerville (influenced by the ideas of such reform-minded scholars of the time as Roger Bacon) they eventually point towards a more human explanation involving the protection of the Catholic Church's control over society by means of censorship.

Eco describes a text as '*a machine for producing possible worlds*' (Eco 1981: 246), and that most certainly can be said of *The Name of the Rose*, which weaves together these various concerns to construct a narrative world that is very convincing indeed. As far as the reader–text relationship goes, the reader may choose to emphasise one set of codes over the many others that the text offers and interpret the text weighted towards that end. But the reader nevertheless has to stay within the particular network of codes laid down by the text: the text sets the terms of reference for interpretation.

What William eventually uncovers in *The Name of the* Rose is a conspiracy by certain members of the Church hierarchy to prevent ideas potentially dangerous to their authority from gaining wider currency. The conspiracy centres on a supposedly lost work by Aristotle outlining a theory of comedy to complement his work on tragedy, *The Poetics*, the only known source of his aesthetic theory (as it still is to this day). If this work on comedy were to be more widely known, the head librarian of the abbey Jorge believes, then it could lead to authority being mocked and thus to a decline in the power of the Catholic Church. The masses would no longer fear the priesthood, as the Church wishes them to do in order to maintain its superiority over them. To take such a position is to side with Plato, whose aesthetic theory, as outlined by the figure of his teacher Socrates in *The Republic*, demanded that poets be prevented from producing any works not in complete accordance with the state's official ideology or in any way disrespectful to those implementing it. In Plato's planned commonwealth, such figures would be regarded as a threat to public order and would be banished. What was required of the creative artist, as in Soviet Russia under the regime of socialist realism, was essentially propaganda serving the needs of the ruling class.

Eco's subsequent fictional output is similarly playful in the way it mixes popular literary genres and narrative tropes with more obviously intellectual concerns, often drawing heavily on semiotic theory. Conspiracy also often plays a major part, as in *Foucault's Pendulum* and *The Prague Cemetery*, with Eco demonstrating how little real substance conspiracies actually have, how gullible the public is to take any of them seriously and how they prey on our prejudices. (Conspiracy is often seen to be a recurrent trope of postmodern fiction, as Brian McHale amongst others has pointed out, but Eco is one of the few to poke fun at the practice.) In the latter work, the Protocols of the Elders of Zion (a document claiming a massive, centuries-long, Jewish conspiracy to take control of the world through infiltrating its key institutions) emerge from the murky underworld of espionage and counter-espionage that stretches across the major European empires of the nineteenth century, and are devised mainly because various secret services are searching for a scapegoat to cover their own failings. Since the Protocols play to a long-running tradition of anti-Semitism in Christian societies, they prove to be very successful in this regard, deflecting attention away from the abuses of power by their rulers to which the population as a whole is being subjected. The promotion of conspiracies becomes an unacknowledged state policy.

Eco's fiction in general presents a practical illustration of his semiotic theories, without falling into the trap of being pedantic and using the fiction purely to make abstruse theoretical points: it is far more than just 'novels of ideas'. From the point of view of post-modern aesthetics, he is a master at the art of double-coding, and that may well prove to be his most lasting legacy as an author.

Eco's major writings

Eco, Umberto, *A Theory of Semiotics*, London and Basingstoke: Macmillan, 1977.

——, *The Role of the Reader: Explorations in the Semiotics of Texts* [1979], London: Hutchinson, 1981.

——, *The Name of the Rose* [1980], trans. William Weaver, London: Secker and Warburg, 1983.

——, *Reflections on 'The Name of the Rose'*, trans. William Weaver, London: Secker and Warburg, 1984a.

——, *Semiotics and the Philosophy of Language*, Bloomington, IN: Indiana University Press, 1984b.

——, *Foucault's Pendulum* [1988], trans. William Weaver, London: Secker and Warburg, 1989.

——, *The Search for the Perfect Language* [1993], trans. James Fentress, Oxford and Cambridge, MA: Blackwell, 1995a.

——, *The Island of the Day Before* [1994], trans. William Weaver, London: Secker and Warburg, 1995b.

——, *Baudolino* [2000], trans. William Weaver, London: Secker and Warburg, 2002.

——, *The Prague Cemetery* [2010], trans. Richard Dixon, London: Harvill Secker, 2011.

References and further reading

Aristotle, *The Poetics*, trans. T. A. Sinclair, Harmondsworth: Penguin, 1962.
Barthes, Roland, *S/Z* [1970], trans. Richard Miller, London: Jonathan Cape, 1975.

McHale, Brian, *Postmodernist Fiction*, London and New York: Methuen, 1987.
——, *Constructing Postmodernism*, London and New York: Routledge, 1992.
Plato, *The Republic*, trans. Desmond Lee, Harmondsworth: Penguin, 2nd edition, 1974.
Saussure, Ferdinand de, *Course in General Linguistics* [1916], ed. Charles Bally, Albert Sechehaye and Albert Reidlinger, trans. Wade Baskin, London: Peter Owen, 1960.

PAUL K. FEYERABEND (1924–94)

Along with Thomas Kuhn, Feyerabend has been a highly controversial figure in the area of the philosophy of science, challenging existing preconceptions of how science works as a discipline, particularly its claims to objectivity, which he thinks are unsustainable once one looks back into scientific history without any preconceptions. Feyerabend is, however, by far the most provocative of the two thinkers, proclaiming at one point that as far as the development of scientific method is concerned the best principle to operate by is '*anything goes*' (Feyerabend 1978a: 23), which is hardly how most practising scientists would conceive of the concept. His best-known book is in fact entitled *Against Method*, and it takes aim at what the author uncompromisingly calls 'the naïve and simple-minded rules which methodologists take as their guide' (Feyerabend 1978a: 17). He is particularly harsh on Karl Popper in this respect, accusing him of theoretical 'simplemindedness' (Feyerabend 1987: 191).

Feyerabend goes so far as to claim that science is actually closer to myth than either its practitioners or philosophers of science would ever admit (and 'a second-rate myth' at that (Feyerabend 1978a: 44)), which suggests a postmodern perspective where narratives are either useful or not rather than true or not – as Jean-François Lyotard also pictures them in *The Postmodern Condition*. It also represents an intriguing twist on Kuhn's notion of alternating paradigms and revolutions throughout scientific history (see *The Structure of Scientific Revolutions*): Feyerabend's model sounds more like a condition of permanent revolution. For the notion of scientific truth to be debunked in this way would be anathema to most scientists, for whom narrative has little or no role to play in their work, being a concern for the arts and humanities instead: in their interpretation, what they deal with is systematically accumulated data generated by methodically conducted experiments.

Against Method kicks off in particularly provocative fashion: 'The following essay is written in the conviction that *anarchism*, while perhaps not the most attractive *political* philosophy, is certainly excellent medicine for *epistemology*, and for the *philosophy of science*' (Feyerabend 1978a: 17). The problem with philosophy of science from this point of view is that it is too neat, that it tends to favour a teleological concept of scientific history, whereas for Feyerabend it is '[a] complex medium sustaining surprising and unforeseen developments', which 'defies analysis on the basis of rules which have been set up in advance and without regard to the ever-changing conditions of history' (Feyerabend 1978a: 18). We would be better advised to see scientific history as 'chaotic', rather than to tidy it up in the manner that scientific education does – and tidying up involves an unholy alliance of 'interests, forces, propaganda and brainwashing techniques' (Feyerabend 1978a: 19, 25) that Feyerabend is adamant should always be resisted. Yoking together Lenin and Einstein to back up his argument only serves to underline Feyerabend's determinedly iconoclastic approach to his subject.

Feyerabend's alternative, anarchistic, methodology for science is structured on the 'anything goes principle'. Unless rules are consistently broken and theories ignored there will be no growth in scientific knowledge, Feyerabend believes, and it is his contention that this is what has always been happening: the official line on scientific history amounts to an idealisation of the real, invariably chaotic, state of affairs. Nor does Feyerabend think that we have to pin down the notion of 'progress' in any way, arguing that it will mean various things to various people and that it is not really necessary to discriminate between these: '*my thesis is that anarchism helps to achieve progress in any one of the senses one cares to choose*' (Feyerabend 1978a: 27). In other words, 'anything goes'.

Feyerabend thinks that scientists should feel under an obligation to keep developing counter-inductive theories, rather than to reinforce existing ones. His rationale is that 'there is not a single interesting theory that agrees with all the known facts in its domain' (Feyerabend 1978a: 31), and that this should be regarded as an open invitation to find other ways of accounting for the discrepancies. We can note something like this happening these days in physics, with some scientists beginning to contemplate other possibilities than the standard model of physics, which has various acknowledged gaps in it, while others of their colleagues are just as bent on finding what is needed to complete the standard model: there is at best an uneasy truce operating between the two sides at present. The latter are starting from the point of a firm belief in the theories that go to make up the standard model, which for Feyerabend means that the theory is implicated in what it finds. As Feyerabend would interpret it, that means those who are attempting to shore up the standard model are proceeding 'from the *inside*', when what would be more useful would be the development of 'an *external* standard of criticism' containing 'a set of alternative assumptions' (Feyerabend 1978a: 32). The greater the proliferation of new theories and new sets of assumptions, the better for science as Feyerabend sees it. Seeking consistency with existing theories – 'saving the phenomena', as its critics call the practice – merely entrenches the establishment who support these theories, thus preventing progress from being made: '*variety of opinion is necessary for objective knowledge*' (Feyerabend 1978a: 46). In Feyerabend's view, nothing at all should be ruled out.

It could be objected that ruling nothing out and following the anything goes principle would open the door to theories like intelligent design, which few scientists think even qualifies as scientific. Intelligent design theorists, however, insist that their theory should merit equal consideration and be taught as an alternative worldview alongside theories like Darwinian evolution, an argument which is currently raging in the American educational system, where intelligent design has made it onto the curriculum in some states. From a Feyerabendian position it could be argued back that intelligent design seeks consistency with biblical texts and so is, if anything, more reductive in its method than most standard scientific theories: neither are its supporters much prepared to countenance 'alternative assumptions'. Whether anything at all useful could be gleaned from intelligent design has to be very doubtful, but if support for it makes scientists look more carefully at their own theories, then it might just be possible to claim that it is serving a useful purpose of some kind.

Science in a Free Society continues the argument, with the aim of demonstrating 'that rationality is one tradition among many rather than a standard to which traditions must conform', and that furthermore '*[a] free society is a society in which all traditions have equal rights and equal access to the centres of power*' (Feyerabend 1978b: 7, 9). The privileged position that science has in our society is unwarranted, therefore, and it undermines the democratic principles on which that society ostensibly is founded. The book also includes a closing section in which Feyerabend replies to some of the critics of *Against Method*, with the provocative title of 'Conversations with Illiterates'. The latter turns into a diatribe against the more negative of his reviewers, who spur him on to claim that 'incompetence, having been standardized, has now become an essential part of professional excellence. We no longer have incompetent professionals, we have professionalized incompetence' (Feyerabend 1978b: 183). The book makes a strong case for opening out science to the general public, arguing, as one of its sections does, that 'Laymen can and must supervise science' (Feyerabend 1978b: 96; Donna Haraway makes similar noises in *Modest Witness*), and that science should be treated as an ideology, which '*prevails not because of its comparative merits, but because the show has been rigged in its favour*' (Feyerabend 1978b: 102).

Farewell to Reason sets out to problematise our notions of 'Reason' and 'Objectivity', on the grounds that '[t]he habit of objectivising basic beliefs or the results of research becomes nonsensical in a world that contains some form of complementarity and in all societies adapted to close social contact' (Feyerabend 1987: 9). 'Reason' and 'Rationality' are terms that for Feyerabend amount to nothing more than adhering to rules laid down by some authority, and he is scathing of how they 'can be connected with almost any idea or procedure and then surround it with a halo of excellence' (Feyerabend 1987: 10). (Popper's 'critical rationalism' comes in for repeated attack over the course of his writings.) Being rational then becomes agreement with whatever the authority in question believes, whereas 'irrational' signals disagreement. Since universal truths have proved to be so divisive (the history of religion alone would confirm this), Feyerabend pushes the case for relativism, arguing that this provides us with a far better basis for social interaction, constituting as it does 'an attempt to make sense of the phenomenon of cultural variety' (Feyerabend 1987: 19). Variety, diversity and pluralism are causes this writer is always concerned to promote as strongly as he can, and he takes science to be notably deficient when it comes to these.

Feyerabend is at once an invigorating and exasperating thinker. He encourages us to take a non-teleological view of scientific history, and this is very valuable; but he does seem to want to push his ideas to extremes that are not always very defensible. While he is keen to emphasise that he should not be considered anti-science, he does have a distinct tendency to overstate the case with regard to current scientific practice, dismissing most of it as the province of self-interested 'law-and-order methodologies' (Feyerabend 1978a: 172). Neither is he likely to convert the scientific profession to the idea that '[w]ithout "chaos" no knowledge. Without a frequent dismissal of reason, no progress' (Feyerabend 1978a: 179); that would be to its members to provide far too much latitude to crank theorists. However, his main point, that theories should always be subjected to opposition, remains very defensible, and he can certainly be classified as a committed opponent of there being any scientific metanarrative, which he dismisses as '*one of the many forms of thought that have been developed by man, and not necessarily the best*' (Feyerabend 1978a: 295). Whether law-and-order methodologies are quite as much of a factor in the current scientific world as they were in the past, however, does have to remain somewhat questionable.

Feyerabend's major writings

Feyerabend, Paul K., *Against Method: Outline of an Anarchistic Theory of Knowledge* [1975], London: Verso, 1978a.
——, *Science in a Free Society*, London: NLB, 1978b.
——, *Realism, Rationalism and Scientific Method: Philosophical Papers, Volume I*, Cambridge: Cambridge University Press, 1981.
——, *Problems of Empiricism: Philosophical Papers, Volume II*, Cambridge: Cambridge University Press, 1981.
——, *Farewell to Reason*, London and New York: Verso, 1987.
——, *Three Dialogues on Knowledge*, Oxford and Cambridge, MA: Blackwell, 1991.
——, *Killing Time: The Autobiography of Paul Feyerabend*, Chicago and London: University of Chicago Press, 1995.
——, *Conquest of Abundance: A Tale of Abstraction Versus the Richness of Being*, ed. Bert Tepstra, Chicago and London: University of Chicago Press, 1999.
——, *Knowledge, Science and Relativism: Philosophical Papers, Volume III*, ed. John Preston, Cambridge: Cambridge University Press, 1999.
——, *The Tyranny of Science* [1996], Cambridge and Malden, MA: Polity Press, 2011.

References and further reading

Haraway, Donna J., *Modest Witness@Second Millennium Meets Oncomouse: Feminism and Technoscience*, New York and London: Routledge, 1997.
Kuhn, Thomas, *The Structure of Scientific Revolutions*, 2nd edition, Chicago and London: University of Chicago Press, 1962.
Lyotard, Jean-François, *The Postmodern Condition: A Report on Knowledge* [1979], trans. Geoff Bennington and Brian Massumi, Manchester: Manchester University Press, 1984.

MICHEL FOUCAULT (1926–84)

Foucault's analyses of cultural history created considerable controversy when they first came out, and have continued to stimulate debate in the academy ever since, despite doubts being expressed by more conventional historians as to the reliability of his data as well as his particular interpretation of those. As Edward Said has remarked, Foucault 'writes neither philosophy nor history as they are commonly experienced' (Said 1975: 288), although he does succeed in combining these two disciplines to create a strikingly new perspective on the development of Western society from classical times to the modern period. Foucault himself sought to avoid such academic pigeonholing, describing his practice in *The History of Sexuality*, a monumental three-volume study of the subject, as 'not the work of a "historian"', but 'a philosophical exercise' on his part 'to learn to what extent the effort to think one's own history can free thought from what it silently thinks, and so enable it to think differently' (Foucault 1987: 9). In terms of his overall intellectual orientation, he was just as evasive, declaring in an interview that 'I have never been a Freudian, I have never been a Marxist and I have never been a structuralist' (Foucault 1988: 22).

Despite his dislike of being labelled, it does not seem unreasonable to think of Foucault as an anti-totalising thinker in the post-structuralist–postmodernist vein; one who rejects authoritarian systems and universal theories, preferring to present them as based purely on the exercise of power, and used by those in power to maintain that power for their own personal ends. Since such systems, or 'discourses', as Foucault came to conceive of them, rely heavily on tradition for their justification – ruling institutions coming to seem the natural order of things after a while – this means they can be challenged, which is a point that all poststructuralists and postmodernists are making as strongly as they can within their own area of expertise. Power, for such thinkers, being explicitly inegalitarian and exploitative in nature, can and should be resisted, and Foucault remains deeply concerned with the issue of power over the course of his career and how it is expressed in its particular historical era (or '*episteme*', in Foucault's terminology).

Foucault specialises in what he calls 'archaeologies', suggesting that this is the way historical study should be conducted nowadays, showing more concern with discontinuities and ruptures, with what does not fall into a pattern rather than with what forms one. Unifying schemes and ideas are losing their credibility for such thinkers. Whereas archaeology once 'aspired to the condition of history' to make sense of its generally very disparate findings, Foucault claims that the relationship is now being reversed, and that 'in our time history aspires to the condition of archaeology' (Foucault 2002: 8). *The Archaeology of Knowledge* argues that we can no longer rely on 'those divisions or groupings with which we have become so familiar' (Foucault 2002: 24), by which he means such standard categories as authors, works, and historical movements. 'The frontiers of a book are never clear cut' (Foucault 2002: 25), and the same goes for the other standard divisions and groupings we find in traditional accounts. As for authors, Foucault downgrades them to the status of 'a function of discourse' (Foucault 1977b: 124).

Foucault adopts an archaeological approach when he delves into the history of sexuality to overturn the standard view of human sexuality – during his lifetime anyway – as being defined by hetero-sexuality, with all other forms of sexual expression to be treated as deviations from this norm. It was an attitude that resulted in various kinds of discrimination against homosexuals around the globe. Foucault insists, on the other hand, that a closer study of classical culture will reveal that homosexuality was considered entirely within the normal range of sexual expression in the Greek classical era, and that this even extended to relations between men and boys. Liaisons of the latter kind were hedged about with various conventions and, as Foucault notes, became something of 'a theme of anxiety for Greek thought' (Foucault 1987: 187), but nevertheless they were both common and publicly accepted. So too was what we now refer to as bisexuality; but in such a society, Foucault contends, homosexuality or bisexuality are simply not meaningful terms.

It was only gradually throughout the later Roman period, particu-larly after the advent of Christianity as the official state religion, that heterosexuality came to be declared the norm and all other forms of sexual expression were eventually outlawed, and even criminalised (as is still the same case in several countries even today). Heterosexuality turned into the dominant discourse within the public sphere in the West. Until modern times that discourse has retained its power over Western societies, driving homosexuality underground, and it is only in the later decades of the twentieth century that this came to be openly questioned through the greater assertiveness of gay culture and the subsequent rise of gay and queer theory. Foucault's point is that history indicates to us that it is convention which dictates sexual practices, and that there is no 'natural law' of what these must be. It is through the work of such theorists as Foucault that queer theory has come to take inspiration, even if his analysis of sexual history is probably far neater than it ever was in reality. On that latter score, James Davidson in *Courtesans and Fishcakes* felt the need to draw attention to the thriving heterosexual culture in ancient Athens in order to strike a balance with such readings (although also drawing inspiration from Foucault's concept of discourse to construct his argument overall).

Foucault's archaeologies tend to show that in the modern world order we have become ever more closely policed by those in power, such that normative codes of behaviour have been imposed right across the social spectrum and not just in areas like sexuality. Madness, illness and crime have all been subject to this policing regime on the part of those in power, as evidenced for Foucault by the creation of the modern asylum, prison and hospital systems, all with authoritative figures in control of their operations. It is through such systems that control is maintained over the mass of the population by the socio-political elite, thus entrenching and safeguarding their own position (a similar argument could be put forward regarding the education system too, for that matter; which is effectively what the Marxist theory of hegemony does). *Madness and Civilization* outlines how asylums were developed in European societies from the seventeenth century onwards, in what Foucault christened 'The Great Confinement' (Foucault 1967: 38–64); although the individuals so confined had been relatively free to roam the streets in medieval times, and even afforded a certain amount of official protection on the grounds of being God's 'innocents'. Foucault speaks of the 'Church's solicitude for the insane' during the pre-modern period, because it felt that madness contained 'a difficult but an essential lesson: the guilty innocence of the animal in man' (Foucault 1967: 82). What the socio-political elite now wanted, however, was to put a check on such displays of difference, by containing it within institutions which could then be kept subject to centralised control and regulation. This rigorous new discourse was to be forced on the populace: 'A sensibility was born which had drawn a line and laid a cornerstone, and which chose – only to banish' (Foucault 1967: 64). Foucault made a point throughout his life of championing the cause of groups such as prisoners, feeling an affinity with marginalised and socially ostracised groups of this kind: the 'different' of contemporary Western culture.

Foucault's concept of discourse has been enormously influential within both the humanities and the social sciences, providing commentators and critics with a very flexible framework for the analysis of the workings of power in any age (Edward Said's *Orientalism* being a particularly notable example of its application in terms of Western colonialism, and Judith Butler's *Gender Trouble* about gender relations). He describes discourse as consisting of the 'delimitation of a field of objects, the definition of a legitimate perspective for the agent of knowledge, and the fixing of norms for the elaboration of concepts and theories' (Foucault 1977b: 199). Discourse could be seen as a theory of how hegemony is implemented by the ruling group at any one time, but without the deterministic imperative lying behind the Marxist version of the concept, with its notion of a class struggle ineluctably heading towards the 'dictatorship of the proletariat' in a post-capitalist Marxist utopia. No such pattern can be discerned by Foucault, nor by his postmodernist peers, when looking back on the historical record: except that of socio-political elites striving their hardest to maintain themselves in power for their own personal benefit.

There is a distinctly anti-humanist strand to Foucault's thought that resists the historical schemes favoured by theories such as Marxism, as expressed most memorably in his closing remarks to *The Order of Things*:

> As the archaeology of our thought easily shows, man is an invention of recent date. And one perhaps nearing its end. If those arrangements were to disappear as they appeared, if some event of which we can at the moment do no more than sense the possibility – without knowing either what its form will be or what it promises – were to cause them to crumble, as the ground of Classical thought did, at the end of the eighteenth century, then one can certainly wager that man would be erased, like a face drawn in sand at the edge of the sea.
>
> (Foucault 1994: 387)

Foucault can identify no particular line of development in history therefore, and that is a viewpoint that recurs consistently throughout poststructuralist and postmodernist thought, which regards random-ness and contingency as far more important factors. Whereas Marxism sees a specific trajectory to historical events that social revolutionaries can take advantage of in order to bring about the socio-political change they desire, thinkers like Foucault see an open future that lies beyond our power to predict or to manipulate to any meaningful extent, making him yet another figure who can be filed under the heading of post-Marxism.

Foucault's major writings

Foucault, Michel, *Madness and Civilization: A History of Insanity in the Age of Reason* [1961], trans. Richard Howard, London: Tavistock, 1967.
——, *The Birth of the Clinic: An Archaeology of Medical Perception* [1963], trans. A. M. Sheridan Smith, New York: Vintage, 1973.

——, *Discipline and Punish: The Birth of the Prison* [1975], trans. Alan Sheridan, Harmondsworth: Pelican, 1977a.

——, *Language, Counter-Memory, Practice*, ed. Donald Bouchard, trans. Donald Bouchard and Sherry Simon, Ithaca, NY: Cornell University Press, 1977b.

——, *The History of Sexuality: Volume I. An Introduction* [1976], trans. Robert Hurley, Harmondsworth: Penguin, 1981.

——, *The History of Sexuality: Volume II. The Use of Pleasure* [1984], trans. Robert Hurley, Harmondsworth: Penguin, 1987.

——, *Politics Philosophy Culture: Interviews and Other Writings 1977–1984*, ed. Lawrence D. Kritzman, trans. Alan Sheridan *et al.*, New York and London: Routledge, 1988.

——, *The History of Sexuality: Volume III. The Care of the Self* [1984], trans. Robert Hurley, Harmondsworth: Penguin, 1990.

——, *The Order of Things: An Archaeology of the Human Sciences* [1966], trans. Alan Sheridan, New York: Vintage, 1994.

——, *The Archaeology of Knowledge* [1969], trans. A. M. Sheridan Smith, London and New York: Routledge, 2002.

References and further reading

Barthes, Roland, 'The Death of the Author', in *Image-Music-Text*, ed. and trans. Stephen Heath, London: Fontana, 1977.

Butler, Judith, *Gender Trouble: Feminism and the Subversion of Identity*, London and New York: Routledge, 1990.

Davidson, James, *Courtesans and Fishcakes: The Consuming Passions of Ancient Athens*, London: Fontana, 1998.

Said, Edward, *Beginnings: Intention and Method*, Baltimore, MD and London: Johns Hopkins University Press, 1975.

——, *Orientalism: Western Conceptions of the Orient* [1978], 2nd edition, Harmondsworth: Penguin, 1995.

CLIFFORD GEERTZ (1926–2006)

Geertz was one of the leading anthropologists of the twentieth century, and his theories have been adapted for use in various other areas of intellectual enquiry, with postmodernists finding support in his work for their own commitment to pluralism and difference. He was one of the founders of 'cultural anthropology', which sought to understand cultures from the inside, as much as that is possible by the studies of incoming observers, as opposed to describing them from a Western-centric outlook. To understand another culture through its actions and the contexts in which these appeared was to develop what Geertz called a 'thick description' of it; whereas merely to describe and catalogue another culture was to provide only a 'thin description'. From the standpoint of cultural anthropology the structural anthropology of Claude Lévi-Strauss, given its concern with identifying common features applying across cultures (an assumed 'deep structure' of the kind that structuralist thinkers were always trying to find, whatever their particular discipline might be), was a source of thin descriptions alone. What Geertz saw himself as striving to achieve in his work was 'a new diagnostics, a science that can determine the meaning of things for the life that surrounds them' (Geertz 1983: 120). He also acknowledged, however, that cultural anthropologists were as prone to bias as anyone else working in the field, referring to 'the ungetroundable fact that all ethnographical descriptions are homemade, that they are the describers' descriptions, not those of the described' (Geertz 1988: 144–5).

In his early career in the 1950s and 1960s Geertz undertook extensive field work studies in places like Indonesia, leading to several books on the culture of the area which helped to establish cultural anthropology as a viable discipline. In *The Religion of Java*, for example, he catalogued in detail the diverse religious practices of the society, with their intriguing combination of influences from various cultures as well as a myriad of local variations to be added in to that mix: 'I have tried in the following pages to show how much variation in ritual, contrast in belief, and conflict in values lie concealed behind the simple statement that Java is more than 90 per cent Moslem' (Geertz 1960: 7). Indeed, what Geertz's field work finds in this instance is a considerable degree of antagonism between the three main religious variants in the town of Modjokuto, where he and his wife lived for over a year, although there are also many shared values which help to keep this antagonism in check, ensuring that the society as a whole attains a workable level of stability. Given that Modjokuto is a small town of only 20,000 inhabitants, one can see the level of detail that Geertz feels it is necessary to accumulate before drawing any conclusions from his studies.

Agricultural Involution: The Processes of Ecological Change in Indonesia went on to explore how larger historical processes affected life right down to the most local of levels, such as that of the country's peasant population. As Geertz saw it, the objective was 'to utilize the insights derived from microsociological analysis for understanding macrosociogical problems' (Geertz 1963a: xviii). Geertz approaches his topic, broadly speaking, from an ecological standpoint, but warns against imposing from the outside any notion of how ecosystems are supposed to work: 'How much of the past growth and present state of Indonesian culture and society is attributable to ecological processes is something to be determined, if at all, at the end of the inquiry, not at the beginning of it' (Geertz 1963a: 11). To let the data lead in this way is to build up a thick description of a culture; to come in with a ready-made notion of ecosystems and measure the data against that is to remain at the level of thin – although there is always that qualification to be made with Geertz that thick should not be taken to mean 'comprehensive'. Geertz remains the most careful of theorists, never allowing himself to be drawn into going past his data – that being his main accusation against the structuralist school.

Geertz can be defined as an anti-ethnocentrist, rejecting the notion of objectivity in anthropological studies on the grounds that this generally involves an assumption on the part of the anthropologist of the superiority of his or her home culture (generally Western, of course, especially in the aftermath of colonialism). Anti-ethnocentrism refuses to treat any culture as innately superior to any other, and to postmodernists this is to align oneself with pluralism and difference, central pillars of the postmodernist ethos. Geertz also leans towards postmodernism when he attacks the principle of 'grand theories' as a method of explaining cultures, as he does in uncompromising fashion in his late book *Local Knowledge*: 'Though those with what they take to be a big idea are still among us, calls for a "general theory" of just about anything social sound increasingly hollow, and claims to have one megalomanic' (Geertz 1983: 4). This is a thinker who, as Fred Inglis puts it, always 'seeks to *respond* to human peculiarity' (Inglis 2000: 2) rather than to make it fit into any preconceived scheme. There is a clear parallel to be noted here with Jean-François Lyotard's rejection of the claims of the 'grand narratives' of Western society in his seminal study *The Postmodern Condition*, and his support for 'little narratives' instead (Lyotard 1984: 60). There is a general drift towards the local to be noted in postmodern thought, and a suspicion of the universalising theory – whatever the area of study may be.

The influence of cultural anthropology can be seen in theories such as new historicism, as in the work of one of its major thinkers, the literary critic Stephen Greenblatt. In *Renaissance Self-Fashioning* Greenblatt similarly turns his attention to the practices of daily life, as experienced by particular individuals, to discover what they reveal about the larger historical processes we can discern as being underway from our later vantage point.

The bias towards difference and particularity in cultural anthropology differentiates Geertz's work sharply from the structuralist anthropology school of figures like Lévi-Strauss, where the emphasis is on finding common elements that apply across cultures and then cataloguing the patterns they appear to exhibit. Lévi-Strauss felt there was just such an underlying pattern to be found in creation myths, and took these as proof of a 'deep structure' lying beneath cultures around the globe (see his *The Savage Mind*, for example). Geertz is deeply sceptical of the value of this method, complaining that, for Lévi-Strauss, '[i]t is all a matter of shuffling discrete (and concrete) images – totem animals, sacred colors, wind directions, sun deities, or whatever – so as to produce symbolic structures capable of formulating and communicating objective (which is not to say accurate) analyses of the social and physical worlds' (Geertz 1993: 353). While conceding that the resultant structures can sometimes be interesting up to a point, and often quite ingenious in the connections they go on to make between various cultures, Geertz feels compelled to add that others can be dismissed as 'triumphs of self-parody' (Geertz 1993: 355) on Lévi-Strauss's part. Lévi-Strauss's approach, Geertz contends, 'annuls history' in the way that it 'replaces the particular minds of particular savages in particular jungles with the Savage Mind immanent in us all' (Geertz 1993: 355). So it is the theory, not the data, that is leading the way to conclusions in Lévi-Strauss's work. It is such a commitment to a 'deep structure' in structuralist thought that we find Jacques Derrida complaining about in works like *Writing and Difference*. As far as both thinkers are concerned, the outcome is a mechanical form of analysis which leads to predictable conclusions, because they are largely predetermined by the theory's underlying assumptions. The structuralist knows what he is looking for before he begins, and is seeking confirmation for his thesis; whatever does not provide that confirmation is all too likely to be sidelined as irrelevant data.

Rather than processing data through a pre-existing scheme in the manner of the structural anthropologist, Geertz insists that we need to immerse ourselves in a culture's codes so that we can come to recognise the many subtle nuances of their 'structures of signification' (Geertz 1993: 9). This is what underpins the technique of 'thick description', a concept that he adapts from the philosopher Gilbert Ryle, and he regards it as the primary task of the ethnographer – ethnography being for Geertz the basis of social anthropology. (Geertz is always keen to make connections between anthropology and philosophy, as his late book *Available Light* makes clear.) Unless the anthropologist is well versed in the microscopic details of a culture his or her large-scale interpretations will always be questionable to Geertz: 'the anthropologist characteristically approaches such broader interpretations and more abstract analyses from the direction of exceedingly extended acquaintances with extremely small matters' (Geertz 1993: 21). As an example of how this approach works, Geertz explains how a village election can be read as a particularly telling illustration of a larger pattern in the national culture of Indonesia, being 'a specific manifestation of a more comprehensive pattern which has a very large, in some cases virtually infinite, number of such embodiments and manifestations' (Geertz 1963a: 154). In such specific manifestations, Geertz contends, 'the paradigm is made flesh' (Geertz 1963a: 154), enabling us to appreciate both the general and the local implications of, in this case, a particular local election at a particular point in Indonesian history. The microsociological and the macrosociological are here seen to be in interaction.

It is this emphasis on the inner details of a culture that informs new historicism, which equally homes in on, and then builds out from, such 'small matters' in its critical analyses. And Geertz does insist on exceedingly extended acquaintance, warning against any large-scale generalisations based on the evidence of some particular location, such as taking one village in a country to be representative of that entire country. As he pithily puts it: 'Anthropologists don't study villages (tribes, towns, neighbourhoods ...); they study *in* villages' (Geertz 1993: 22). Again, we note that sensitivity to the factor of difference above all else.

Geertz's major writings

Geertz, Clifford, *The Religion of Java*, Chicago and London: Chicago University Press, 1960.

——, *Agricultural Involution: The Processes of Ecological Change in Indonesia*, Berkeley, Los Angeles and London: University of California Press, 1963a.

——, *Peddlers and Princes: Social Change and Economic Modernization in Two Indonesian Towns*, Chicago: University of Chicago Press, 1963b.

——, *Islam Observed: Religious Development in Morocco and Indonesia*, New Haven, CT: Yale University Press, 1968.

——, *The Social History of an Indonesian Town* [1965], Westport, CT: Greenwood Press, 1975.

——, *Negara: The Theatre State in Nineteenth-Century Bali*, Princeton, NJ: Princeton University Press, 1980.

——, *Local Knowledge: Further Essays in Interpretive Anthropology*, New York: Basic Books, 1983.

——, *Works and Lives: The Anthropologist as Author*, Stanford, CA: Stanford University Press, 1988.

——, *The Interpretation of Cultures: Selected Essays* [1973], London: Fontana, 1993.

———, *Available Light: Anthropological Reflections on Philosophical Topics*, Princeton, NJ: Princeton University Press, 2000.

References and further reading

Derrida, Jacques, *Writing and Difference* [1967], trans. Alan Bass, Chicago: University of Chicago Press, 1978.

Greenblatt, Stephen, *Renaissance Self-Fashioning: From More to Shakespeare*, Chicago and London: University of Chicago Press, 1980.

Inglis, Fred, *Clifford Geertz: Culture, Custom and Ethics*, Cambridge and Oxford: Polity Press, 2000.

Lévi-Strauss, Claude, *The Savage Mind*, trans. Rodney Needham, London: Weidenfeld and Nicolson, 1966.

Lyotard, Jean-François, *The Postmodern Condition: A Report on Knowledge* [1979], trans. Geoff Bennington and Brian Massumi, Manchester: Manchester University Press, 1984.

KENNETH J. GERGEN (B. 1935)

Gergen is a social psychologist who has been very prominent in developing the theory of social constructionism, particularly in terms of emphasising its postmodern qualities. 'Constructionism is one of the more challenging outcomes of postmodern thought' (Gergen 1994a: 242), Gergen contends, in that it calls into question our traditional conceptions of truth and knowledge, and along with those, as Jean-François Lyotard had so famously claimed in *The Postmodern Condition*, the grand narratives that legitimate them and provide them with their apparent authority. Social constructionism acknowledges that we construct a series of narratives about the world and that these are in a constant process of negotiation. It also points out that those narratives will differ around the world and that we should not assume that the ones we happen to use are the only way of describing reality; that is, we should always be on the lookout for any lapse back into an assumption of 'cultural imperialism'. In Gergen's words, 'as we presume the reality and truth of our own beliefs, so do we trample on the realities of others' (Gergen 1999: 17). It is the interaction between human beings that determines how these narratives work and they are always subject to change on that basis: as Gergen neatly summarises it, 'I am linked, therefore I am' (Gergen 2009: 400). To be human is to be embedded in a network of narratives.

For social constructionists, being perpetually subject to change is a healthy sign, indicating an openness to new ideas and a refusal to become trapped in dogmatic attitudes. That is also very much the message to emerge from thinkers like Lyotard and Jacques Derrida, for whom there is no way of guaranteeing how events will turn out in the future, or assuming that any grand narrative can provide a method for us doing so. Gergen asks us to embrace the postmodern in this positive manner, arguing that it should be treated as 'the beginning of a brave new dialogue, dangerous yes, but one both exciting and profound in consequence' (Gergen 1999: 19).

Gergen is also one of the founders of the Taos Institute, an organisation designed to spread the ideas of social constructionism for the public good. They describe themselves as

> a community of scholars and practitioners concerned with the social processes essential for the construction of reason, knowledge, and human value. We are a non-profit ... organization committed to exploring, developing and disseminating ideas and practices that promote creative, appreciative and collaborative processes in families, communities and organizations around the world.
>
> (http://www.taosinstitute.net)

With Gergen as President, the Institute runs various programmes, both in the education sector and in the community, as well as engaging in publishing. Gergen's wife, Mary Gergen, is also a leading figure in this enterprise, and has published with her husband as well as under her own name.

Social constructionism was originally outlined by Peter L. Berger and Thomas Luckmann in their 1966 book *The Social Construction of Reality*: 'The basic contentions of this book are that reality is socially constructed and that the sociology of knowledge must analyze the processes in which this occurs' (Berger and Luckmann 1971: 13). The authors acknowledge a debt to Marx, establishing social constructionism as a left-leaning theory with an emphasis on the social group rather than the individual. The notion that our social reality is what we make it fits in well with postmodernism's worldview, since it implies that narratives can always be altered and that we need not consider ourselves to be perpetually under the sway of any authoritarian metanarrative. It is at the opposite end of the spectrum from the selfish and divisively individualistic behaviour that the current economic paradigm, neoliberalism, insists is the natural way for human beings to act, with its commitment to competitiveness above all else. This is to assume an unchanging human nature over time, which neither social constructionists nor postmodernists would accept is the case.

Gergen's attitude towards truth and knowledge echoes some of the more playful aspects of postmodern thought as found in writers like Derrida, Lyotard and the team of Gilles Deleuze and Félix Guattari, as in statements like the following: 'constructionist views function as an invitation to a dance, a game, or a form of life' (Gergen 1994a: 79). Gergen also notes, in his guise as Taos Institute President, that 'the most exciting and creative movement in any given field takes place at the margins. At the edge one is not playing by fixed rules, but borrowing, melding, and re-shaping. In a word, one is playing' (http://taos.publishpath.com/a-message-from-the-taos-institute-president). In terms of organisations, that means their goals and objectives should not be seen as fixed, but, instead, as in an ongoing state of negotiation and reconstruction as relationships within the organisation alter – as they invariably will even over quite short periods of time. There are particular parallels to be noted here to the concepts of nomadism (Deleuze and Guattari, *A Thousand Plateaus*) and svelteness (Lyotard, 'A Svelte Appendix'); a similar sense that all beliefs and practices should be treated as provisional only, and be as lightly held and supported as possible. No system should allow itself to become dogmatic in its beliefs and practices, defending these at all costs, because that will not be making the best of the talents of those working within it, who will be deterred from putting forward any new or radical ideas. The more hierarchical an organisation becomes, in other words, the less adaptable it will be in terms of changing socio-political circumstances – and these ought to be considered a permanent part of the landscape. To be dogmatic is to go against the grain of how human beings actually interact with each other and construct ideologies in what can be considered a rather *bricolage* fashion that can alter – even from day to day.

This could be seen as raising critical questions for corporate organisations since they believe their primary goal is the creation of increasing levels of profit, for both owners and shareholders, by means of carefully calculated strategies which are generally devised by higher management and then delivered in top-down fashion to the rest of the workforce. The point is, however, that organisations are social entities rather than just profit-making ones, so social constructionism, like postmodern theory in general, is challenging the assumptions underlying institutional authority and how it is implemented. There is at least an implicit critique of corporate metanarrative contained within a theory like social constructionism; an awareness that corporate organisations are often resistant to change if it in any meaningful way seems to undermine their metanarrative, and the power relationships that lie behind these (generally patriarchal in nature; see du Toit 2006).

Social constructionism has quite significant implications for business studies, therefore, particularly in the area of organisation theory. Gergen has specifically addressed this topic in 'Organization Theory in the Postmodern Era' (in the collection *Rethinking Organization*) and in a co-authored essay with Tojo Joseph Thatchenkery, 'Organizational Science in a Postmodern Context' (in the collection *In the Realm of Organization*). In the former, Gergen argues that organisation theory has grown out of romanticism and modernism in turn, but that these are now being undermined by 'the postmodern turn within the intellectual sphere' (Gergen 1992: 208). It is a turn of which Gergen entirely approves, feeling that it offers exciting new possibilities for theorising the organisation 'in ways that open new options for action' (Gergen 1992: 218), such as a reassessment, and ideally reconfiguration, of the power relationships within the organisation. Gergen is strongly of the opinion that it is a good thing when power is diffused throughout the organisation rather than monopolised by higher management, and all in favour of organisational consensus being kept under perpetual challenge. Again, it is the social aspect of the organisation that is emphasised – how it responds to the many discourses that it contains inside it, and how it relates to the broader concerns to be found in the world outside. In the latter essay, Gergen and Thatchenkery argue the case for organisational science in general taking its lead from social constructionism, identifying a modernist bias still pervading the field into the twenty-first century, preventing new realities from emerging within organisations.

In *The Saturated Self*, Gergen turns his attention to what he feels is a growing problem in the postmodern world, the sheer volume of communication systems and information that we are being constantly bombarded with. It is all too easy under this bombardment to feel like a 'self under siege' (Gergen 2000: 1). If anything we are now over-linked with a network of narratives, leading to an increasing sense of dislocation between our inherited notions of the self and the demands made on us by the 'state of social saturation' (Gergen 2000: 3) we find ourselves in. This is to be considered the less positive side of the postmodern condition.

Gergen is highly critical of the methods deployed generally in the social sciences, regarding these as biased towards the production of general principles and universal laws based on empirical research findings. He feels there is no justification for such principles and considers himself to be engaged in a 'shift from an empiricist to a post-empiricist philosophy of science, from a structuralist to a post-structuralist view of language, and from a modernist to a post-modernist worldview' (Gergen 1994a: xii) in his own work. Gergen also insists, much in the way that Derrida does with deconstruction, that social constructionism should be seen as a method and not as a set theory: 'social constructionist ideas do not carry a banner proclaiming their own truth. It is just such banners that invite the erecting of boundaries' (http://taos.publishpath.com/a-message-from-the-taos-institute-president). Reflecting on the work of the Taos Institute, he points out that the question his associates there are always asking themselves when investigating any phenomenon is, '[i]f we take this idea on, what happens next?' (http://taos.publishpath.com/a-message-from-the-taos-institute-president), and insists that they are genuinely open as to what that might turn out to be and where their researches might lead. Again, this seems to be in tune with the sceptical spirit of postmodernism as exemplified by the work of such as Derrida and Lyotard, who firmly reject the idea of there being any overarching grand narrative that we can always appeal to for answers in any walk of life.

Gergen's major writings

Gergen, Kenneth J., 'Organization Theory in the Postmodern Era', in Michael Reed and Michael Hughes (eds), *Rethinking Organization: New Directions in Organization Theory and Analysis*, London: Sage, 1992, pp. 207–26.

——, *Toward Transformation in Social Knowledge*, 2nd edition, London: Sage, 1994a.

——, *Realities and Relationships: Soundings in Social Construction*, Cambridge, MA: Harvard University Press, 1994b.

——, *An Invitation to Social Construction*, London: Sage, 1999.

——, *The Saturated Self: Dilemmas of Identity in Contemporary Life*, 2nd edition, New York: Basic Books, 2000.

——, *Social Construction in Context*, London: Sage, 2001.

——, *Relational Being: Beyond Self and Community*, New York: Oxford University Press, 2009.

Gergen, Kenneth J. and K. E. Davis (eds), *The Social Construction of the Person*, New York: Springer-Verlag, 1985.

Gergen, Kenneth J. and Mary M. Gergen, 'Social Construction and Research as Action', in P. Reason and H. Bradbury (eds), *The Sage Handbook of Action Research: Participative Inquiry and Practice*, 2nd edition, London: Sage, 2008, pp. 159–71.

Gergen, Kenneth J. and Tojo Joseph Thatchenkery, 'Organizational Science in a Postmodern Context', in Robert C. H. Chia (ed.), *In the Realm of Organization: Essays for Robert Cooper*, London and New York: Routledge, 1998, pp. 15–42.

References and further reading

Berger, Peter L. and Thomas Luckmann, *The Social Construction of Reality: A Treatise in the Sociology of Knowledge* [1966], Harmondsworth: Penguin, 1971.
Deleuze, Gilles and Félix Guattari, *A Thousand Plateaus: Capitalism and Schizophrenia* [1980], trans. Brian Massumi, London: Athlone Press, 1988.
du Toit, Angélique, *Corporate Strategy: A Feminist Perspective*, London and New York: Routledge, 2006.
Lyotard, Jean-François, *The Postmodern Condition: A Report on Knowledge* [1979], trans. Geoff Bennington and Brian Massumi, Manchester: Manchester University Press, 1984.
——, 'A Svelte Appendix to the Postmodern Question', in *Political Writings*, trans. Bill Readings and Kevin Paul Geiman, London: UCL Press, pp. 25–9.
'The Taos Institute', http.//www.taosinstitute.net (accessed 2 May 2012).
——, http://taos.publishpath.com/a-message-from-the-taos-institute-president (accessed 2 May 2012).

WILLIAM GIBSON (B. 1948)

Gibson is an author whose work is very much concerned with the impact of the new technology on thought and culture. He operates mainly within the science fiction genre, although not in a genre-bound or clichéd fashion, and his fictions tend to be set in either a dystopian present or a not too distant future. As Bruce Sterling puts it in his Introduction to a collection of Gibson's short stories:

> He is opening the stale corridors of the genre to the fresh air of new data[.] ... SF has survived a long winter on its stored body fat. Gibson, along with a broad wave of inventive, ambitious new writers, has prodded the genre awake and sent it out on recce for a fresh diet.
>
> (Sterling, in Gibson 1995: 12)

It is a notably 'information-dense' world, as Graham Sleight aptly has described it (Introduction to Gibson and Sterling 2011: 3), that Gibson chronicles, where knowledge is power – and for that reason much fought over by Gibson's characters. The protagonist of the short story 'Johnny Mnemonic', reflecting on the background to that power struggle, notes that 'it's impossible to move, to live, to operate at any level without leaving traces, bits, seemingly meaningless fragments of personal information. Fragments that can be retrieved, amplified' (Gibson 1995: 30). In *Idoru*, Colin Lainey, a 'netrunner' collecting information on celebrities to detect patterns in them, is described as someone whose researches involve becoming embroiled 'in the deeper realms of data that underlay the worlds of media' (Gibson 2011a: 94), data that can be used in exposés of those celebrities' lives. It is not just an information-dense but a surveillance-dense world as well, and much of Gibson's fiction is about trying to evade that surveillance while engaged in some legally or morally dubious enterprise. Gibson's early work helped to establish the genre of 'cyberpunk', while a later collaborative effort with another cyberpunk author Bruce Sterling can be classified as part of what came to be known as 'steampunk'. Gibson himself drew inspiration from the punk movement in music in the 1970s and 1980s.

Gibson's best-known work is probably *Neuromancer*, which envisages a world where humans can transfer their consciousness directly into computer programs while positioned at the terminal, leaving the 'meat' of their physical body behind while they explore the mysterious world of cyberspace – a term coined by Gibson himself. As so often in Gibson, it is the underside of the information society that we see much of the time, rather than the bright and shiny world of new gadgets, machinery and processes that we find in so much mainstream science fiction. The gadgets, machinery and processes do exist in Gibson, to expedite entry into cyberspace, for example; but when not in cyberspace *Neuromancer*'s characters inhabit a rather grimy, run-down, ghetto-like section of their world, where crime is rife and personal security always at risk. One exception in *Neuromancer* is the visit the main characters make to Freeside, a series of self-governing colonies out in space, engineered to look like glamorous locations on Earth. As one of the characters describes the French-themed 'Rue Jules Verne', 'It's just a big tube and they pour things through it. ... Tourists, hustlers, anything' (Gibson 1993: 149). Given the popularity of places like Disneyland in our own world, Freeside simply seems like an extension of that principle. The way that Dubai has developed in the last few decades also rather intriguingly echoes Freeside in many ways, down to the creation of artificial-land colonies stretching out into the sea.

Cyberspace is described at one point by the voice-over on a television programme that the narrative's main character, Case, is briefly watching as 'a consensual hallucination experienced daily by billions of legitimate operators in every nation, by children being taught mathematical concepts. ... A graphic representation of data extracted from the banks of every computer in the human system. Unthinkable complexity' (Gibson 1993: 67). Those entering cyberspace, software cowboys as they are dubbed (such as Case), are searching for information on behalf of their clients, and it can be a dangerous business coping with the often deadly security systems set up to protect institutional information – the 'ice', as the cowboys refer to these. At one point in the action one of the best-known cowboys, the Dixie Flatline, who has technically suffered 'brain-death' several times already, finally cannot be recovered from yet another episode of this and finds his consciousness trapped in cyberspace with nothing left to return to in real life. He is reduced to being a 'construct', 'a bunch of ROM' (Gibson 1993: 159), and it is in that form that Case encounters him when he seeks him out as a partner on his assignments. As a construct, the Flatline exists only in the most tenuous sense, aware of what is going on only when brought into play by a program manipulated by others, and with no memory of the past. Eventually, Dixie asks Case for a favour: 'This scam of yours, when it's over, you erase this goddam thing' (Gibson 1993: 130).

Case's health has been ruined by his exploits as a cowboy, and he is surviving by being engaged in several criminal enterprises, such as drug dealing, that often put his life at risk. He is rescued from this lifestyle by a shady character named Armitage who pays for his health to be restored in order to employ him as a software cowboy again, although this comes with a threat to Case's life if he fails to keep his side of the bargain. Case is only too happy to return to what for him feels like his natural element, and we are plunged back into the weird world of cyberspace, with its many dangers: 'This was it. This was what he was, who he was, his being. He forgot to eat' (Gibson 1993: 76). The point of Case's exploits in cyberspace is to hack into security systems, so that they regard him as a natural part of their functioning and allow him to override their programs in the quest to gather sensitive information. *Neuromancer* raises the spectre of artificial intelligence (AI) systems becoming more powerful than human beings, and perhaps even exerting domination over them – as with the system Case finds himself up against, Wintermute. It is a worry that has become more widespread amongst those working in that field in the interim, when our dependence on computer-run systems in our daily life (all our utilities and transport networks, such as air travel) has become progressively greater.

Gibson has moved into a more recognisably contemporary world in his recent novels, although these still have a distinctly dystopian and alien quality about them, as in *Pattern Recognition*, and its sequels *Spook Country* and *Zero History*, where Western cities like London, Paris and Vancouver are presented as dark and dangerous locales which the protagonists negotiate with a certain amount of trepidation. What they are searching for is information that their competitors do not yet have, in order to stay ahead of the field, even if it is not exactly clear to everyone involved what could be done with the information itself once brought under their control. The assumption is just made that it will always pay, somehow or other, to be in possession of whatever new information comes along. In *Spook Country* Hollis Henry, an ex-rock star, is hired by Hubert Bigend, head of the Big Ant corporation, an 'innovative global advertising agency' (Gibson 2011b: 77) as its Wikipedia entry describes it, to write a magazine article about 'locative art', virtual representations of past events at their place of occurrence. These include events such as the death on the streets of Los Angeles of Hollywood film stars like River Phoenix, or the writer F. Scott Fitzgerald suffering a heart attack. The technical background to locative art comes from experiments with tracking by the military, and leads Hollis Henry into a complicated plot involving a search for a mysterious shipping container, an example of the 'anomalous phenomena' (Gibson 2011b: 108) that so fascinate Bigend.

Gibson has also had a fruitful collaboration with fellow cyberpunk author Bruce Sterling in *The Difference Engine*, a narrative set in Victorian times based on the assumption that many more recent inventions, such as the computer, had been introduced then through the work of one of the key pioneers of this field, Charles Babbage. In keeping with the character of Victorian technology, computers are steam-driven, and also of the mainframe variety that they initially had in the twentieth century. As a result of their introduction, lectures can even be accompanied by an early version of PowerPoint. It is a highly imaginative piece of work, which maintains a strong sense of period flavour despite the presence of so many modern inventions in it. Victorian morality and social attitudes are still there (one of the protagonists, Sybil Gerard, is a 'fallen woman'), while characters can also voice thoroughly postmodern sentiments about the cultural importance of knowledge: 'But they can't ever take what you *know*, now can they, Sybil? They can't ever take that' (Gibson and Sterling 2011: 20). As usual in Gibson, it is information that rules, and the more of this you possess, the greater the power you can wield over others – and the greater the lengths you will go to in order to gain possession. It is just such a cultural mix of past and present that will be developed by the steampunk movement. The fact that the authors give us a past age with a more up-to-date technology represents an interesting twist on double-coding, which does the opposite, bringing elements of the past into the present.

Gibson's work was much touted in the 1980s and 1990s, and there is no denying that he was instrumental in carving out a new direction and set of concerns for science fiction that have been highly influential. The extent to which his work will continue to exert such an appeal into the future, however, might be more problematical. Science fiction of any era has a tendency to date very fast, and what can be cutting-edge to one generation can come to seem merely quaint just a generation or two down the line once the boundaries of technology have been pushed considerably further on. It is noticeable that Gibson's later work is less generic in this respect, and more concerned with the interaction of the characters and the emotional turmoil they have to go through in tracking down information in its bewildering variations. It also displays a higher level of irony in the way that it mocks the foibles and pretensions of corporations in the information game, such as the Big Ant set-up and its relentless seeking out of the very latest in information technology – even if it can hardly say what its commercial application might ever turn out to be. Bigend himself is clearly being held up for satire, and eventually comes to seem like someone increasingly out of his depth in terms of his understanding of what is going on around him in the world of information. Information, eventually, surpasses the understanding of all of us in a particular generation, so a character like Bigend becomes rather poignantly symbolic of our individual inability to keep pace with technological innovation.

Gibson's major writings

Gibson, William, *Mona Lisa Overdrive*, New York: Bantam, 1988.
——, *Neuromancer* [1984], London: HarperCollins, 1993.
——, *Virtual Light*, London: Penguin, 1994.
——, *Burning Chrome and Other Stories* [1986], New York: HarperCollins, 1995.
——, *All Tomorrow's Parties*, New York: Viking, 1999.
——, *Pattern Recognition*, London: Penguin, 2004.
——, *Zero History*, New York: Putnam, 2010.
——, *Idoru* [1996], London: Penguin, 2011a.
——, *Spook Country* [2007], London: Penguin, 2011b.
Gibson, William and Bruce Sterling, *The Difference Engine* [1990], London: Gollancz, 2011.

PHILIP GLASS (B. 1937)

Glass is one of the leading lights of musical minimalism, and has a rich and varied oeuvre to his name, ranging from operas through orchestral works, concertos and film scores. He is probably best known by the music-listening public for his operas, such as *Einstein on the Beach*, *Satyagraha* and *Akhnaten* (the three works forming 'The Portrait Trilogy'), which have gained a worldwide following, although increasingly over the years his film scores have been bringing his work to the attention of a much wider audience than opera alone reaches. To date he has also produced nine symphonies, although these have not had as much impact as the rest of his work in terms of public or critical acclaim. Along with Steve Reich, he is considered to be one of the most influential composers of his time, and also like Reich he founded his own band early in his career, the Philip Glass Ensemble, as an outlet for performance of his own works. The band has continued to perform periodically.

Minimalism is a style that developed in reaction to musical modernism, and particularly the serial method of composition that had become something of a paradigm in the world of academic music departments over the course of the twentieth century. Serial music rejected the Western tradition of tonality based on seven-note scales, and instead insisted that all twelve notes of the octave had to be played before any of them could be repeated (hence the other names by which it is known, twelve-tone or atonal), without at any time forming a recognisably tonal chord. The resultant highly intellectual and abstract style was never very popular with the concert-going public (a few key works excepted), although it had some dedicated devotees who regarded it as the future of serious music. It did take root in the academy, however, becoming *the* modernist style that young musicians were expected to embrace, leading to the production of several generations of serially trained composers whose work had very little success in the concert hall. Indeed, as Derek B. Scott has noted, 'it became common for a composition tutor to find students earnestly composing a type of music that they would never dream of actually going to a concert hall to hear' (Scott 2011: 122–32). More to the point, few of the public would dream of going to hear it either (unless it was buried in a programme with more popular works, not always a well-received method). Minimalism, on the other hand, is largely tonal, although generally lacking in the development (of theme and musical idea) associated with traditional Western classical music, as exemplified by such composers as Mozart or Beethoven in their symphonies and concertos. Wim Mertens has described Glass's approach as 'based on additive structure principles' (Mertens 1983: 67) rather than systematic development in the classical style.

Minimalism in its early days also relied very heavily on rhythm, usually insistently repetitive in form, to make its impression, with shifts of key generally being few over the course of a composition. Eventually, in the hands of composers like Glass, Reich, John Adams and Michael Nyman (to name some of its best-known and most successful practitioners), it developed into quite a popular style with a youthful audience, drawing on elements of jazz and rock music to increase its appeal to that constituency. Linda Hutcheon has noted how composers like Glass set out to achieve 'communication with the audience through simple repetitive harmonies' (Hutcheon 1989: 9), in a desire to widen the base for a classical music audience – although the term 'classical' is becoming rather loose in this context. Glass has turned out to be one of the most distinctive, and prolific, voices of the minimalist movement, and has been in particular demand in recent years as a film composer.

Glass's score for the film *Koyaanisqatsi* (a Hopi Native American phrase meaning 'life out of balance') is one of the most striking efforts of his earlier career, and forms the backdrop to a work consisting of a series of images comparing unspoiled nature with the environmental despoliation created by humankind. Speeded-up images of urban traffic, for example, are meant to convey the relentless, almost mindless, pace of late twentieth-century life, and come accompanied by Glass's music at its most frenetic. Since the film lacks either dialogue or plot, it is the music that dominates and is likely to make the greatest impact on the viewer. Glass went on to collaborate on two further projects with the filmmaker Godfrey Reggio, but without the same success that *Koyaanisqatsi* enjoyed. Since then, his film scores have gravitated towards more conventional Hollywood fare.

Glass has made a point of disregarding the distinction between popular and classical music, adapting albums by David Bowie and Brian Eno (*Low* and *Heroes*) into symphonic form in his *Low Symphony* and *Heroes Symphony* respectively. In fact, Eno had been influenced by Glass's music to some extent in his contribution to the *Low* album, indicating the kind of cross-over between styles and genres that minimalism has tended to inspire – and that Glass has always actively encouraged. Earlier, he had set the lyrics of such popular artists as Paul Simon and David Byrne to music in *Songs from Liquid Days*, and he has continued to collaborate with pop and rock figures over the course of his career. The minimalist school in general had a notable effect on the development of pop music in the later twentieth century, influencing styles such as house music, which has similarly insistent rhythms to those found in the work of Glass, Reich and company. In an interview just before his seventy-fifth birthday, speaking about a recent collaborative effort he had undertaken with several pop musicians, Glass emphasised that 'I felt completely comfortable working with people in pop music. I didn't think of it as a higher or lower art form. ... We fought to break down those barriers, and those barriers are gone, there's no battle' (in Wolfe 2012).

Glass's overall reputation still rests largely on his work as an opera composer, however, and the 'Portrait Trilogy' is right at the centre of that output. Each instalment is a portrait of a figure who had a significant impact on his world. *Einstein on the Beach* created a stir in operatic circles on its first performance, departing quite radically from the conventions of the opera form and challenging the audience in various ways, such as being both very long and virtually plotless. The opera lasts around five hours, consisting of four acts interspersed with five interludes (or 'knee plays' as they are dubbed), and the audience is permitted to come and go as it pleases during its performance – not surprisingly, since the work was conceived to be performed without any intervals. Setting various texts to music, including poems by an autistic youth whom Glass had come to know, Christopher Knowles, it is certainly an expansive piece by the standards of early minimalism, and the composer continues on in like manner for the rest of the 'Portrait Trilogy'. In a book tracing the development of minimalism into the 1990s, K. Robert Schwarz has described the move to larger forms like opera as Glass's 'maximalist' phase (Schwarz 1996: 130). Glass himself felt that *Einstein* represented the culminating point of his early musical style, remarking in an interview:

> It's curious because at the time most people experienced it as the beginning of something, but for me it was the end. It was the end of a period that had gone on for 10 years and it was a summation of a way of thinking about the musical language, in terms of rhythm and harmony and melody.
>
> (Glass, in Sillito 2012)

Rather disarmingly, he also said that he would not be unduly worried if some of the audience were to fall asleep during the piece if it proved to be too much for their attention span.

Satyagraha, meaning 'truth-force' (Mahatma Gandhi's name for the technique of non-violent resistance that he developed as a way of challenging the colonial authorities), is based on Gandhi's stay in South Africa before he returned to India to become the figurehead of Indian nationalism against British rule of the subcontinent. Glass felt that the work marked a change in his style from the early works, and one can note a more lyrical tone coming into play, both here and in *Akhnaten*. The text is adapted from the ancient Sanskrit work the *Bhagavad Gita*, part of the longer epic called the *Mahabharata*, and, in an exotic touch on the composer's part, is actually sung in that language. Each of the work's three acts features a famous historical figure silently observing the scene unfolding on stage: Ravindranath Tagore, Leo Tolstoy and Martin Luther King Jr, respectively.

Akhnaten, the last piece in the 'Portrait Trilogy', is a highly ambitious work with a dramatic orchestral score and some very challenging writing for the voice (Akhnaten is sung by a counter-tenor, lending an unearthly feel to some of the arias). The score utilises several languages, including Hebrew and ancient Akkadian, and even ends with descriptions taken from a contemporary tourist brochure, in English, of the landscape in Egypt associated with Akhnaten's reign – the ruins of Amarna, Akhnaten's capital. Amongst the texts that are set in the work is Akhnaten's own 'Hymn to the Sun', and extracts from the *Egyptian Book of the Dead* (Glass does seem to be attracted to such esoteric texts).

Glass has continued to work in the opera medium since the trilogy, and even turned Jean Cocteau's film *La Belle et la Bête* into a quasi-opera by removing its soundtrack, including the musical score by the French composer Georges Auric, and writing his own score for it to be performed as the now-silent film was projected. As he remarked of this intriguing experiment, 'as far as I know no one has actually opera-ized a movie' (quoted in Schwarz 1996: 164).

Minimalism can, however, become a very predictable style and Glass's music does not always escape that danger, with his film scores eventually coming to sound very similar to each other: for all their immediate surface excitement, insistent rhythms and repeated patterns can become a cliché pretty quickly, and they do seem to predominate in these scores. Although that style can be very successful in helping to build up a sense of tension in a film, it does not necessarily render the score all that interesting outside that context. The works in the 'Portrait Trilogy', however, despite all the difficulties they pose in staging them, do seem to have entered the operatic repertoire and established Glass's name.

Glass's major works

Glass, Philip, *Einstein on the Beach*, 1976.
———, *Satyagraha*, 1979.
———, *Koyaanisqatsi*, 1981.
———, *Akhnaten*, 1984.
———, *Songs from Liquid Days*, 1986.
———, *Violin Concerto*, 1987.
———, *The Voyage*, 1992.
———, *Low Symphony*, 1992.
———, *La Belle et la Bête*, 1993.
———, *Heroes Symphony*, 1997.

References and further reading

Hutcheon, Linda, *The Politics of Postmodernism*, London and New York: Routledge, 1989.

Mertens, Wim, *American Minimal Music* [1980], trans. J. Hautekeit, London: Kahn and Averill, 1983.

Schwarz, K. Robert, *Minimalists*, London and New York: Phaidon Press, 1996.

Scott, Derek B., 'Postmodernism and Music', in Stuart Sim (ed.), *The Routledge Companion to Postmodernism*, 3rd edition, London and New York: Routledge, 2011, pp. 122–32.

Sillito, David, 'Have a Sleep During *Einstein on the Beach*', *BBC News, Entertainment and Arts*, http://www.bbc.co.uk/news/entertainment-arts-17958400, 4 May 2012 (accessed 11 October 2012).

Wolfe, Zachary, 'Remixing Glass', *New York Times Magazine*, http://www.nytimes.com/2012/10/07/magazine/philip-glass-and-beck-discuss-collaborating-on-rework.html?_r=0, 10 July 2012 (accessed 9 October 2012).

STEPHEN GREENBLATT (B. 1937)

A noted Renaissance scholar and critic, Greenblatt is one of the leading figures in the critical movement of new historicism, which enjoyed a particular vogue in academic literary studies during the 1980s and 1990s. He is best known for his study of early modern culture, *Renaissance Self-Fashioning: From More to Shakespeare*, which established new historicism as an important new critical method. New historicism, and its companion theory cultural materialism, sought to establish links between literary works and other writings of their time, being very much influenced by the work of Michel Foucault and also by the cultural anthropology of Clifford Geertz. The latter emphasised the importance of getting down to the micro level of any culture if we were to understand it properly; thus a village election in Indonesia could be treated as 'a specific manifestation of a more comprehensive pattern' (Geertz 1963: 154). In similar fashion, new historicists like Greenblatt often make use of ephemeral, non-fictional texts when analysing major literary figures like Shakespeare and Marlowe. In the case of Foucault, new historicists find him inspiring for his strikingly counter-historical approach to cultural analysis. Foucault's concern with the effect of power structures at the margins of society is yet another example of going down to the micro level.

Greenblatt was reacting against the spread of deconstructive techniques in literary studies in the American academy in the later twentieth century, when they were much in favour, arguing that the analyses they generated were lacking in a sense of historical context (a criticism also levelled earlier against new criticism). In *Practicing New Historicism*, jointly written with Catherine Gallagher, the authors note, somewhat bemusedly, that new historicism is often criticised as under-theorised, when from their point of view it was 'the simultaneous fascination with theory and resistance to it that has shaped from the start our whole attempt to rethink the practice of literary and cultural studies' (Gallagher and Greenblatt 2000: 2). They voice their antipathy to the notion of abstract systems of thought which are then backdated onto the past, their own critical writings being firmly opposed to such a procedure. They also speak of the 'liberating effect' (Gallagher and Greenblatt 2000: 20) on them of Geertz's work, such as the concept of 'thick description' outlined in *The Interpretation of Cultures*. What they also take from Geertz is a fondness for the anecdote as a way in to analysis (something found in Foucault, too, as in *The Order of Things*); the assumption being that anecdotes serve to bring out the importance of the micro level in the overall scheme of things.

Building on a generally recognised point amongst scholars that the early modern period saw 'a change in the intellectual, social, psychological, and aesthetic structures that govern the generation of identities', *Renaissance Self-Fashioning* proceeds to examine the social tensions that this change, with the attendant 'complex interaction of meanings' (Greenblatt 1980: 1, 3), brought in its wake. Literature's role in this process is central to the study, with Greenblatt adopting an anthropological approach in order to put together a thick description of its social context. His concern is to bring out 'both the social presence to the world of the literary text and the social presence of the world in the literary text' (Greenblatt 1980: 5). This sounds a large-scale project, but Greenblatt is unapologetic in pursuing it through a small selection of texts and authors, picking those he regards as 'arresting figures who seem to contain within themselves much of what we need' (Greenblatt 1980: 6). In each case, Greenblatt argues, self-fashioning looms large.

Self-fashioning is held to involve some key 'governing conditions' (Greenblatt 1980: 9), such as the lack of a strong sense of social identity in one's background, the requirement for the self to submit to some higher authority (monarchy or church, for example) and the need to assert oneself against a threatening alien force. Competing authorities form a backdrop to the period Greenblatt is concerned with, and defending one's particular choice of authority can lead to the development of a power so strong that it comes to threaten that very entity: 'Hence self-fashioning always involves some experience of threat, some effacement or undermining, some loss of self' (Greenblatt 1980: 9).

An incident from Thomas More's early life – his attendance at a dinner party given by Cardinal Wolsey – that he later worked up into a story mocking the cardinal, is taken to constitute a 'distillation of More's long career in the dangerous, glittering world of Renaissance politics' (Greenblatt 1980: 12), which Greenblatt proceeds to unpick in terms of his subject's life and writings. Although More joins in praise of the cardinal's recent oration, as the cardinal demands of the company present, he is doing so merely to further his own ambition, and there is a sense of amusement and irony behind his presentation of his own part in the scene. Above all to Greenblatt it reveals More's attraction to power (also a major concern of Foucault's), and it is that attraction that ultimately leads to his death when he clashes with the greater power of the king. A fictionalised anecdote becomes the way in to an understanding of More's social position. It is just such a juxtaposition of micro and macro that becomes so characteristic of new historicist criticism and Greenblatt deploys the technique throughout his writings. Thus he cites a police spy report on Christopher Marlowe as an entry into the subject of atheism in Elizabethan/Jacobean culture, and a medical report on hermaphroditism for that of sexual ambiguity – a recurrent theme in Shakespeare's plays.

Greenblatt also looks at the case of a lawyer (James Bainham), prosecuted by More in his role as Lord Chancellor for his Protestant beliefs, as a further illustration of the tensions that could arise in the self-fashioned individual. More on this occasion acts with cruelty towards Bainham as a heretic, as his position demanded of him in an age of religious turmoil; but this did clash with the more generous side of his nature that contemporaries could speak so well of, and that history has tended to emphasise since. Again, biographical details are held to help open up the subject's literary output. Greenblatt finds the tension between More's public and private persona coming through in fictionalised guise in *Utopia*, where in the opening debate 'More isolates, on the one hand, his public self and, on the other, all within him that is excluded from this carefully crafted identity, calls the former *Morus* and the latter *Hythlodaeus* and permits them to fight it out' (Greenblatt 1980: 36). In Greenblatt's interpretation, this amounts to a staging of More's public career, and how he had to struggle to reconcile what this required of him with his private beliefs: the 'threat' and 'loss of self' that are taken to be intrinsic to the process of self-fashioning register clearly. The awkward and threatening relationship to power is also very evident in the plays of Christopher Marlowe and William Shakespeare. Marlowe, whose life is marked by an overt sense of 'recklessness', is described as 'deeply implicated in his heroes' (Greenblatt 1980: 220); whereas in Shakespeare's case 'his plays offer no single timeless affirmation or denial of legitimate authority and no central, unwavering authorial presence' (Greenblatt 1980: 254).

Shakespeare has been an ongoing concern of Greenblatt's and he has written extensively about him, as in *Shakespearean Negotiations, Hamlet in Purgatory, Will in the World* and *Shakespeare's Freedoms*, in each case paying very close attention to historical context and the place of Shakespeare's work within this. *Shakespearean Negotiations* looks at the author's plays as 'the products of collective negotiation and exchange' (Greenblatt 1988a: vii) taking place in his society. Greenblatt is concerned to explore the effect on a writer like Shakespeare of the ruptures present in the Elizabethan and Jacobean world, the 'cracks, conflict, and disarray' (Greenblatt 1988a: 2) that belie any notion of unity there. Power is always being contested, and Greenblatt warns us that we should 'resist the integration of all images and expressions into a single master discourse' (Greenblatt 1988a: 2–3) – very much a postmodern sentiment. Texts will carry traces of this contestation, and that is to be one of the new historicist's primary tasks, exploring 'the half-hidden cultural transactions through which great works of art are empowered' (Greenblatt 1988a: 4). Authors are to be seen as responding to, and being inspired by, the 'social energy' (Greenblatt 1988a: 6) of their time. Greenblatt notes several types of exchange of this social energy – 'Appropriation', 'Purchase', 'Symbolic Acquisition', for example – and their collective impact leads him to the conclusion that '[t]here can be no appeals to genius as the sole origin of the energies of great art' (Greenblatt 1988a: 12).

In *Will in the World* Greenblatt reminds us that theatre 'is a highly social art form, not a game of bloodless abstractions' (Greenblatt 2005: 11), and he ranges around in the events in Shakespeare's life, public and private, that provided the social energy that then became encoded in his plays. *Hamlet in Purgatory* explores the impact of the changing notions of purgatory in Protestant culture, where it was attacked as a false doctrine, on that play. *Hamlet* provides yet another example of the channelling of social energy into fictional form, with the ghost's condition suggesting that of purgatory, indicating that it was still a topical issue even though the doctrine had been removed from Church of England theology in 1563. *Shakespeare's Freedoms* explores the relationship of freedom and constraint in his work, seen in the boundaries and limits that his characters are so often brought up against.

Greenblatt's critical writings are consistently historically informed, and he provides a corrective in that respect to the various formalist schools of critical theory that had proved so popular over the course of the twentieth century, from structuralism and new criticism through to deconstruction. His adaptation of Geertz's anthropological techniques is striking, although the micro–macro juxtaposition and the use of anecdote can become a somewhat predictable method after a while. Nevertheless, his work is very valuable in its insistence on the importance of a historical consciousness in literary studies, and in the arguments it puts forward against the danger of assuming master narratives in any historical period. There is always difference and pluralism to be taken into account, as well as contestation of power.

Greenblatt's major writings

Greenblatt, Stephen, *Renaissance Self-Fashioning: From More to Shakespeare*, Chicago and London: University of Chicago Press, 1980.

——, *Marvelous Possessions: The Wonder of the New World*, Oxford and New York: Clarendon Press, 1981.

——(ed.), *The Power of Forms in the English Renaissance*, Norman, OK: Pilgrim Books, 1982.

——, *Shakespearean Negotiations: The Circulation of Social Energy in Renaissance England*, Oxford: Clarendon Press, 1988a.

——(ed.), *Representing the English Renaissance*, Berkeley, CA: University of California Press, 1988b.

——, *Learning to Curse: Essays in Early Modern Culture*, New York and London: Routledge, 1990.

——, *Hamlet in Purgatory*, Princeton, NJ: Princeton University Press, 2002.
——, *Will in the World: How Shakespeare Became Shakespeare*, London: Pimlico, 2005.
——, *Shakespeare's Freedoms*, Chicago and London: University of Chicago Press, 2010.
Gallagher, Catherine and Stephen Greenblatt, *Practicing New Historicism*, Chicago and London: University of Chicago Press, 2000.

References and further reading

Foucault, Michel, *The Order of Things: An Archaeology of the Human Sciences* [1966], trans. Alan Sheridan, London: Tavistock, 1974.
Geertz, Clifford, *Agricultural Involution: The Processes of Ecological Change in Indonesia*, Berkeley, Los Angeles and London: University of California Press, 1963.
——, *The Interpretation of Cultures: Selected Essays* [1973], London: Fontana, 1993.

PETER HALLEY (B. 1953)

Halley is both a practising artist and an art theorist, whose writings are an invaluable source of information about the impact of postmodern and poststructural theory on the New York art scene of the late twentieth century. It was a scene where many artists enthusiastically embraced postmodern concepts as a source of inspiration for their work, often referencing figures like Jean Baudrillard, Michel Foucault and Guy Debord, even if, as in Baudrillard's case, the theorists themselves did not necessarily feel all that enthusiastic about the appropriation that was being made of their concepts. The art that Halley and others (Jeff Koons, Sherrie Levine and Ross Bleckner, for example) produced in this period was labelled as 'simulationist', or 'neo-geo', and attempted to relate art to cultural and critical theory in order to extend the concerns of thinkers like the above and so make statements about contemporary culture. Halley is very much influenced by the ideas around in recent theory, and describes his art as 'extremely intertextual' (Siegel 1985) in intent.

Halley considered himself to be something of a modernist, but he took a very different view of what that term meant than the doyen of modernist art theory, Clement Greenberg, one of the great defenders of abstraction in art (see, for example, his *Collected Essays and Criticism*): 'I disagree with Greenberg in just about everything in terms of his ideas about what's important in a work of art' (Siegel 1985).

Halley insisted that 'I don't think of my art as abstract at all' (Siegel 1985), and saw the use of geometric shapes in his paintings as representing and commenting on certain critical aspects of the culture around him rather than simply drawing attention to matters of form and colour. The audience was expected to read things into the paintings, a reaction of which most abstract artists disapprove. Yet while he did express some reservations about postmodernism, Halley acknowledged the particular influence of both Foucault and Baudrillard on his artistic practice, and took theory very seriously; indeed, the art critic Jeanne Siegel remarked that '[h]e prefers to be thought of as a theorist' (Siegel 1985). Revealingly enough, Halley himself commented in an interview with Siegel that he found 'reading Baudrillard is very similar to looking at Andy Warhol's paintings' (Siegel 1985).

Halley felt that theory enabled him better to understand elements that were already present in his paintings, and so to realise these more explicitly: 'I think of myself as not a very good conceptualizer. So when I read Foucault's *Discipline and Punish*, some of the things I was trying to get at in the paintings were very clearly conceptualized there and it helped me make conscious my own feelings about the subject' (Siegel 1985). Baudrillard's concepts of simulation and seduction had a similar effect on him. Halley's early work used Day-Glo acrylic colours (one commentator referring to the effect as 'lurid elegance' (Halley 2001: 8)) to produce geometrically composed works in a minimalist style, explaining that he thought of these as 'simulated colors' (Siegel 1985) and that it was only when he read Baudrillard that he recognised the wider implications of his choice of material. Siegel insightfully suggests that we should see Halley as 'a synthesizer within a post-modern dialectic' (Siegel 1985).

Halley's first collection of essays reveals him as someone trying to assimilate the ideas coming through from poststructuralist and postmodernist theorists, and to work out their implications for contemporary artistic practice in America, including his own. In 'Against Post-Modernism', Halley emphasises that modernism is a more varied form of expression than Greenberg defines. It is a point well worth making, given the immense influence that Greenberg exercised within the postwar art world in America, where he had effectively set the terms of reference as to what constituted modernism. This affected not just artistic practice in the period but the buying habits of both collectors and art galleries as well, in the process turning into something approaching an orthodoxy. Halley identifies a different trend in the history of modernism to what he regards as the 'idealist' strain that Greenberg championed. This other modernism is based on an attitude of relativism and doubt, rather than what Halley considers to be the cultural imperialist notions motivating Greenbergian modernism, which he interprets as an expression of America's emergence as the world's dominant economic power: 'an artistic equivalent for America's post-war aspirations to leadership of the western and developing nations' (Halley 2000: 27). As Halley points out elsewhere in the essay 'Nature and Culture', modernist artists were assumed to be playing 'a vanguard, heroic role' (Halley 2000: 63) in this enterprise. Halley suggests that if we go back to the work of the Spanish writer Ortega y Gasset we can find a source for the kind of modernism he is advocating, Ortega promoting the notion of liberalism as an antidote to the shift towards authoritarian government in the 1920s, with communism in control in Russia and fascism rearing its head elsewhere in Europe. Liberalism is seen to enshrine the idea of relativism, ensuring respect for and tolerance towards the beliefs of others.

Halley feels that this other strand of modernism is what is informing practice on the current scene, and that it can be found not just in painting but in pop music and film too. Although some commentators are now beginning to label the change of attitude that is occurring as postmodern, Halley prefers to see it as a distinct form of modernism in its own right, one that challenges the assumptions lying behind the abstract expressionist form of modernism that Greenberg so admired. One of the consequences of living in a period 'of economic adversity and uncertainty', as Halley sees it, is that it will encourage some artists to adopt a position of 'intense thought and doubt' (Halley 2000: 45) about the world around them. What he hopes is now imminent is 'a modernist resurgence in the arts' (Halley 2000: 46). If he still wants to retain the term 'modernism', however, Halley makes it clear that he is opposed to the ideals of contemporary modernity, 'the ruthless modernity preached and practiced by the postwar American corporation' (Halley 2000: 49).

Halley specifically tackles the growing influence of poststructuralist thought at the time in 'Nature and Culture'. He is intrigued by poststructuralist concepts, although unclear as to how they can be incorporated into artistic practice, wondering, for example, if '[t]he practice of simulation by the artists can be seen as an endorsement of the culture of simulacra' (Halley 2000: 71). This would make artists collusive with a system that Halley feels should be the subject of criticism. He is also somewhat surprised that Baudrillard's ideas seem to be finding more favour than Foucault's, considering the latter to be the more penetrating thinker of the two, with his 'bleak excavation of the spaces of regimentation' (Halley 2000: 72) in our society. Foucault directs us towards pressing social issues in a way that Baudrillard does not, and Halley warns that for all poststructuralism's undoubted merits in undermining the belief system of modernity, we need also to be on the lookout for whatever 'negative results it may engender' (Halley 2000: 72). The tendency to regard power as a unified entity is for Halley one such negative result, and one that could lead artists to turn their backs on social commentary.

Halley regards his geometric painting as a transformation of minimalist style into an art carrying social significance. Minimalism for him 'was really to do with issues about social and industrial development and the modern landscape, rather than being hermetic the way minimal artists thought it was' (Siegel 1985). What to minimalists was purely a series of geometrical shapes suggested to him instead actual industrial landscapes – smokestacks, for instance, as well as, even more sombrely, prisons and cells. Jails, he points out, 'came about as a way of describing the minimalist square as a confining structure' (Siegel 1985). This is a culturally very resonant notion, suggestive of institutional power and its surveillance techniques, amongst other things (see, for example, *Prison with Underground Conduit*, 1985, in Halley 2001). Foucault, of course, held that over the last few centuries we had developed into a surveillance society, describing in books like *Discipline and Punish* how institutions such as prisons and asylums became a means of exercising ever greater power over the population. Thus Halley can assert that '[i]nformed by Foucault, I see in the square a prison; behind the mythologies of contemporary society, a veiled network of cells and conduits' (Halley 2000: 25). The allusion to such ideas substantiates Halley's point about his painting not being abstract, as in the minimalists' case, but rather 'diagrammatic' (Siegel 1985). He does regard himself, in both his writings and paintings, as a commentator on post-industrial society. Even the Day-Glo colours are supposed to be read in this manner, representing for Halley 'the afterglow of radiation' (Halley 2000: 23).

Halley is one of the most theory-aware artists of his generation, and the body of writing he has produced over his career makes him a particularly rich source for the examination of the relationship between art and theory. Many artists can be suspicious of theorists, feeling that they can read things into their work that are not there, or that they themselves knew nothing about. Other artists might well feel impelled to raid fashionable theories for some ideas and then apply these in a superficial manner to their practice, just in order to attract critical attention. Halley, on the other hand, is clearly someone drawn to theory as a means of enhancing and deepening his art, rather than someone imposing a theory on it merely to follow a cultural trend: the impetus to give his paintings theoretical significance was there before the work of Foucault and Baudrillard came to his attention. It is more a case of him seeking out theories to integrate his work into so that the ideas latent there could find their fullest expression. Crucially, too, he shows a sceptical turn of mind, and does not just take theories over wholesale, directing us to their weak points as well as their strong. His work puts modernism into dialogue with postmodern thought, and demonstrates another route to constructing a postmodern aesthetic than the double-coding approach popularised by Charles Jencks in *The Language of Post-Modern Architecture*. Perhaps altermodernism, as outlined by Nicolas Bourriaud (see Bourriaud 2009), might be interpreted as an expression of the 'modernist resurgence' that Halley was seeking back in the 1980s.

Halley's major writings and works

Halley, Peter, *Recent Essays 1990–1996*, New York: Edgewise Press, 1997.

——, *Collected Essays 1971–1987* [1988], Zurich and New York: Bruno Bischofberger Gallery and Sonnabend Gallery, 2000.

——, *Paintings*, London: Waddington Galleries, 2001 (Introduction by Alex Coles).

Hough, Jessica, Monica Montagut, Anthony Vidler and Peter Halley, *Revisiting the Glass House: Contemporary Art and Modern Architecture*, New Haven, CT: Yale University Press, 2008.

References and further reading

Baudrillard, Jean, *Simulations*, trans. Paul Foss, Paul Patton and Philip Beitchman, New York: Semiotext(e), 1983.

——, *Seduction* [1979], trans. Brian Singer, London and Basingstoke: Macmillan, 1990.

Bourriaud, Nicolas (ed.), *Altermodern: Tate Triennial*, London: Tate Publishing, 2009.

Foucault, Michel, *Discipline and Punish: The Birth of the Prison* [1975], trans. Alan Sheridan, Harmondsworth: Pelican, 1977.

Greenberg, Clement, *The Collected Essays and Criticism: Perceptions and Judgements, 1939–44*, vol. 1, ed. John O'Brian, Chicago and London: University of Chicago Press, 1986.

Jencks, Charles, *The Language of Post-Modern Architecture* [1975], 6th edition, London: Academy Editions, 1991.

Siegel, Jeanne, 'Artist/Critic of the Eighties, Part One: Peter Halley and Stephen Westfall, Interview and Text', *Arts Magazine*, September 1985, pp. 72–6, www.peterhalley.com/ARTISTS/PETER.HALLEY/INTERVIEW.FR2.1985.Siegel.htm (accessed 2 November 2012).

DONNA J. HARAWAY (B. 1944)

Haraway's description of her career path and interests indicates the kind of interdisciplinarity that she promotes, and practises, in her work:

> Trained in molecular and developmental biology, I identify as a historian of science. I have applied for a visa for an extended stay in the permeable territories of anthropology – as a resident alien or a cross-specific hybrid, naturally. But my real home is the ferociously material and imaginary zones of technoscience.
>
> (Haraway 1989: 49)

There is invariably a feminist dimension to Haraway's work as well, and she is best known for her championship of the 'cyborg' concept, suggesting that, if it were embraced enthusiastically enough, this could provide a way of overcoming the gender discrimination that is still so evident in our culture. (The term was originally devised by the scientist Manfred E. Clynes in 1960.) In her provocative words ending 'A Cyborg Manifesto', 'I would rather be a cyborg than a goddess' (Haraway 1991: 181). Cyborgs, 'a hybrid of machine and organism' (Haraway 1991: 149), far outstrip the power and ability of the human alone, and for Haraway they hold out the promise of erasing the imbalance between the sexes.

Haraway's intention in the 'Cyborg Manifesto' is 'to build an ironic political myth faithful to feminism, socialism, and materialism' (Haraway 1991: 149) around the notion of the cyborg. What the cyborg represents for her is a new, more positive relationship between women and technoscience, something that she calls for consistently throughout her writings. She counsels feminists to make the most of what technological advance can offer instead of rejecting it as a male-dominated field, using whatever new processes and products come on stream to further the cause of breaking down gender boundaries. Science and technology are always in a process of change, and for Haraway that means they help to demonstrate the pointlessness of universal theories: 'There is no drive in cyborgs to produce total theory[.] … [T]he production of universal, totalizing theory is a major mistake that misses most of reality, probably always, but certainly now' (Haraway 1991: 181). The anti-universalising bias is very much in the spirit of postmodernism, with Haraway regarding the 'Cyborg Manifesto' as 'an effort to contribute to socialist-feminist culture and theory in a postmodernist, non-naturalist mode' (Haraway 1991: 150) designed to stir up controversy. 'The cyborg', she further asserts, 'is a kind of disassembled and reassembled, postmodern collective and personal self. This is the self feminists must code' (Haraway 1991: 163).

Haraway has had her critics from within feminism, who have complained that the cyborg concept is highly questionable, not to mention highly impractical, as a method of improving women's social status. For such critics, the cyborg notion can hardly stand as a programme for political action in the immediate future, thought-provoking though it undoubtedly is. Susan Bordo, for example, cannot envisage how such a concept could work in practice, nor how it would serve to further the feminist cause in any meaningful way:

> What sort of body is it that is free to change its shape and location at will, that can become anyone and travel anywhere? If the body is a metaphor for our locatedness in space and time and thus for the finitude of human perception and knowledge, then the postmodern body is no body at all.
>
> (Bordo 1990: 145)

As Sue Thornham puts it, Haraway could 'be accused of replacing a narrative of liberation directed at change in the real world with a utopian fantasy' (Thornham 2011: 46).

Utopian fantasy notwithstanding, there is a sense in which cyborgisation can be said merely to represent an extension of processes that are already well under way in our society. As Haraway notes, medical science is making more and more use of machine parts to replace faulty parts of the human body, as with heart pacemakers, and artificial organs are now in regular use. That can only become a more common practice in future as technology develops, but whether this either could or should lead to the development of full-blown cyborgs as Haraway conceives of them is more contentious. The loss of humanity this almost undoubtedly would have to involve were we to move towards full-blown cyborgisation of our bodies would prove very problematical to many. Jean-François Lyotard's argument against the threat posed by the 'inhuman' in the book of that name indicates the kind of fears that the prospect of a machine- or computer-led future can arouse, and it is precisely this kind of future, Lyotard warns, that the forces of technoscience are trying to engineer.

For Lyotard technoscience is a threat, whereas Haraway invites us to consider the opportunities it could offer us to reconstruct our culture and its fixed notions of gender roles and abilities (although she is by no means an uncritical supporter of the technoscientific enterprise, as her book *Modest Witness* reveals). Biological definition would no longer hold much weight as an argument for a patriarchal form of society if women could access an equal amount of power to men and encourage women to become more involved with the world of technoscience, with the goal of rendering it less of a masculinist province.

Haraway delves deeply into the relations between women and technoscience in *Modest Witness@Second Millennium Meets Oncomouse: Feminism and Technoscience*, describing the book as consisting of 'cascading accounts of humans, nonhumans, technoscience, nation, feminism, democracy, property, race, history, and kinship' (Haraway 1997: 2). Noting how prejudices of various kinds – anti-Semitism and racism, for example – had flourished even during periods of intellectual and scientific advancement in the past, and perhaps could even be considered as products of cultural phenomena like the Renaissance and the Scientific Revolution, she sets out to explore what similar socio-political problems are emerging in the technological revolution of our time, the era of the Net. Technoscience is held to transcend the concerns of modernity quite dramatically, with Haraway observing that 'the ferocity of the transformations lived in daily life throughout the world are undeniable' (Haraway 1997: 4). Presenting herself as a 'modest witness', she takes on the role of 'spy and scout' (Haraway 1997: 6) on the Net, in order to try and work out just where these transformations might be leading us, and what new structures of domination might be hidden in the Net's expansion. We need to be aware that technoscience brings with it both opportunities and dangers, as we would expect from a system that has effectively been turned into the servant of free market capitalism.

For a start, Haraway is none too happy with the way that in the USA 'technoscience is a millenarian discourse' (Haraway 1989: 10), with overtly Christian overtones, particularly about achieving salvation through being a devout follower of the discourse and never questioning its aims or overall ideological orientation. This is precisely the kind of metanarrative that Lyotard warns us so strongly against in *The Postmodern Condition*. Haraway also points out that modern science is a metanarrative that traditionally has been a masculine preserve that actively works to exclude women – and this despite the fact that '[g]ender is always a relationship, not a performed category of beings or a possession that one can have' (Haraway 1989: 28). How to evade that metanarrative and turn technoscience into a more socially responsible practice is one of the book's main themes, with Haraway's 'modest witness' describing how the metanarrative works and manages to exert the power over us that it does.

Modest Witness constitutes both a critique and a defence of tech-noscience, therefore: a critique not of the enterprise itself, which has had many laudable successes that clearly have been of significant benefit to the human race, but of the way it has developed and its failure to transcend its ideological limitations. Haraway is particularly concerned to point out the extent to which technoscience is driven by the principles of free market capitalism, which means that it views nature as essentially an entity waiting to be manipulated and exploited by humankind. This attitude has led to some very dubious schemes such as the development of the 'oncomouse', a mouse raised specifi-cally to be used for testing purposes in cancer research. Oncomice are sold openly on the market, being perceived there as just another technoscientific product. There has been little in the way of public discussion about such developments, with technoscience treating them purely as technical challenges; and of course the corporations involved stand to make a lot of money out of such products. Whether the creation of those products is always desirable, or ethical, is put to one side in a system which is heavily geared towards profit.

How far technoscience would be willing to go in order to generate profit is something that Haraway is clearly very worried about, and she argues for more checks and balances to be built into the system, which in the main tends to regard itself as above politics and thus not in need of any public approval. Kazuo Ishiguro's novel *Never Let Me Go* offers a chilling vision of where this attitude could ultimately lead, with a group of humans being bred solely for the purpose of becoming organ donors to others, ultimately at the expense of their own lives. Haraway declares that 'I oppose patenting of animals, human genes, and much plant genetic material' (Haraway 1989: 62), but wants more informed public debate on such issues, rather than leaving the decision on whether to follow up such lines of enquiry to corporate technoscience, with its profit-driven bias.

Haraway has had a long-running interest in the relations and interactions between species, which she has followed up in a series of books from *Primate Visions* through to *When Species Meet*. *Primate Visions* is unashamedly polemical, designed to make us rethink the relationship we have constructed with primates in the modern world.

Primates, she claims, 'existing at the boundaries of so many hopes and interests are wonderful subjects with whom to explore the permeability of walls, the reconstitution of boundaries, the distaste for endless socially informed dualisms' (Haraway 1989: 3). The objective here, as it so often proves to be in Haraway's work, is 'to set new terms for the traffic between what we have come to know historically as nature and culture' (Haraway 1989: 15). This is an author for whom boundaries are always more permeable than tradition would lead us to believe.

Haraway's major writings

Haraway, Donna J., *Primate Visions: Gender, Race, and Nature in the World of Modern Science*, New York and London: Routledge, 1989.

——, *Simians, Cyborgs, and Women: The Reinvention of Nature*, London: Free Association Books, 1991.

——, *Modest Witness@Second Millennium Meets Oncomouse: Feminism and Technoscience*, New York and London: Routledge, 1997.

——, *The Companion Species Manifesto: Dogs, People and Significant Otherness*, Chicago: Prickly Paradigm Press, 2003.

——, *When Species Meet*, Minneapolis, MN: University of Minnesota Press, 2008.

References and further reading

Bordo, Susan, 'Feminism, Postmodernism, and Gender-Scepticism', in L. J. Nicholson (ed.), *Feminism/Postmodernism*, London and New York: Routledge, 1990, pp. 133–56.

Clynes, Manfred E. and Nathan S. Kline, 'Cyborgs and Space', *Astronautics*, September 1960, pp. 26–7 and 74–5.

Ishiguro, Kazuo, *Never Let Me Go*, London: Faber, 2005.

Lyotard, Jean-François, *The Postmodern Condition: A Report on Knowledge* [1979], trans. Geoff Bennington and Brian Massumi, Manchester: Manchester University Press, 1984.

——, *The Inhuman: Reflections on Time* [1988], trans. Geoffrey Bennington and Rachel Bowlby, Oxford: Blackwell, 1991.

Thornham, Sue, 'Postmodernism and Feminism', in Stuart Sim (ed.), *The Routledge Companion to Postmodernism*, 3rd edition, London and New York: Routledge, 2011, pp. 37–49.

DAVID HARVEY (B. 1935)

Harvey is an urban geographer whose work offers an interesting new dimension on the impact of modernism and capitalism on the city.

He is also a prominent commentator on the phenomenon of post-modernity, and has been a consistent campaigner against authoritarian socio-political systems from a Marxist position – if of a fairly open-minded variety – throughout his career. A Marxist bias notwith-standing, his politics now might best be described as 'popular front' in orientation, seeking a general left-wing response to the dominance of neoliberalism in the realms of politics and economics. Neoliberalism is for Harvey one of the most destructive forces in the current world order, and he has been an uncompromising critic of it. Harvey's Marxist-inclined theories on urban geography can be found in several of his works, such as *Social Justice and the City*, *The Urban Experience*, *Spaces of Capital*, *Spaces of Global Capitalism* and, most recently, *Rebel Cities*. His working premise in these books is that cities 'are founded upon the exploitation of the many by the few', and that this is a legacy of capitalism that we are still struggling to overcome: 'A gen-uinely humanizing urbanism has yet to be brought into being' (Harvey 1973: 314). Nor is there much likelihood of that emerging from a neoliberal economic system.

Harvey's work on postmodernity starts from the premise that '[t]here has been a sea-change in cultural as well as in political-economic practices since around 1972. This sea-change is bound up with the emergence of new dominant ways in which we experience space and time' (Harvey 1990: vii), and he sets out to capture what this means for our culture in *The Condition of Postmodernity*. He is one of the first commentators to regard postmodernism as a short-lived phenom-enon, arguing in this book, published in 1990, that its influence is on the wane. One can understand why a Marxist would wish this was so, given their general dislike of 'isms' other than their own (espe-cially one claiming, as Jean-François Lyotard did so confidently in *The Postmodern Condition*, that the days of such 'grand narratives' had now passed), but it has proved to be a very premature judgement. Nevertheless, Harvey does provide an illuminating critical overview of what postmodernity looked like as a cultural phenomenon at that point.

For Harvey, postmodernism has its roots in a growing unease about how modernity and capitalism were developing, an unease that spawned the counter-cultural movements of the 1960s that were so influential in the various uprisings around the world in 1968, perhaps most notably in the *événements* in Paris: 'Somewhere between 1968 and 1972 ... we see postmodernism emerge as a full-blown though still incoherent movement out of the chrysalis of the anti-modern move-ment of the 1960s' (Harvey 1990: 38). While Harvey acknowledges that there are many positive aspects to postmodernism, such as its commitment to difference, he does feel that its conception of modernism and what it represented is drastically oversimplified. If there is anyone to blame for the ills of current society, then it is capitalism rather than modernism which should stand accused, because modernism, too, has many positive aspects to its name. Indeed, what Harvey wants to emphasise is the degree of continuity that exists between modernism and postmodernism, whereby postmodernism is to be conceived of as a state of crisis that has arisen within modernism/modernity rather than something with its own distinct identity. It is a crisis that manifests itself in an extreme form of nihilism which renders postmodernism politically impotent: as a theory it offers us nothing concrete with which to fight the evils of late capitalism, leaving it free to extend its influence. As we would expect of a Marxist thinker, Harvey finds this completely unacceptable, concluding that 'postmodernism is dangerous for it avoids confronting the realities of political economy and the circumstances of global power' (Harvey 1990: 117). It is a not unreasonable criticism, and Fredric Jameson makes similar noises in *Postmodernism, or the Cultural Logic of Late Capitalism*.

Harvey makes another not unreasonable criticism that, for all their appeals to relativism, postmodern philosophers are ultimately assuming the truth of their own statements and thus undermining the relativistic stance which differentiates their theory from the grand narratives they are engaged in critiquing. Without implicitly making such an assumption, the theories of such as Lyotard and the deconstructionist movement would have no radical import at all – and Harvey remains clearly unimpressed by their claims on that score. Postmodernity, he concedes, may have the capacity to evolve into something else, perhaps even something more radical; but Harvey puts his faith instead in 'a renewal of historical materialism and of the Enlightenment project' (Harvey 1990: 359) as a way of challenging capitalism. The increasing dominance of neoliberalism in the interim, however, hardly suggests this renewal has materialised yet.

Harvey has been particularly critical of neoliberalism, which he regards as the source of many of our contemporary social and political ills. His study *A Brief History of Neoliberalism* is an impassioned indictment of the impact of neoliberal economics on almost every area of our life in the early twenty-first century; for Harvey this has been entirely negative and is to be deplored. Whereas the ideas of John Maynard Keynes initially had held sway in the West in the postwar era, recommending government intervention in the economy to stimulate demand when the economy faltered (as it so memorably did in the Great Depression of the 1930s when Western economies collectively stagnated after the boom years of the 1920s), those of Friedrich Hayek and Milton Friedman had come to dominate from the later 1970s onwards, providing the theoretical basis for the widespread adoption of neoliberal economics by the majority of Western governments. Friedman's book *Capitalism and Freedom* came to take on almost iconic status with world economic leaders, and its doctrines were even promoted by them in the developing world as the new way forward to achieve lasting economic prosperity; although countries like Argentina found the new regime socially extremely painful, being reduced to bankruptcy, and even widespread use of barter, in the early 1990s by its rigorous implementation in the face of widespread public protest.

Neoliberal economics prescribed free markets with minimum government legislation (the less the better from this standpoint) and, very specifically, no government intervention during market downturns – no matter how tough the impact of these might be on the general public. The belief in the 'invisible hand' of the market to correct such periodic crises was unshakeable in such theorists. The result has been to turn the world economy into something of a rollercoaster, culminating in the credit crisis of 2007–8, which as yet is still largely unresolved. Nevertheless, despite the need for massive government intervention to prevent complete meltdown in the world economy when the crisis first broke, most Western governments are still putting their faith several years later in neoliberal economics to provide the route out of the problem that neoliberalism caused in the first place. Harvey's criticisms of neoliberalism from before the crisis had occurred can look very prescient indeed; although their lessons are yet to be heeded properly by the political and financial elite, who have basically turned a blind eye to them.

Harvey is deeply worried by the extent of neoliberalism's hold on the public mind, noting how it 'has become incorporated into the common-sense way many of us interpret, live in, and understand the world' (Harvey 2005: 3). That hold can be explained in large part by neoliberalism's ability to present itself as the defender and guarantor of personal freedom and individualism, even though the theory's main effect has been to increase the power of large corporations such as the multinationals. Only organisations of that size and financial power are able to take advantage of the looser regulations governing the global flow of capital that neoliberal's champions have so tirelessly campaigned for in the last few decades.

One of the great mysteries of capitalism, especially for a Marxist-inclined thinker like Harvey, is how it has managed to survive so many crises over the modern era, with a series of large-scale economic depressions reaching back into the nineteenth century seeming to offer the right kind of conditions for social revolution. It was this unexpected resilience that led to the development by Marxist theorists of the concept of hegemony, to be taken apart by Ernesto Laclau and Chantal Mouffe in *Hegemony and Socialist Strategy* as little more than a convenient excuse for Marxism's predictive failures. Harvey addresses this problem in *The Enigma of Capital: And the Crises of Capitalism*, written in the aftermath of the financial crash of 2007. There he criticises Western politicians for their failure to recognise the culpability of neoliberalism in the crisis, being content instead to engineer 'a botched return to the sort of capitalism that got us into the mess in the first place' (Harvey 2010a: 221). The credit crisis has also prompted Harvey to write *A Companion to Marx's* Capital, in an attempt to reassess its relevance to our economic lives. He senses a desire to move away from the abstraction and academicism of so much Marxist thought in the twentieth century, to 'practical engagements' with the theory that might lead to a better understanding of the current crisis: that is, for a more pragmatic approach to Marxism.

Harvey's call for some kind of a broad front to campaign against neoliberal capitalism is deliberately phrased in the most general terms which allow space for the diversity and plurality that are so central to the postmodern outlook: 'Perhaps we should just define the movement, our movement, as anti-capitalist or call ourselves the Party of Indignation, ready to fight and defeat the Party of Wall Street and its acolytes and apologists everywhere' (Harvey 2010a: 260). There is a definite attempt here to strike a balance between traditional leftist views and the 'radical democracy' strain to postmodern thought, the grand narrative and the little narrative approach respectively. In a way, however, that does bring out the failure of both positions to have any really substantial effect in the political arena of late, despite the crisis that neoliberalism has generated in the form of the credit crunch and its long and very drawn-out aftermath, which gives every appearance of being with us for some considerable time yet.

Harvey's major writings

Harvey, David, *Social Justice and the City*, London: Edward Arnold, 1973.
——, *The Urban Experience*, Baltimore, MD: Johns Hopkins University Press, 1989.

——, *The Condition of Postmodernity: An Enquiry into the Origins of Cultural Change*, Cambridge, MA and Oxford: Blackwell, 1990.
——, *Spaces of Capital: Towards a Critical Geography*, Edinburgh: Edinburgh University Press, 2001.
——, *A Brief History of Neoliberalism*, Oxford: Oxford University Press, 2005.
——, *Spaces of Global Capitalism: Towards a Theory of Uneven Geographical Development*, London and New York: Verso, 2006.
——, *The Limits to Capital*, 2nd edition, London and New York: Verso, 2007.
——, *The Enigma of Capital: And the Crises of Capitalism*, London: Profile, 2010a.
——, *A Companion to Marx's* Capital, London and New York: Verso, 2010b.
——, *Rebel Cities: From the Right to the City to the Urban Revolution*, London and New York: Verso, 2012.

References and further reading

Friedman, Milton, *Capitalism and Freedom*, 2nd edition, Chicago: University of Chicago Press, 1982.
Jameson, Fredric, *Postmodernism, or the Cultural Logic of Late Capitalism*, London: Verso, 1991.
Laclau, Ernesto and Chantal Mouffe, *Hegemony and Socialist Strategy: Towards a Radical Democratic Politics*, London: Verso, 1985.
Lyotard, Jean-François, *The Postmodern Condition: A Report on Knowledge* [1979], trans. Geoff Bennington and Brian Massumi, Manchester: Manchester University Press, 1984.

LINDA HUTCHEON (B. 1947)

Hutcheon is a literary critic best known for developing the concept of metafiction in relation to postmodern literature, a topic she has pursued in several books, including one on the contemporary fiction of her own country, Canada. Hutcheon's particular interest, as far as postmodernism goes, lies in what she calls 'historiographic metafiction'; that is, 'novels which are both intensely self-reflexive and yet paradoxically also lay claim to historical events and personages' (Hutcheon 1988a: 5). These become the basis for the 'poetics of postmodernism' she outlines in the book of that name (Hutcheon 1988a), one of her most important contributions to the debate over postmodernism. Hutcheon has also written several works on opera in collaboration with her husband, Michael Hutcheon, a doctor with an interest in the representation of death and disease in the opera form.

She first explores the world of metafiction in *Narcissistic Narrative*, describing it as 'fiction about fiction – that is, fiction that includes within itself a commentary on its narrative and/or linguistic identity'

(Hutcheon 1980: 1), although she shies away from discussing it in terms of postmodernism at this stage. Postmodernism is only just coming into general usage as a cultural signifier in literary circles in North America at this point (it was far better known in the field of architecture, where it was rapidly spawning a new aesthetic with enthusiastic followers), partly because of the efforts of such as the novelist John Barth in his two influential articles 'The Literature of Exhaustion' and 'The Literature of Replenishment', where it was argued that modernism had reached something of a dead end. Although metafiction clearly appeals to the postmodern sensibility, Hutcheon points out that it is a term with a much larger range than just the postmodern, as well as one that can be backdated into literary history. (She will go on in *A Poetics of Postmodernism* to cite as earlier examples of metafiction Laurence Sterne's *Tristram Shandy*, in the mid-eighteenth century (a novel claimed as a predecessor at various times by both modernists and postmodernists), Cervantes' *Don Quixote* and even the work of Homer.) Hutcheon soon turns her attention to the postmodern in detail, however, and to the critical role played in postmodern literary practice by historiographic metafiction: fiction that 'problematizes the very possibility of historical knowledge' (Hutcheon 1988a: 106).

Although Hutcheon is sceptical of the notion that postmodernism constitutes a new cultural paradigm, she nevertheless believes that it represents a significant new direction in the arts that must be taken very seriously and merits having a poetics ascribed to it. She takes inspiration in the first instance from its impact in architectural practice, acknowledging the influence of Charles Jencks's works on the topic on her thought (as in *The Language of Postmodern Architecture*). From postmodern architecture we can learn the 'urgent need, in both artistic theory and *practice*, to investigate the relation of ideology and power to all of our present discursive structures' (Hutcheon 1988a: 36). Hutcheon's proposed poetics is designed to make us pay attention to how postmodern fiction at its best does just that – and she considers historiographic metafiction to be the most thought-provoking in this regard. She emphasises that her poetics is based on what is actually happening in the world of fiction-writing, so it is descriptive rather than prescriptive in the manner of such theories as Marxism (which has a tendency to lay down rules for what fiction should be to further its political cause, as in the infamous 'socialist realism'). What marks out historiographic metafiction for Hutcheon is the presence of parody, irony, self-reflexivity, and, paradoxically enough for a genre that is deliberately concerned to blur the line between fiction and history, a sense of historical grounding – even if it takes the form of 'a historical consciousness mixed with an ironic sense of critical distance' (Hutcheon 1988a: 201). Those are characteristics to be found in works like Gabriel García Márquez's *One Hundred Years of Solitude*, or Günter Grass's *The Tin Drum*.

After working through a wide range of contemporary novels, Hutcheon ultimately concludes that what she has constructed is as much a 'problematics' as a poetics of postmodernism: 'a set of problems and basic issues that have been created by the various discourses of postmodernism' (Hutcheon 1988a: 224). Postmodernism leads us to query all sorts of assumptions that we had formerly taken for granted, such as those 'between fiction and non-fiction, and ultimately, between art and life' (Hutcheon 1988a: 224–5). For Hutcheon, postmodernism is more effective at raising questions than it is at providing set answers, which is part of the reason why it receives attacks from both the right and the left of the political spectrum, who want something more from cultural theory than to be presented with a host of contradictions and paradoxes. It is because it is so successful at revealing the ideology that lies behind the dogmatism of both the left and the right, however, that we should value postmodern thought. What left and right take to be evidence of bad faith, Hutcheon claims to be a virtue, since contradiction and paradox open new lines of enquiry rather than fitting the world to a preconceived image, a besetting sin of political life in general, as she notes. The more our sense of certainty is shaken up the better, and postmodernism continues to do that, through the creative arts as well as theory.

Hutcheon goes on in *The Politics of Postmodernism* to look more closely at the issue of representation in postmodernism and the politics lying behind it, firmly emphasising, as she does throughout her writings on the subject, that '[p]ostmodern art cannot but be political' (Hutcheon 1989: 3). It is political in drawing our attention to the ideology underpinning representation across all the arts (although Hutcheon concentrates on fiction and photography in this particular instance). While conceding that postmodernism 'has no effective theory of agency that enables a move into political action', a failing the theory has never really managed to overcome, she nevertheless feels that 'it does work to turn its inevitable ideological grounding into a site of de-naturalizing critique' (Hutcheon 1989: 3); which is to say that postmodernism makes us realise that all the structures of our society are cultural rather than natural, developed by humanity for particular purposes. Being merely constructs means that those structures can be changed if it is decided they have outlived their original purpose – a point insisted upon by the major theorists of the postmodern, who are at pains to make us realise that, no matter what metanarratives and their supporters may claim, power is always ephemeral.

Hutcheon is critical of Fredric Jameson's assumption, in a journal article that was later to be worked up into a full-length book, that postmodernism should be regarded as 'the cultural logic of late capitalism' (Jameson 1991). Her argument is that postmodernism is quite aware that it is to some degree complicit in that system, even if only on the basis that it can never get outside it, but that it is also engaged in critiquing it from within. Representation in postmodernism is to be understood as marked by that mixture of complicity and critique, and Hutcheon feels that Jameson has simply missed this – a blindness he shares with Marxist critics in general. At least part of the misunderstanding has been caused, Hutcheon suggests, by a confusion between postmodernism, a set of cultural practices, and postmodernity, a socio-historical condition. Critics often tend to use these terms interchangeably, although we should see the former as a response to the latter. Hutcheon's concern is, therefore, 'to show that critique is as important as complicity in the response of cultural postmodernism to the philosophical and socio-economic realities of postmodernity' (Hutcheon 1989: 26).

Hutcheon is also particularly interested in the relationship between postmodernism and feminism – or, more precisely, 'feminisms', since it cannot be regarded as a unified movement with a common agenda. What all feminisms do agree upon, however, is the need for radical social change to improve the position and status of women in society, and that is not something postmodern theory, with its well-documented failings when it comes to political agency, can guarantee. Nevertheless, Hutcheon feels it can be one of the tools that feminism uses when it comes to subjects like representation. Cindy Sherman's self-portraits, in settings that suggest genres like Hollywood film noir, are an example of how to use a postmodern approach to score feminist points on this topic, since they 'are so self-consciously posed that the social construction of the female self, fixed by the masculine gaze, is both presented and ironized' (Hutcheon 1989: 156). The irony in this instance stems from the fact that it is Sherman herself who has set the whole scene up, photographing herself in such a way that it all but forces the masculine gaze to view her in a stereotypical manner. Yet, effective though such work can be, feminism will always want to go beyond the aims of postmodernism to realise its objectives, given that these are more explicitly politically motivated and goal-directed in character.

Overall, Hutcheon takes a very measured approach to post-modernism, avoiding the adoption of political extremes, as well as the often apocalyptic visions of the postmodern world offered by such thinkers as Jean Baudrillard, for whom we are trapped in a world of simulacra that have long since destroyed any notion of the 'real' (a somewhat naïve notion, in her opinion). She takes a much more positive line on how postmodernism is developing, arguing that it is making us examine our cultural and political assumptions anew, and that this is always a highly valuable activity in which to engage. Its mixture of complicity and critique means that it retains a subversive edge, even when it is being exploited for commercial purposes, and in that sense it escapes for her the charge of being late capitalism's cultural logic.

Hutcheon's major writings

Hutcheon, Linda, *Narcissistic Narrative: The Metafictional Paradox*, Waterloo, ONT: Wilfred Laurier University Press, 1980.

——, *A Theory of Parody: The Teachings of Twentieth-Century Art Forms*, New York: Methuen, 1985.

——, *A Poetics of Postmodernism: History, Theory, Fiction*, London and New York: Routledge, 1988a.

——, *The Canadian Postmodern: A Study of Contemporary Canadian Fiction*, Toronto: Oxford University Press, 1988b.

——, *The Politics of Postmodernism*, London and New York: Routledge, 1989.

——, *Splitting Images: Contemporary Canadian Ironies*, Toronto: Oxford University Press, 1991.

——, *Irony's Edge: The Theory and Politics of Irony*, London and New York: Routledge, 1994.

——, *A Theory of Adaptation*, London and New York: Routledge, 2006.

Hutcheon, Linda and Michael Hutcheon, *Opera: Desire, Disease, and Death*, Lincoln, NE: University of Nebraska Press, 1996.

——, *Opera: The Art of Dying*, Cambridge, MA: Harvard University Press, 2004.

References and further reading

Barth, John, 'The Literature of Exhaustion' [1967], in Malcolm Bradbury (ed.), *The Novel Today: Writers on Modern Fiction*, Manchester: Manchester University Press, 1977, pp. 70–83.

———, 'The Literature of Replenishment' [1980], in *The Friday Book: Essays and Other Non-Fiction* [1980], Baltimore, MD and London: Johns Hopkins University Press, 1984, pp. 193–206.

Cervantes, Miguel de, *Don Quixote* [1605, 1615], trans. John Rutherford, London: Penguin, 2003.

Grass, Günter, *The Tin Drum* [1959], trans. Breon Mitchell, London: Vintage, 2010.

Jameson, Fredric, *Postmodernism, or the Cultural Logic of Late Capitalism*, London: Verso, 1991.

Jencks, Charles, *The Language of Postmodern Architecture* [1975], 6th edition, London: Academy Editions, 1991.

Márquez, Gabriel García, *One Hundred Years of Solitude* [1967], trans. Gregory Rabassa, London: Picador, 1978.

Sterne, Laurence, *The Life and Opinions of Tristram Shandy* [1759–67], ed. Ian Campbell Ross, Oxford: Oxford University Press, 1983.

LUCE IRIGARAY (B. 1930)

With a background in psychoanalysis and philosophy, Irigaray is a prominent figure in the development of difference feminism, applying deconstructionist techniques to the topic of gender relations. Difference feminism, as its name implies, insists on emphasising strongly the difference between the two sexes: 'Sexual difference', Irigaray claims, 'is one of the major philosophical issues, if not the issue, of our age' (Irigaray 1993a: 5). It is a position that has led some feminists to advocate lesbian separatism as a way of resolving gender problems once and for all, and separatism is at least implicit in Irigaray who regards difference as intrinsic to women's sexual and psychological make-up. '"She" is indefinitely other in herself' (Irigaray 1985b: 28), in her poetic description, meaning that female identity is to be conceived of as diffuse and plural. Masculine identity, on the other hand, tends to be more focussed and intent on dominating its environment – to the detriment of women. 'Female sexuality', for Irigaray, 'has always been conceptualized on the basis of masculine parameters' (Irigaray 1985b: 23), which puts women in the inferior position, as if their bodies had been designed purely to serve male needs. Women therefore find themselves trapped in a 'sexual imaginary' as 'only a more or less obliging prop for the enactment of man's fantasies' (Irigaray 1985b: 25). Western culture for this thinker is incorrigibly phallocentric in its organisation and attitudes. Nothing short of a fundamental change in the social order will be enough to rectify this situation, and Irigaray's injunction as to how to bring this about is uncompromising: 'Women, stop trying' (Irigaray 1985b: 203).

The divide between men and women that there is for a theorist like Irigaray becomes very evident when she reflects on the nature of female discourse:

> It is useless, then, to trap women in the exact definition of what they mean, to make them repeat (themselves) so that it will be clear; they are already elsewhere in the discursive machinery where you expected to surprise them. They have returned within themselves. Which must not be understood in the same way as within yourself. They do not have the interiority that you have, the one you perhaps suppose they have. Within themselves means *within the intimacy of that silent, multiple, diffuse touch.* And if you ask them insistently what they are thinking about, they can only reply: Nothing. Everything.
>
> (Irigaray 1985b: 29)

Given such a difference between the sexes it seems unlikely that there can be much in the way of meaningful interaction between them; it is almost as if they inhabited different worlds, and one can understand why this would alienate not just male readers but also many feminists. Not all feminists accept the biological essentialism that informs such comments, nor would be willing to create separate spheres of development rather than strive to achieve equality in the world that we know, and continue to share. What Irigaray's conception of women is concerned to do, however, is to remove women from the reach of the patriarchal grand narrative; while simultaneously also suggesting that biological essentialism does not entail an equivalent female grand narrative with a power-seeking imperative behind it. Being female is a condition that, like meaning in Jacques Derrida, can never be pinned down, nor summed up at any one point. If it can be defined as essentialism, then it would seem to be essentialism without an essence. As in deconstruction, there is never full presence in the female being, it is always in a state of flux and change that resists precise definition: men can only sound one-dimensional in comparison.

Sexual difference is Irigaray's central theme and it recurs throughout her oeuvre, as in *Speculum of the Other Woman, This Sex Which Is Not One, An Ethics of Sexual Difference* and *Je, Tu, Nous: Towards a Culture of Sexual Difference. Speculum* takes issue with psychoanalysis for its role in helping to reinforce the phallocentric bias in Western culture. Freud is the foremost villain, with Irigaray taking him to task for the claim that when it comes to working out gender relations it is women who are the problematical gender in need of explanation.

Freud is accused of a completely wrong-headed conception of female sexuality whose influence is still with us today. The problem is that male sexuality is taken as the standard against which female sexuality must be analysed, so that, as Irigaray points out, 'the little girl is therefore a little man. ... A little man with a smaller penis. A disadvantaged little man' (Irigaray 1985a: 26), as is brought out in Freud's concept of 'penis envy'. Women are to be characterised for what they lack, so female sexuality is reduced to being 'merely the *other side* or even the *wrong side* of male sexualism' (Irigaray 1985a: 51).

Consistently throughout *This Sex Which Is Not One* Irigaray points out critical differences between the psychology of men and women that would seem to render discourse between them at best extremely difficult. Women are said to be more tactile than men, less responsive to visual stimuli when it comes to sexual attraction; they have less predictable and goal-oriented characters; they do not think of other human beings as mere commodities to be exploited (a particular characteristic of patriarchal societies for the author). Freudian theory and its legacy are again subjected to searching analysis, with the post-Freudian Jacques Lacan, for example, being criticised for failing to question concepts like 'penis envy'. Psychoanalysis is compared to a 'negative theology' (Irigaray 1985b: 89), in that it tells us only what female sexuality is not, what it lacks.

Irigaray has been criticised by other feminist theorists such as Judith Butler, who argues that she is indeed proceeding from a position of biological essentialism, which Butler herself feels is not in women's best interests. To assume, as Irigaray does, that a monolithic patriarchy suppresses 'the feminine as a site of subversive multiplicity' (Butler 1990: 19) is to suggest that separatism would be the logical solution to the problem of male–female relations, something to which Butler is very much opposed, being more concerned to blur the lines between genders. American and English feminists have generally been more interested in achieving equality of status and treatment with men. Irigaray is asserting herself against that interpretation of feminism in *An Ethics of Sexual Difference*, on the grounds that '[a] revolution in thought and ethics is needed if the work of sexual difference is to take place' (Irigaray 1993a: 6). If this was to be achieved, then 'man and woman may once again or at last live together, meet, and sometimes inhabit the same place' (Irigaray 1993a: 17). Those feminists campaigning for sexual equality would no doubt find that 'sometimes' more than a bit half-hearted.

Je, Tu, Nous addresses the equality-oriented school of feminist thinking very directly: 'To demand equality, as women is, it seems to me, a mistaken expression of a real objective' (Irigaray 1993b: 12), and that real objective has to be the recognition and institutionalisation of sexual difference within our society. Equality with men would be pointless given the difference between the sexes, Irigaray arguing that the only important thing is for women to be equal to each other. That would be to reject the phallocentric model which has dominated our history, and which traps women into certain roles: wife, childbearer, mother, etc. Even if they strive to be equal with men in the workplace by their performance of their job, that does not alter the imbalance of power between the sexes; instead they merely take on the character of men for the duration. Achieving social justice for women is not just a case of overcoming the economic inequalities that undoubtedly exist between the sexes in a patriarchal culture; it is more a matter of 'changing the laws of language and the conceptions of truths and values structuring the social order' (Irigaray 1993b: 22). Neither will revolutionary theorists like Marx help much on this score, Marxist feminists notwithstanding, since he too is fully imbued with the ideology of patriarchy and phallocracy.

Irigaray has also come under attack from Alan Sokal and Jean Bricmont in their controversial book attacking the understanding displayed of science by postmodern and poststructuralist thinkers, *Intellectual Impostures*. In *To Speak Is Never Neutral*, as a case in point, Irigaray describes herself a feeling 'irritated and amused by the language of science', arguing that effectively it denies the existence of sexual difference and gendered subjects: 'We end up with the paradox: scientific studies proves the sexuality of the cortex, while science maintains that discourse is neuter' (Irigaray 2002a: 1, 3). For Sokal and Bricmont, however, Irigaray is guilty of a series of 'scientific confusions' which are used to underpin 'more general philosophical considerations of a vaguely relativist nature' (Sokal and Bricmont 1998: 112) in her work. They also accuse her of 'the most blatant sexist stereotypes' (Sokal and Bricmont 1998: 112) in identifying rationality with men and emotional subjectivity with women. To their mind, that is to exclude women from any attempt to redress the imbalance in power between the sexes, which would be against the spirit of feminism: 'Simone de Beauvoir must be turning in her grave' (Sokal and Bricmont 1998: 113) being how their critique of her curtly closes.

The impetus of Irigaray's work overall is to bring sexual difference and sexed identity to the forefront of public debate, and she is adamant this is a critical factor that is not being given the priority it should be. For her, they are at the very centre of her being and experience: 'The whole of my body is sexuate. My sexuality isn't restricted to my sex and to the sexual act' (Irigaray 1993b: 53). Unless this is more generally taken on board, by feminists as much as anyone, then there will be no progress made in gender relations: 'All the egalitarian slogans keep pushing us further back' (Irigaray 1994: xi), she contends. Irigaray has also looked outside the West for other ideas of how to achieve a condition supporting sexual difference, and in *Between East and West* has taken some inspiration from Eastern cultures in that respect. While difference feminism undoubtedly remains an extreme position on the spectrum of feminist thought, it is nevertheless a thought-provoking contribution to the ongoing debate on gender relations, and it also succeeds in demonstrating that deconstruction has much wider applications in public life than many of its critics have been willing to admit.

Irigaray's major writings

Irigaray, Luce, *Speculum of the Other Woman* [1974], trans. Gillian C. Gill, Ithaca, NY: Cornell University Press, 1985a.

——, *This Sex Which Is Not One* [1977], trans. Catherine Porter, with Carolyn Burke, Ithaca, NY: Cornell University Press, 1985b.

——, *An Ethics of Sexual Difference* [1984], trans. Carolyn Burke and Gillian C. Gill, London: Athlone Press, 1993a.

——, *Je, Tu, Nous: Towards a Culture of Sexual Difference* [1990], trans. Alison Martin, New York and London: Routledge, 1993b.

——, *Thinking the Difference: For a Peaceful Revolution* [1989], trans. Karin Montin, London: Athlone Press, 1994.

——, *Democracy Begins Between Two* [1994], trans. Kirsteen Anderson, London: Athlone Press, 2000.

——, *To Speak Is Never Neutral* [1985], trans. Gail Schwab, London: Athlone Press, 2002a.

——, *The Way of Love*, trans. Heidi Bostic and Stephen Pluhácek, London and New York: Continuum, 2002b.

——, *Between East and West: From Singularity to Community* [1999], trans. Carolyn Burke, New York and Chichester: Columbia University Press, 2003.

——, *Sharing the World: From Intimate to Global Relations*, London and New York: Continuum, 2005.

References and further reading

Butler, Judith, *Gender Trouble: Feminism and the Subversion of Identity*, New York and London: Routledge, 1990.

Sokal, Alan and Jean Bricmont, *Intellectual Impostures: Postmodern Philosophers' Abuse of Science*, London: Profile Books, 1998.

FREDRIC JAMESON (B. 1934)

A highly respected cultural commentator and film theorist, Jameson's roots are in Marxism, which has brought him into conflict with postmodern theory, most notably in his book *Postmodernism, or the Cultural Logic of Late Capitalism*, one of the most sustained and thoughtful attacks on it from a left-oriented thinker. (It is a line of argument he continues on with in *A Singular Modernity*, where he insists that modernity is still with us into the twenty-first century.) It is a point well made, in that neoliberal economic theory is an example of modernity at its most streamlined (although Jameson is no fan of neoliberalism). As Jameson counsels, 'it is easier to denounce historical narratives ... than it is to do without them' (Jameson 2002: 5), and throughout his writings he treats postmodernism as a development from, rather than a break with, modernism and modernity.

Yet Jameson is not completely dismissive of postmodernism and can also see some value in it as a project, as his Foreword to the English edition of Jean-François Lyotard's *The Postmodern Condition* would certainly suggest. Postmodernism, he concedes, having run through various forms it can take, 'is a rich and creative movement, of the greatest aesthetic play and delight' (Jameson 1984: xviii). It is only when we come to consider its political implications that Jameson feels the need to express deep reservations about the movement's motivation and validity, which he decides are counter-productive to the goals of the left and as such are all to the benefit of the capitalist system. We must not be misled into thinking that 'aesthetic play and delight' alone will ever bring down an entrenched ideology.

Jameson's Marxism, an unusual enough attribute for an American intellectual to display these days, comes across very strongly in his instruction to cultural commentators that they should '[a]lways historicize!' (Jameson 1981: 9). It is this lack of historicisation which, he contends, puts a question mark over postmodernism, undercutting any notion of it being a revolutionary kind of theory (a criticism Marxists had made previously about literary theories such as 'new criticism', with its insistence on the internal autonomy of texts and rejection of external socio-political considerations). The tendency towards an apolitical attitude of so many postmodernists plays right into the hands of capitalism in Jameson's opinion, since that system has a vested interest in making itself seem to be the natural order of things rather than a historical phenomenon which is open to challenge. Postmodernism for this critic does not meaningfully enough question the status quo, a point he feels comes out in what he terms the 'repressed or buried symbolic narrative' (Jameson 1984: xviii) of Lyotard's *Postmodern Condition*, which provides no specific method based on real-life political action through which to undermine the dominant late capitalist order. Lyotard's call for the data-banks of the information age to be thrown open to the general public is for Jameson at best a 'protopolitical' (Jameson 1984: xx) stance to adopt, when he is convinced that something altogether more radical in character is required to shake up the system to any really significant effect and create a new sense of oppositionally minded class consciousness. For that reason, as Jameson goes on to expound in what is probably his best-known work, postmodernism is to be considered the 'cultural logic of late capitalism' (Jameson 1991a), although that is hardly how its more radical theorists would like to picture it. At best, postmodernism to Jameson amounts to little more than sniping from the sidelines, an irritant to the system perhaps, but a fairly minor one that it can tolerate quite easily.

While it is a fair point to call attention to postmodernism's somewhat diffuse political intentions, it is more debatable whether these are merely a product of the hegemony exercised by a system that most postmodern thinkers regard with considerable suspicion themselves. There is a distinct suggestion that Jameson feels they are guilty of a certain naïveté although that would be a harsh assessment of a figure such as Lyotard, who is almost painfully aware of the gap between theory and practice in political life, turning that into one of the primary concerns of his writing. What Lyotard is concerned to avoid, however, is turning postmodernism into yet another grand narrative that becomes intolerant of other viewpoints.

Jameson's line is that postmodernism becomes the cultural logic of late capitalism by its sheer suspicion of revolutionary theories like Marxism, lumping them all indiscriminately under the heading of grand narrative and thus to be avoided at all costs (although Lyotard's more complex reaction to capitalism on occasion praises its sheer energy, if without ever turning him into an out-and-out supporter of the system). Few postmodern theorists have anything much good to say about Marxism in the aftermath of the 1968 *événements* (see Lyotard's notorious attack on it in *Libidinal Economy*, for example, or Jean Baudrillard's in *The Mirror of Production*), but the loss of faith in mass action this induces in them leaves capitalism's power base largely untouched, for all their continuing anti-bourgeois sentiments. It is never very clear in postmodern thought exactly how political change is going to be achieved across the whole social spectrum, although the desire for that to occur is plainly evident in its major figures – and never more so than in Lyotard, with his call for us to 'wage a war on totality' (Lyotard 1984: 82). Postmodern thinkers are sincerely striving to inspire a radical change of consciousness that leaves the current political system bereft of mass support, but that is a notoriously diffi-cult goal to achieve without a worked-out political programme behind it – essentially Jameson's point. In consequence, he is moved to insist that 'postmodernism is not the cultural dominant of a wholly new social order (the rumor about which, under the name of "post-industrial society," ran through the media a few years ago), but only the reflex and the concomitant of yet another systemic modification of capitalism itself' (Jameson 1991a: xii). Not only that, but Jameson also goes on to claim that 'postmodern culture is the internal and superstructural expression of a whole new wave of American military and economic domination throughout the world: in this sense, as throughout class history, the underside of culture is blood, torture, death, and terror' (Jameson 1991a: 5).

Postmodernism is characterised for Jameson by the following key features: 'a new depthlessness', a 'weakening of historicity', 'a whole new type of emotional ground tone', and 'the deep constitutive relationship of all this to a whole new technology' (Jameson 1991a: 6). The depthlessness reveals itself in the notion of the simulacrum; the weakening of historicity in the turn away from historicisation; the new ground tone in the return of interest in theories of the sublime, based on a belief in limitations to human reason; the technology in the development of a whole new range of communication and media forms, which have become the basis for a new generation of cor-porations with considerable geopolitical power. This to Jameson is 'the bewildering new world space of late or multinational capital' (Jameson 1991a: 7) which has spawned the postmodern outlook.

Critical though he is of postmodernism and its obsessive concern with the present moment at the expense of any sense of historical process, Jameson can still find a value in it in terms of what it reveals about our current cultural condition of late capitalism. As he notes, when he finds himself getting tired of all its many faults, he can nevertheless also find himself 'pausing to wonder whether any other concept can dramatize the issues in quite so effective and economical a fashion' (Jameson 1991a: 418). Faint praise though it may be, postmodernism has its role to play in Jameson's Marxist scheme all the same.

Jameson has made some very interesting observations about the effect of the postmodern aesthetic on filmmaking, seeing it as gen-erating what he has dubbed the 'nostalgia film' (Jameson 1998: 7). This genre can involve films about the past – the fairly recent past of

George Lucas's *American Graffiti*, for example – but also the same director's apparently futuristic *Star Wars* films, which seek to replicate the effect of the Saturday afternoon serials of the 1930s, 1940s and 1950s. While the younger audience 'can take the adventures straight', an older audience 'is able to gratify a deeper and more properly nostalgic desire to return to that older period and to live its strange old aesthetic artefacts through once again' (Jameson 1998: 8). Much of Steven Spielberg's work, such as the Indiana Jones films (*Raiders of the Lost Ark* etc.), would fall into this category too, the director deploying pastiche in a very knowing way. Another source for the nostalgia film genre has been comic books, and it is noticeable that Hollywood is continuing to exploit the tradition of superheroes and superheroines found there right through into the new century, with several 'franchises' in profitable operation. Jameson takes quite a moralistic line on this genre, describing it as 'an alarming and pathological symptom of a society that has become incapable of dealing with time and history' (Jameson 1998: 10). Films like these, and postmodern artistic activity in general for Jameson, add little to social or political debate, and that will always constitute a failing for a Marxist. There is more than a suggestion in Jameson of postmodernism being culturally parasitic, and he cannot see it as representing the kind of clean break historically that would endow it with its own distinctive identity, in the realm of either art or politics.

There is no denying that Jameson's critique of postmodernism carries a considerable amount of weight, and postmodernism, or at least some postmodernists, can be held guilty of a lack of historicisation as he claims; but his own Marxist commitment is open to criticism too. In order to continue to present Marxism as a liberating socio-political force, one has to treat it as an ideal which has been misinterpreted and maltreated by most of its major exponents in the twentieth century, from the Bolsheviks onwards. Communism has to be classified as a distortion of that ideal, which begs the question as to why that happened – and happened quite as often as it did. Neither the Soviet nor the Maoist system offers much encouragement to budding revolutionaries now in this respect, neither having a very attractive track record, and postmodernism is unwilling to extend Marxism the benefit of the doubt that Jameson patently still does.

Jameson's major writings

Jameson, Fredric, *Marxism and Form: Twentieth-Century Dialectical Theories of Literature*, Princeton, NJ: Princeton University Press, 1971.

——, *The Prison House of Language*, Princeton, NJ: Princeton University Press, 1972.

——, *The Political Unconscious: Narrative as a Socially Symbolic Act*, London: Methuen, 1981.

——, Foreword to Jean-François Lyotard, *The Postmodern Condition: A Report on Knowledge* [1979], trans. Geoff Bennington and Brian Massumi, Manchester: Manchester University Press, 1984, pp. vii–xxi.

——, *Late Marxism*, London: Verso, 1990.

——, *Postmodernism, or the Cultural Logic of Late Capitalism*, London: Verso, 1991a.

——, *Signatures of the Visible*, London: Routledge, 1991b.

——, *The Cultural Turn: Selected Writings on the Postmodern, 1983–1998*, London and New York: Verso, 1998.

——, *A Singular Modernity: Essay on the Ontology of the Present*, London and New York: Verso, 2002.

——, *Archaeologies of the Future: The Desire Called Utopia and Other Science Fictions*, London and New York: Verso, 2005.

References and further reading

Baudrillard, Jean, *The Mirror of Production* [1973], trans. Mark Poster, St Louis, MO: Telos, 1975.

Lucas, George (dir.), *American Graffiti*, Universal Studios, 1973.

——(dir.), *Star Wars*, Twentieth Century Fox, 1977.

Lyotard, Jean-François, *The Postmodern Condition: A Report on Knowledge* [1979], trans. Geoff Bennington and Brian Massumi, Manchester: Manchester University Press, 1984.

——, *Libidinal Economy* [1974], trans. Iain Hamilton Grant, London: Athlone Press, 1993.

Spielberg, Steven (dir.), *Raiders of the Lost Ark*, Paramount Pictures, 1981.

CHARLES JENCKS (B. 1939)

Jencks has to count as one of the most influential voices in the development of postmodern theory, and he is one of the few thinkers grouped under this heading who is more than happy to be defined as a postmodernist and to act as an unashamed champion of the post-modern ethic. Architecture has proved to be one of the primary sources of inspiration for postmodern theory, and it was Jencks more than anyone who helped to identify a rationale for postmodernism as a cultural movement and for its rejection of the ideology informing modernism and modernity. His concept of 'double-coding', whereby architects were encouraged to appeal both to the general public and to their professional peers ('radical eclecticism' (Jencks 1991: 12, 13) as Jencks described the technique), soon became widely adapted across the other arts, to the extent that it has now become one of the cornerstones of the postmodern aesthetic, found throughout the world of the arts. In the architectural world itself it has become extremely influential, and urban areas throughout the West bear testament to its ongoing impact on the architectural profession. There is a distinct difference to be noted between the buildings erected in the late twentieth/early twenty-first century and those of the earlier twentieth century, between postmodernist playfulness and modernist severity, and Jencks has been at the forefront of this change as one of its most vocal advocates for the greater part of his career.

As interpreted both by Jencks himself and by the postmodern creative community, double-coding has evolved into a self-conscious dialogue with the past, both in terms of style and themes, in order to create a greater sense of familiarity with the material on the part of the general audience. Architects predictably want to make a name for themselves in their profession and the majority will gravitate towards doing what meets with peer approval, wins prestigious national and international prizes, etc.; the general public, on the other hand, can be very conservative about such matters and more likely to want their surroundings to stay much the same as always and to keep changes in their home townscape or cityscape to a minimum. Double-coding's brief is to see these conflicting desires reconciled so that there is no longer such a gulf between architect and public, since the latter, after all, will be the everyday users of their buildings. Architecture differs from the other arts in this way in being a practical discipline that the general public cannot avoid having contact with: you can choose not to go into museums, galleries, theatres and concert halls, but you can hardly fail to be aware of them as buildings as you go about your daily business in city or town. Radical eclecticism was meant to make such encounters more pleasant for the general public.

Whether radical eclecticism can escape the charge of being super-ficial or even just plain reactionary as a method has been a subject of much debate since Jencks first floated it, and it is not without its critics. It can encourage a kind of laziness in creative artists, as Gilbert Adair amongst others has noted when he speaks of creative artists treating the past as little more than 'a mammoth lucky dip' into which they can 'plunge ... and scoop out' (Adair 1992: 17) whatever takes their fancy as a candidate for pastiche. The implication is that double-coding reduces the amount of creative input required to produce artistic artefacts; that it tends to be slick and superficial rather than to have any great artistic depth.

Jencks is notorious for his highly provocative, although also clearly tongue-in-cheek, pronouncement detailing the end of modernism:

> [W]e can date the death of Modern Architecture to a precise moment in time. ... Modern Architecture died in St. Louis, Missouri on July 15, 1972 at 3.32 p.m. (or thereabouts) when the infamous Pruitt-Igoe scheme, or rather several of its slab blocks, were given the final *coup de grâce* by dynamite. Previously it had been vandalised, mutilated and defaced by its black inhabitants, and although millions of dollars were pumped back, trying to keep it alive (fixing the broken elevators, repairing smashed windows, repainting), it was finally put out of its misery.
>
> (Jencks 1991: 23)

Jencks's point was that the demolition of Pruitt-Igoe amounted to a gesture of defeat by modernism; an acknowledgement that its social engineering schemes simply were not working as originally intended, and possibly never would. Those schemes were in fact proving to be counter-productive in generating anti-social behaviour and a sense of alienation amongst the inhabitants of their buildings – no matter how well intended their design had been. Le Corbusier had been one of the staunchest advocates of modernism as social engineering, and his ideas, outlined in the 1920s and 1930s in works like *Towards a New Architecture*, had become deeply engrained in the modernist architectural aesthetic, which became entranced by his idea of tower blocks 'opening on every side to air and light' (Le Corbusier 1946: 61). Such buildings would possess all the benefits of modern technology to make life easier and more pleasant for their inhabitants, and it was assumed that in the process they would help to forge a new kind of community spirit.

Postwar town planning throughout Western Europe was firmly committed to this modernist aesthetic and felt it was being put into practice in the construction of large-scale housing estates consisting of numerous tower blocks – such as Pruitt-Igoe. The assumption was that the public would welcome the opportunity to escape the crowded and unsanitary conditions left behind by the explosive growth brought on by full-scale industrialisation, not to mention extensive recent wartime damage, and it is probably true to say that at least some did in the early years of the exercise (as Owen Hatherley has eloquently argued in his book *Militant Modernism*). It is easy to forget that there was a great deal of social idealism behind the tower block movement, and it could be argued that postmodernism tends to underestimate this. The Pruitt-Igoes of this world were never less than well intended, even if there was an authoritarian, and somewhat patronising, element to those intentions.

Pruitt-Igoe may have gone now, but most major cities in Western Europe still have many examples of the tower block concept, which, well intended or not, all too often are just as vandalised and deeply unpopular with their inhabitants as Pruitt-Igoe became. There was a huge gap between the professional and the public perception of such buildings that Jencks felt demanded an entirely new approach to architecture, the postmodern, which was to be far less doctrinaire than modernism had become and more in tune with public taste. Jencks has proved to be a tireless campaigner for that cause, and an inspiration to a new generation of architects, who have proceeded to put his ideas into practice around the globe.

Jencks has, however, also written very sympathetically about Le Corbusier, in his book *Le Corbusier and the Tragic Vision of Architecture*. There he pays homage to Le Corbusier's 'undeniable creative potency' and the 'moral stature and strength' (Jencks 1973: 7) that he brought to modern architecture. Le Corbusier comes across as a character constantly struggling against social convention, who presents overall 'a tragic view through his life and architecture' (Jencks 1973: 180). Despite all the faults of the architectural modernism that he was so central in developing, Le Corbusier is still for Jencks a figure to be admired, and he does note a more humanist side to his character beginning to emerge in the post-World War Two period, despite his turn to what has been dubbed the 'Brutalist' style in architecture. It is the Brutalist style that Jencks is attacking above all in *The Language of Post-modern Architecture*, but his respect for Le Corbusier is evident in the revised version of his study on him, published twenty-seven years after the original under the title *Le Corbusier and the Continual Revolution in Architecture*.

It is worth noting that Jencks has to some extent modified his conception of postmodernism in recent years, and in his book *Critical Modernism* refers to it as a reform movement emerging from within modernism itself. We can now speak of a 'Modernism 2', therefore, which will be a more flexible movement than 'Modernism 1' was, without the authoritarian side that marred the former. A similar move towards a reformed modernism can be found in Nicolas Bourriaud and his concept of the altermodern (see Bourriaud 2009).

Jencks is a practising architect, whose speciality is landscape design, in a method he calls 'landforming', which he outlines in *The Garden of Cosmic Speculation*. The book takes its title from a work of that name in Dumfries, Scotland, described on Jencks's website as follows:

> Covering thirty acres in the Borders area of Scotland, the garden uses nature to celebrate nature, both intellectually and through the senses, including the sense of humor. A water cascade of steps recounts the story of the universe, a terrace shows the distortion of space and time caused by a black hole, a 'Quark Walk' takes the visitor on a journey to the smallest building blocks of matter, and a series of landforms and lakes recall fractal geometry.
>
> (http://www.charlesjencks.com?#!projects)

Jencks sees his work as echoing the underlying laws of nature in the forms and shapes it takes, and one could even see this (if perhaps a bit fancifully) as an instance of double-coding between the earth's past and present. It is also characteristic of the postmodern ethos that Jencks draws attention to the playful aspects of his creations, the 'sense of humor' that is built into them in contradistinction to the general seriousness of the modernist architectural temperament, as displayed in Pruitt-Igoe and its ilk, with their social engineering imperative. Another work designed for the Scottish National Gallery of Modern Art in Edinburgh, 'Landform Ueda', won the prestigious Gulbenkian Prize for Museums in 2004.

Jencks is still active as a landscape architect in 2013 as this book is being written, and continuing to draw complimentary notices for his work. It is not always the case that a theorist can put his or her theories into practice (or chooses to, for that matter), but Jencks has put himself up for judgement in that way, providing a valuable insight into his overall architectural vision. Postmodern thought is often criticised for being anti-humanist in tone and orientation, but Jencks could not be accused of that; there is a deeply humanistic quality to his work, in terms of both his writing and his landscaping projects.

Jencks's major writings

Jencks, Charles, *Le Corbusier and the Tragic Vision of Architecture*, London: Allen Lane, 1973.

——, *What Is Post-Modernism?*, London: Academy Editions, 1986.

——, *Post-Modernism: The New Classicism in Art and Architecture*, London: Academy Editions, 1989.

——, *The Language of Post-Modern Architecture* [1975], 6th edition, London: Academy Editions, 1991.

——, *Heteropolis*, London: Academy Editions, 1993.

——, *Le Corbusier and the Continual Revolution in Architecture*, New York: Monacelli Press, 2003a.

——, *The Garden of Cosmic Speculation*, London: Frances Lincoln, 2003b.

——, *The Iconic Building: The Power of Enigma*, London: Frances Lincoln, 2005.

——, *Critical Modernism: Where Is Post-modernism Going?*, London: John Wiley, 2007.

——, *The Story of Post-modernism: Five Decades of the Iconic and Critical in Architecture*, London: John Wiley, 2011.

References and further reading

Adair, Gilbert, *The Postmodernist Always Rings Twice: Reflections on Culture in the 90s*, London: Fourth Estate, 1992.

Bourriaud, Nicolas, 'Altermodern', in Nicolas Bourriaud (ed.), *Altermodern: Tate Triennial*, London: Tate Publishing, 2009, pp. 11–24.

Hatherley, Owen, *Militant Modernism*, Winchester and Washington, DC: Zero Books, 2008.

Le Corbusier, *Towards a New Architecture* [1923], trans. Frederick Etchells, London: Architectural Press, 1946.

REM KOOLHAAS (B. 1944)

Koolhaas is one of the leading architects of his generation, and one of the founders of the Office for Metropolitan Architecture (OMA), a highly regarded practice that has won several major commissions around the world, such as the EuroLille station on the Channel Tunnel route from London to Paris. He also worked as a journalist and film scriptwriter in his early career in Holland. Along with such other figures as Peter Eisenman and Bernard Tschumi, Koolhaas is usually classified as part of the Deconstructivist movement in architecture, which took inspiration from the work of Jacques Derrida and his theory of deconstruction; although at best this is a fairly loose description of the style that evolved from that. Koolhaas's buildings have proved to be very controversial, often challenging the public's expectations of how they should be used, which is a characteristic of the Deconstructivist approach to architecture (also found particularly in the work of Eisenman). Koolhaas has an iconoclastic streak to his character, exemplified as early as his choice of topic for a public presentation on his degree programme at the Architectural Association School in London in the early 1970s. Entitled 'The Berlin Wall as Architecture', it prompted one of his teachers to ask him pointedly after delivering it, 'Where do you go from here?' (Koolhaas and Mau 1998: 231).

Deconstructivists tend to be critical of postmodern architecture, and in many ways it is easier to relate their work to modernism, although it is clearly not modernism as the major proponents of the style conceived of it. Neither does it cast itself in the heroic light that the modernist movement did, as is made clear in *Small, Medium, Large, Extra Large*, by Koolhaas and his co-author Bruce Mau, who emphasise the elements of randomness and lack of control in architects' careers:

> [T]hey are confronted with an arbitrary sequence of demands, with parameters they did not establish, in countries they hardly know, about issues they are only dimly aware of, expected to deal with problems that have proved intractable to brains vastly superior to their own. Architecture is by definition a *chaotic adventure*.
>
> (Koolhaas and Mau 1998: xix)

This contrasts dramatically with the vision of modernists like Le Corbusier, who considered themselves to be engaged in a radical re-engineering of the world to fit both their aesthetic and social aims, and brooked little interference with their often grandiose schemes. Koolhaas and Mau, however, set about making 'disclosures about the conditions under which architecture is now produced' in order to come to an accommodation 'about what architecture is and what it can do' (Koolhaas and Mau 1998: xix), which sounds like a reaction against the pretensions of high modernism.

As an example of how OMA go about interacting with the building parameters and traditions of the cities they work in, there is the rationale provided for the Netherlands Embassy in Berlin:

> The Netherlands Embassy is a disciplined cube with equally disciplined irregularities which aims to facilitate a better understanding of Berlin, confronting divergent ideas about how the city, with its complexity, heaviness, opacity, and beauty, should build/rebuild. Traditional planning guidelines of the former West Berlin demanded that new buildings in the neighbourhood (the Rolandufer in Mitte) reflect the local 19th century architectural style. Planning officials in the former East Berlin were more open to innovation. As a result, OMA combined an obedient approach

(strictly fulfilling the block's perimeter) with a disobedient one (building an isolated cube).
(http://oma.eu/projects/2003/netherlands-embassy (accessed 26 July 2012))

There is a concern here to ensure that, in keeping with OMA's name, urban regeneration takes account of the metropolitan area in question and its history, and that buildings can, indeed almost must, express a plurality of viewpoints in such a context and not just that of the architect.

There is a recognisably poststructuralist dimension in the work of Koolhaas and his Deconstructivist colleagues, in that they are rejecting the idea of buildings as totalities that represent some metanarrative of architecture, with every detail in them fitting a general scheme that the architect imposes on the project. Like poststructuralist thought in general, the Deconstructivists do not believe that the meaning of artefacts can be pinned down in this way, or that it is possible to exercise complete control over any discourse, let alone a discourse with so many variables involved in it as architecture patently has. So the Netherlands Embassy is fitted into Berlin, not the other way round – as the high modernists would be more likely to assume was the proper way to proceed. The notion of making one's way as best as one can through a 'chaotic adventure' has a definite poststructuralist resonance.

Another example of Koolhaas's work in Guangzhou in southern China, the Times Museum, further indicates the non-standard approach favoured by OMA. The Times Museum was originally commissioned, as part of the Guangzhou Triennial in 2005, to be on the ground floor of a residential building owned by Times Property, one of the sponsors of the Triennial. Koolhaas disagreed with the company's plans, however, and moved the museum to the very top of the building on the nineteenth floor, and then located its offices on the fourteenth floor, with another exhibition area sited on the ground floor, so that the museum was distributed throughout the block and thus, as he saw it, more integrated into the daily life of its inhabitants. Koolhaas's plan was to challenge the traditional notion of museums by creating 'a museum without a shape' (Shen 2012), thus requiring its users to discover new ways of relating to it, as well as to what it stood for as an entity.

Small, Medium, Large, Extra Large is a compendious work comprising a visual tour through OMA's architectural projects, as well as those of various others, with these being grouped according to size, as the title announces. It is intercut with writings, including a marginal column of short reflections lifted from various sources in the form of an A–Z glossary, as well as cartoons, diagrams and even details of the firm's expenditure and travel behaviour. How we are meant to relate all its component parts is unclear. In layout it is very reminiscent of certain of Derrida's writings, such as *Glas*, where we are presented with parallel texts, disconnected fragments, and non-linear narratives that are deliberately devised to prevent the work from adding up to a whole.

Small, Medium is something of a ragbag production, therefore, perhaps designed to echo the chaos that for Koolhaas is an inescapable element of architecture as a practice. In a typically deconstructive gesture the authors inform us that '[t]he book can read in any way' (Koolhaas and Mau 1998: xix). The glossary contains such interesting nuggets as the following from the architect Charles Moore: 'BABOON. I read *The Fountainhead* at an early age and identified with the supercilious bad guy Peter Keating, rather than with that dangerous baboon Howard Roark' (Koolhaas and Mau 1998: 12). Given that Howard Roark was meant by the book's author, Ayn Rand, to be taken as the prototypical picture of the modernist architect as hero, this has to stand as a calculated rejection of the high modernist ethos and the notion that one can make unequivocal aesthetic statements through buildings. What Koolhaas and OMA want to encourage instead is a much more pragmatic approach to architecture, one that steers clear of what is described as 'a method of systematic *idealization*' (Koolhaas and Mau 1998: 208) by most architects, an overestimation of the importance of their particular project and its long-term place in the scheme of, say, a city's existence.

The marginal entry on postmodernism is lifted from a speech given by Richard Meier to the Royal Institute of British Architects (RIBA) in 1998: 'Basically that is what post-modernism is, a moving backwards. It was a process that took from original copies, copies of copies, imitations of interpretations, all timidly following the past. This not only ransacked our past, but more importantly robbed us of our present, obliterating our future' (Koolhaas and Mau 1998: 1048–52). The extent to which this, or any of the A–Z entries for that matter, represents OMA's outlook is hard to say, although it would be consistent with the Deconstructivist ethos in general. Koolhaas's comment on the impression the Berlin Wall made on him was that '*on the eve of postmodernism, here was unforgettable (not to say final) proof of the "less is more" doctrine* ... I would never again believe in form as a primary vessel of meaning' (Koolhaas and Mau 1998: 227). This could be read either as support for or condemnation of modernism; although it does also suggest there is something wrong in the underlying assumptions of both modernism and postmodernism, especially when the latter's plan to overcome the domination of the former revolves around the substitution of one set of formal features for another. 'Double-coding', as formulated by Charles Jencks (see Jencks 1991), sets out to challenge modernist architecture by playing around with its forms, doing its best to destroy the purity of line associated with them on the grounds that this will subvert both their aesthetic and social objectives.

Amongst several other publications, Koolhaas has also gone into detail about how large cities have developed, emphasising the chance dimension to much of it, in *Delirious New York* and *Lagos: How It Works*. What impresses him most of all is the sheer variety such cities involve, both in buildings and lifestyles.

Koolhaas would seem to be just the kind of architect that Robert Venturi, proponent of a vernacular-based architecture as found in locations like Las Vegas, dislikes, complaining of the 'sado–masochistic expressionist applications of Deconstructionism' (Venturi 1996: 8) that are being espoused by certain postmodernist architects. Whether the Deconstructivists would agree with being defined as postmodernist is another issue, but it is fair to regard them as largely having turned their back on high modernism. Perhaps we need to start thinking of postmodernism, in architecture anyway, as a broader church than it has tended to be represented. The Deconstructivists do share with postmodernists the problem of how to reconstruct architecture in the aftermath of modernism's fall from grace, and in some respects they are close to the ideas being expressed by the altermodern movement about the necessity of recapturing some of the spirit of modernism before it hardened into the authoritarian doctrine it subsequently did (see Bourriaud 2009). Certainly, deconstructivism does offer a different route out of modernism than postmodernism – and in many ways a more inventive one.

Koolhaas's major writings

Koolhaas, Rem, *Delirious New York: A Retroactive Manifesto for Manhattan* [1978], New York: Monacelli Press, 1994.
——, *Content*, Cologne: Taschen, 2004.
Koolhaas, Rem and Edgar Cleijne, *Lagos: How It Works*, Zurich: Lars Muller, 2007.

Koolhaas, Rem and Bruce Mau (eds), *Small, Medium, Large, Extra Large: Office for Metropolitan Architecture (S,M,L,XL)* [1995], 2nd edition, New York: Monacelli Press, 1998.

Koolhaas, Rem and Hans-Ulrich Obrist, *Project Japan, Metabolism Talks*, Cologne: Taschen, 2011.

Koolhaas, Rem, Norman Foster and Alessandro Mendini, *Colours* [2001], Basel and Boston: Birkenhauser, 2004.

References and further reading

Bourriaud, Nicolas (ed.), *Altermodern: Tate Triennial*, London: Tate Publishing, 2009.

Derrida, Jacques, 'Living On • Border Lines', in Harold Bloom *et al.*, *Deconstruction and Criticism*, London and Henley: Routledge and Kegan Paul, 1979, pp. 75–176.

——, *Glas* [1974], trans. J. P. Leavey and R. Rand, Lincoln, NE and London: University of Nebraska Press, 1986.

Jencks, Charles, *The Language of Post-Modern Architecture* [1975], 6th edition, London: Academy Editions, 1991.

Rand, Ayn, *The Fountainhead* [1943], London: Penguin, 2007.

Shen, Ruijun, 'A Report on the Times Museum, Guangzhou, China', *Asia Art Archive in America*, 2012, http://www.aaa-a.org/2012/07/09/a-report-on-the-times-museum-guangzhou-china/ (accessed 25 July 2012).

Venturi, Robert, *Iconography and Electronics upon a Generic Architecture*, Cambridge, MA and London: MIT Press, 1996.

Venturi, Robert, Denise Scott Brown and Steven Izenour, *Learning from Las Vegas: The Forgotten Symbolism of Architectural Form*, 2nd edition, Cambridge, MA and London: MIT Press, 1977.

THOMAS S. KUHN (1922–96)

Kuhn's work on the history and philosophy of science has resonated throughout the fields of philosophy and science since the publication of his book *The Structure of Scientific Revolutions* in 1962, where he put forward a controversial conception of scientific history as consisting of a series of paradigms overcoming each other in turn. The argument was that each new paradigm was incommensurable with its predecessor; one had to believe in one or the other. Ptolemaic astronomy, for example, could not be reconciled with Copernican; they had entirely different starting points that excluded the principles and processes of the other, forcing astronomers into one camp or the other. In the case of Ptolemaic astronomy, it had to make so many revisions to the theory to incorporate a series of anomalies that arose over the years (the notorious epicycles added to planetary paths, for example) that it created conditions favourable for a revolution, as astronomers sought to find new ways and new perspectives by which those anomalies could be eradicated. When it reached the stage of epicycles within epicycles, then that search for a new perspective could only intensify: the system was becoming too unwieldy to be proof against, its many modifications creating rather than staving off doubt.

Once a revolution was successful (which often involved waiting for an older generation of scientists to die out, and their beliefs with them) the paradigm that had been overcome was to be relegated to the history books, thenceforth to have no more effect on scientific practice. Scientific practice within a new paradigm was then largely a case of filling in any gaps in the new theory and applying it as widely as possible in order to reinforce its claims to authority. This was what Kuhn came to call 'normal science' (Kuhn 1970: 10), and it was the activity on which most career scientists would spend the greater part of their working lives. Normal science brings to mind the construction of a jigsaw as much as anything else, with scientists gradually filling in the gaps: 'extending the knowledge of those facts that the paradigm displays as particularly revealing' (Kuhn 1970: 24). In the modern era, filling in the gaps was taken to mean coming ever closer to a Grand Unified Theory, where no gaps would be left. It would only be when such applications started to generate significant and persistent anomalies – when, to continue the analogy, the pieces no longer fitted the spaces left – that belief in the theory would begin to waver, paving the way for the possibility of a new revolution. Until that point the new paradigm would make such revisions as were necessary to maintain its dominance within the profession. Paradigms were not given up lightly – too many professional reputations were at stake for that ever to be allowed to happen – so a latter-day version of epicycles, and then epicycles within epicycles when required, would be concocted to save the theory. As long as normal science was getting the results it expected, however, it would continue as usual and would consider itself to be successful: 'it is only during periods of normal science that progress seems both obvious and assured. During those periods, however, the scientific community could view the fruits of its work in no other way' (Kuhn 1970: 163).

Kuhn could point to various examples of revolutions over the course of scientific history since the Copernican, such as those instigated by the work of major scientists like Albert Einstein with the theory of relativity, which postulated a very different form of physics to that developed out of Newtonian mechanics. As Kuhn notes,

Because they provide an economical summary of a vast quantity of information, Newtonian concepts are still in use. But increasingly they are employed for their economy alone, just as the ancient two-sphere universe is employed by the modern navigator and surveyor. They are still a useful aid to memory, but they are ceasing to provide a trustworthy guide to the unknown.

(Kuhn 1957: 265)

Einstein himself was soon to come under pressure from the newly developing field of quantum mechanics, proving that scientific knowledge is in a constant state of internal critique and reformulation: 'a continued and continuing story', as Kuhn sums its history up (Kuhn 1957: 265). We now have a 'standard model' of physics, which has not quite managed as yet to incorporate all the known forces in the universe into a Grand Unified Theory, although the discovery of the Higgs boson holds out the hope that this may be imminent. Nevertheless, the lack of progress on this issue until recently has encouraged some of the scientific community to consider the possibility of new models that would start from a very different set of premises than the old. Should this indeed happen it would institute yet another profound scientific revolution that would demand we reconstruct our picture of the nature of reality according to a new set of co-ordinates. Already the issues of dark matter, dark energy and dark magnetism put the standard model under a considerable amount of strain, and many in the field are beginning seriously to doubt its validity. Even the Higgs boson may not turn out to be the final piece in the jigsaw, with some scientists already questioning whether it is as fundamental as it has been theorised to be.

Kuhn initially made more use of the term 'consensus' to describe the agreed theories and procedures to be found in most scientific eras, but eventually decided that 'paradigm' was 'the missing element' (Kuhn 1977: xix) he needed to structure the argument of *The Structure of Scientific Revolutions*. He conceded that the term soon took on a much wider remit in his work than just 'consensus', referring to the entire body of knowledge that lay behind agreed theories and procedures at any one point, and that this did cause a certain amount of confusion amongst his readers as to which sense was in use at any given point in the argument. It became one of the main aspects of his work picked on by his critics, but it can be defended on the grounds that a scientific consensus does depend on a tradition of ideas. Paradigm certainly carries with it a stronger sense of framework of thought than consensus does.

Kuhn's vision of science as permanently susceptible to revolutions rather than gradual changes as data accumulated over time, although highly congenial to postmodern cultural commentators, has been widely criticised by both philosophers of science and the scientific community more generally. One philosopher who took particular exception to Kuhn's theories was Karl Popper, who had earlier devised a model of scientific practice in which theories were held to be true until proven otherwise according to the dictates of a rigorously applied scientific method. The criterion scientists were recommended to work by was 'falsifiability'. As Popper put it in *The Logic of Scientific Discovery*, if a theory is tested and 'its singular conclusions turn out to be acceptable, or *verified*, then the theory has, for the time being, passed its test: we have found no reason to discard it'; but 'if the conclusions have been *falsified*, then their falsification also falsifies the theory from which they were logically deduced' (Popper 1980: 33). It is probably true to say that most practising scientists felt more comfortable with this kind of notion than they did with Kuhn's more dramatic picture of the scientific landscape, in which entire theoretical systems could be demolished by emerging new ideas and then consigned to oblivion. Kuhn's suggestion was that, whereas such episodes of falsifiability could, and did, take place periodically, they were not what most scientists felt they were doing the bulk of the time. In fact, experimental failures were more likely to be laid at the door of the scientist, not the theory:

> If it fails the test, only his own ability not the corpus of current science is impugned. In short, though tests occur frequently in normal science, these tests are of a peculiar sort, for in the final analysis it is the individual scientist rather than current theory which is tested.
>
> (Kuhn 1972: 5)

There would need to be systematic instances of the theory failing in experimental settings before serious doubt about the theory emerged as an important factor. From the point of view of a Kuhnian, Popper's theory of scientific progress is just a little too neat, and underestimates the complex psychological struggles that are always at work in the scientific enterprise.

The Kuhn–Popper debate soon became central to philosophy of science in the 1960s and 1970s, drawing heated exchanges between proponents, often centring on the precise meaning of the notions of 'paradigm' or 'falsifiability' (see, for example, the various essays in

Lakatos and Musgrave, *Criticism and the Growth of Knowledge*, including contributions from both Kuhn and Popper themselves). In retrospect, however, it could be argued that the respective positions are not necessarily as far apart as they might have seemed at the time. Kuhn himself is at pains to point out what their respective theories have in common: 'On almost all the occasions when we turn explicitly to the same problems, Sir Karl's view of science and my own are very nearly identical' (Kuhn 1972: 1). While Kuhn does go on to specify areas of disagreement in this particular essay, it would nevertheless be perfectly possible to put together an amalgam of the two theories: scientific revolutions might be described as large-scale incidents of falsifiability, for example. What is important to note is that both theories introduce an element of provisionality into scientific practice, even if that element works differently in each case.

Postmodern thinkers, however, have been particularly drawn to the sense of provisionality that is so evident in Kuhn's notion of the paradigm; the sense that no one theory can be considered to hold for all time and to claim any monopoly on truth. Undoubtedly, they have pushed this notion much further than Kuhn himself probably would have wanted, not to mention most of those in the scientific community, who remain in general sceptical of there being such a phenomenon as 'postmodern science', regarding this almost as a contradiction in terms. From such a perspective, postmodern science calls into question almost the whole scientific enterprise as it has developed in modern times, conceiving of it as a far more arbitrary form of enquiry than practising scientists generally experience it to be in their professional lives – particularly those engaged in the tasks attendant on normal science. Neither do most scientists consider their subject to lie within the remit of mere cultural theories, which to their minds are far less rigorous in methodological terms.

Kuhn's major writings

Kuhn, Thomas S., *The Copernican Revolution: Planetary Astronomy and the Development of Western Thought*, Cambridge, MA and London: Harvard University Press, 1957.

——, *The Structure of Scientific Revolutions* [1962], 2nd edition, Chicago and London: University of Chicago Press, 1970.

——, 'Logic of Discovery or Psychology of Research', in Imre Lakatos and Alan Musgrave (eds), *Criticism and the Growth of Knowledge*, Cambridge: Cambridge University Press, 1972, pp. 1–23.

——, *The Essential Tension: Selected Studies in Scientific Tradition and Change*, Chicago and London: University of Chicago Press, 1977.

——, *Black-Body Theory and the Quantum Discontinuity, 1894–1912*, New York: Oxford University Press, 1978.

——, *The Road Since Structure: Philosophical Essays, 1970–1993, with an Autobiographical Interview*, Chicago and London: University of Chicago Press, 2000.

References and further reading

Popper, Karl R., *The Logic of Scientific Discovery* [1935], London: Hutchinson, revised edition, 1980.

ERNESTO LACLAU (B. 1935) AND CHANTAL MOUFFE (B. 1943)

Although Marxism had a long list of internal critics and dissenting voices over the course of the twentieth century, it was Laclau and Mouffe more than anyone else who established post-Marxism as a specific theoretical movement in its own right in their highly controversial book *Hegemony and Socialist Strategy*, published in 1985. This was as it was becoming increasingly clear that the Soviet system was running into considerable difficulties that would culminate in its collapse in the later 1980s, giving the book added resonance in the years immediately following its publication. *Hegemony and Socialist Strategy* laid out a new direction for Marxist thought, away from the dogmatic stance it had increasingly come to adopt over the course of the twentieth century (as evident in the Soviet system) to a more open-minded attitude, where the theory's revolutionary spirit would take precedence over doctrinaire adherence to its concepts and the insistence on an uncritical acceptance of the official Communist Party line regardless of circumstances. Those circumstances simply no longer applied for these two thinkers:

> The 'evident truths' of the past – the classical forms of analysis and political calculation, the nature of the forces in conflict, the very meaning of the Left's struggles and objectives – have been seriously challenged by an avalanche of historical mutations which have riven the ground on which those truths were constituted.
>
> (Laclau and Mouffe 1985: 1)

It was held to be dogmatism more than anything else, exemplified for Laclau and Mouffe by the continual reformulation of the concept of hegemony to cover Marxism's increasingly embarrassing predictive failures, that had led to Marxism's progressive decline in the later decades of the twentieth century and its general loss of appeal to the ranks of social revolutionaries. Marxism had argued that capitalism would eventually collapse when its contradictions became so apparent that the proletariat would rise up against it and defeat it, ushering in a new era in human history when economic exploitation would cease. The longer this took to happen the more awkward it became for the leaders of Marxism, who had to find some way to explain this that did not sound like they were criticising the theory itself, this being why hegemony was developed. Hegemony posited that the capitalist system was able to convince the population at large to accept its values, even though it was not in their best interests to do so. This was achieved by passing on the system's values through the media, as well as the society's education system, thus making the working classes think that those values were the natural order of things. The more successful the establishment was at reinforcing this belief, the less opposition they would have to face and the less likely a revolution became – although for classical Marxists there was no question that ultimately it would come; bourgeois hegemony could not last forever. The new, looser form of Marxism that Laclau and Mouffe were recommending to replace a hegemony-led Marxism was to go under the name of 'radical democracy', and much of the authors' subsequent work, both collaboratively and individually, has been concerned with fleshing out the details of what such a politics would entail.

Laclau and Mouffe pointed out that a series of social movements had sprung up around the globe by the later twentieth century that Marxism could not accommodate within its rigid historical scheme, hence what they called 'the vicissitudes of hegemony' (Laclau and Mouffe 1985: 192). Movements of this nature tended to have a particular remit – ethnic, ecological or sexual, for example – rather than a commitment to a universal idea, and from official Marxism's point of view to amount to little more than special-interest groups obscuring the larger struggle that ought to be the primary concern of revolutionaries, the class struggle. Effectively, what the authors were identifying was the growing importance of identity politics around the globe. Whereas Laclau and Mouffe felt that such movements could be built upon to achieve significant social change (as Jean-François Lyotard also believed was the case with 'little narratives' (Lyotard 1984: 60)), Marxism rejected them on the basis that they did not fit their projections as to how revolutionary change ought to occur. For Marxists the theory was assumed to take precedence over such individual concerns, a policy with which feminists in particular took issue, with one such, Heidi Hartmann, even raising the spectre of a 'divorce' between Marxism and feminism in a provocative essay entitled 'The Unhappy Marriage of Marxism and Feminism' (Hartmann 1981: 2). Clearly, revolutionary thought in general was beginning to doubt the validity of Marxism as a guide to socio-political change.

The heart of *Hegemony and Socialist Strategy*'s argument was the analysis of the various formulations of the concept of hegemony that Marxist theorists had felt the need to have recourse to, over the course of the twentieth century, to explain why capitalist society was proving far more resilient than classical Marxism had envisaged it would. A succession of crises within capitalism (the 'Great Depression' of the 1930s, to take one particularly notable example) did not create the surge of popular support for Marxism that both its founders and major thinkers had believed would inevitably follow such phenomena, when the system's internal contradictions would become publicly apparent, leading to calls for radical change. Hegemony was therefore devised as a way of propping up the Marxist model of historical process despite events not conforming to it, the line being that the process had merely been delayed. For Laclau and Mouffe, however, after so many incidences of delay the theory had to be considered more than somewhat suspect, and they proceeded to find serious fault with all the versions of hegemony that had been put forward by prominent Marxist theorists like Antonio Gramsci and Louis Althusser.

The book was the subject of a series of attacks by several Marxist thinkers, who took exception to the notion that Marxism had somehow been 'cheating', or just plain wrong, in the claims it had been making for its historical vision. Norman Geras, for example, openly accused the authors in the influential *New Left Review* journal of being ex-Marxists, and dismissed their book as 'a product of the very advanced stage of an academic malady, ... theoretically profligate, dissolute' (Geras 1987: 42–3). Another criticism to be raised was that while pluralism was an entirely laudable notion for the authors to promote, the practicalities of it were at best unclear: 'Their notion of an open plural democracy depends crucially on maintaining an unstable equilibrium between different social agents without lapsing either into authoritarian centralisation or fragmentation. An attractive idea, but hard to see how it would work' (Forgacs 1985: 43). Following up on that point, another critic observed that although '[t]he heart of this book is the discourse concerning agency, ... it succeeds only in raising the question, not in providing a solid alternative theory' (Aronowitz 1986/7: 2). That will be a recurrent criticism of Laclau and Mouffe, and indeed the issue of agency remains one of the weak points of postmodern political theory in general: postmodernists are good at telling us what is wrong with our current cultural system, less effective when it comes to providing plans of action as to how to correct such wrongs. So often, as Aronowitz notes of *Hegemony and Socialist Strategy*, there is 'a lack of specificity' (Aronowitz 1986/7: 3) when it comes to outlining the character that such agency must take to bring about significant socio-political change. The problem is that most postmodernist thinkers are suspicious of mass action, which they identify with old-style left politics and its insistence on unity rather than plurality of viewpoints – a unity which all too easily became authoritarian in character. In consequence they shy away from any suggestion of this in their cultural analyses, falling back on some version or other of the 'little narrative' notion.

Laclau and Mouffe replied in similarly robust fashion to Geras in a subsequent issue of *New Left Review*, making it clear they were completely unrepentant and that their promotion of post-Marxism as the way forward for the left was to be considered entirely 'without apologies' (Laclau and Mouffe 1987: 79). The left, they contended, had no choice but to concede Marxism's 'limitations' (Laclau and Mouffe 1987: 106) as a theory rooted in its own historical time, and to move on and revise the theory to take account of changing circumstances that its founder could not have foreseen. The rise of identity politics was a pertinent case in point, and could not simply be dismissed as a bourgeois phenomenon or mere passing fancy. Only by such a change of perspective could the spirit of Marxism be upheld and remain some kind of inspiration to emerging revolutionaries, with Laclau and Mouffe insisting that as far as they were concerned they were carrying on the best traditions of Marxist thought: 'if our intellectual project in this book is *post*-Marxist, it is evidently also post-*Marxist*' (Laclau and Mouffe 1985: 4). Radical democracy was proposed as the method by which that spirit could be maintained while avoiding the dogmatism found in most Marxist thought (most obviously in its Soviet manifestation). It was to be 'a form of politics which is founded not upon dogmatic postulation of any "essence of the social", but, on the contrary, on affirmation of the contingency and ambiguity of every "essence", and on the constitutive character of social division and antagonism' (Laclau and Mouffe 1985: 193).

Much of the authors' writing from *Hegemony and Socialist Strategy* onwards is concerned with the form that radical democracy should take in order to encompass that contingency and ambiguity within a socialist framework, and thus to overcome their critics' complaints about its 'lack of specificity' as a theory. How could plurality be turned into a working reality? In Mouffe's *The Democratic Paradox*, for instance, there is an attempt to outline the kind of pluralism that radical democracy should feature, and it takes the form of agonistic rather than antagonistic relations between competing political positions. Antagonistic relations are what mark out the kind of democracy we currently live under in the West, and for Mouffe it invariably involves compromise, to which she is very much opposed: 'This is the typical liberal perspective that envisages democracy as a competition among elites, making adversary forces invisible and reducing politics to an exchange of arguments and the negotiation of compromises' (Mouffe 2000: 111). Mouffe is critical of any attempt to play down the adversarial side of politics, arguing in *On the Political* that this is what is wrong with the 'Third Way' theory of Anthony Giddens (*Beyond Left and Right*) and the 'cosmopolitanism' of Ulrich Beck (*The Reinvention of Politics*): for her, to adopt either of these positions is to be 'post-political' (Mouffe 2005: 48). Agonism, in contrast, avoids this state of affairs by actively encouraging pluralism through the 'confrontation between democratic political positions', leading to 'real debate about possible alternatives' (Mouffe 2000: 113). The point is to try and convert one's opponent to one's own point of view rather than giving in to the process of compromise, where both points of view are thereby diluted.

Changing antagonism into agonism, elite politics into plural, becomes one of the key tasks in a radical democratic society, otherwise we continue to marginalise much of society from meaningful participation in political life, creating a worrying 'democratic deficit' (Mouffe 2000: 96) that simply builds up trouble for the future. When such deficits occur they invite the rise of totalitarian movements that can hold considerable appeal for the marginalised with no real stake in the political process, leaving them easy to sway: if they are being neglected by the existing system they have nothing to lose in supporting extremism. Both doctrinaire Marxism and fascism traditionally thrive in such situations.

While Mouffe's analysis of standard democratic politics has much to commend it, we are left with the usual problem of agency: how do we convince everyone in the current political process to switch over to a different method of debate than their cultural history sanctions? Involving the whole populace sounds an entirely laudable idea, but the question of how practical it is quickly arises. Political life cannot solely be about debate; there is after all at least some measure of governing to be done, with decisions to be made on behalf of the whole populace. It is reasonable to wonder how many agonistic positions a political system could feature and still be able to form governments with at least some degree of mass support, without which implementing decisions would be extremely difficult. Radical democracy can sound rather like a glorified university-style debating society, and, however sincerely meant, it does not really resolve the pressing issue of agency.

For all her commitment to pluralism Mouffe concedes that there are some political positions that would have to be excluded from a system based on radical democracy. There would have to be agreement amongst participants on basic principles, such as pluralism and agonism, and that would of course not be acceptable to all political parties – communists, fascists and religious fundamentalists propounding theocracy for starters. None of those latter accept that there can, or should, be pluralism in a political system, being convinced that their worldview alone is the correct one and that it admits of no opposition. Groups like that tend to be immune to 'conversion', but exactly how they would be dealt with under radical democracy is unclear – and it would be unrealistic to expect them to disappear altogether. The exact nature of the difference between compromise and conversion calls for some exploration as well: might some conversions be in reality temporary compromises reached for strategic reasons (wily political opponents being only too capable of such actions)? Whether one could always trust a conversion is a moot point, one suspects; especially if they are happening all the time, as we have to assume might well be the case under an agonistic system with constant, impassioned, debate taking place.

Laclau further explores the issues raised in *Hegemony and Socialist Strategy* in *New Reflections on the Revolution of Our Time*, with a sense that the trends noted at the beginning of the earlier book have considerably speeded up in the interim, enough to make it reasonable to talk of a full-scale 'revolution' being underway: 'The last two years have seen the most important epochal mutation that the world has experienced since the end of the Second World War. ... The cycle of events which opened with the Russian Revolution has definitively closed' (Laclau 1990: xi). The reference is to the fall of the Berlin Wall, and with it the collapse of the communist project in Europe. Given the circumstances, Laclau feels that there is an even more pressing need for the left to adopt the post-Marxist stance that both he and Mouffe had been developing, and he opens out more on what this should feature. Laclau's task, as he sees it, is to steer a course between old-style socialism rooted in a statist, interventionist, mentality and free-market fundamentalism rooted in individualism and entrepreneurialism. The fact that the former has been discredited by the sad record of the communist project over the twentieth century does not mean that the other has been vindicated. Some kind of middle way between the two extremes is required: 'social regulation will be a complex and pragmatic process in which state intervention and market mechanisms will combine according to forms that are irreducible to any aprioristic principle' (Laclau 1990: xv).

Creating those conditions has, however, proved very difficult for the left in the period since, and free-market fundamentalism in the guise of neoliberal economics has become more and more the preferred option for Western societies – the recent credit crisis notwithstanding. Giddens's 'Third Way' theory would seem to be much in the same spirit as Laclau's assessment of what is needed (although, as we have noted, Mouffe rejected it as post-political), and New Labour did put it into operation in the UK from its election win in 1997 to at least some extent; but by the end of their period in office it was neoliberalism which was dictating events politically, and it has continued to do so under the new coalition government which replaced New Labour in 2010.

In *The Making of Political Identities*, Laclau's introduction sees 'the avalanche of historical mutations' mentioned in *Hegemony and Socialist Strategy* as manifesting itself in a shift from the competing ideologies of the Cold War to 'a proliferation of particularistic political identities, none of which tries to ground its legitimacy and its action in a mission predetermined by universal history' (Laclau 1994: 1). While the ideological confrontations that marked out modernity may have gone, Laclau concedes that it is still in the balance whether the proliferation he notes will lead to radical democracy or to a new outburst of authoritarianism.

Despite the attempts to flesh out radical democracy as a political system, for many commentators it remains an intriguing idea rather than a fully worked-out political programme that could easily be put into practice, raising precisely the kind of problems listed above. David Howarth, for example, while sympathetic overall to radical democracy as a concept, notes that not enough 'attention is paid to the economic, material and institutional obstacles that block its realisation', and that this leads to the emergence of an unfortunate 'institutional deficit' in the theory (Howarth 2008: 189). It is that tricky issue of agency again: what framework would guarantee that an agonistic-style politics would function as desired, or that a pragmatic middle way could be found between the state and the market? Marxists will always be able to pick holes in such a theory because, as we know, they can be very specific indeed about how to make their system function. Whether or not one agrees with their goals, there is no denying that they offer a structured programme as to how to achieve them and put them into working practice. Marxism lays great emphasis on the need to take over key state institutions and remake them in its own image, leaving nothing up to chance in such cases (hence the refusal to allow independent media to exist in any communist state). There is no institutional deficit to be noted when communism takes over. If nothing else, Marxism has the virtue of clarity, and that does draw adherents in, as it does with fascism too.

Nevertheless, post-Marxism remains an important strand in postmodern thought, ensuring that it does have a strong political dimension that is in dialogue with a left-wing past. Even if it could be said of that thought in general, as Aronowitz does of *Hegemony and Socialist Strategy*, that it is 'a series of *hypotheses* rather than a real theory' (Aronowitz 1986/7: 3), those hypotheses nevertheless did need to be aired and debated in order to shake up moribund movements and traditions. Just how moribund we have discovered in the interim, with the implosion of the Soviet empire and the subsequent eclipse of communism's political influence in the West. Post-Marxism may not have solved the problem of agency, or of how to reconcile 'universality and particularity' (Laclau 1996: vii) into a workable political model, but it has made it clear where the left's efforts would be most profitably applied in a post-communist world.

Laclau and Mouffe's major writings

Laclau, Ernesto and Chantal Mouffe, *Hegemony and Socialist Strategy: Towards a Radical Democratic Politics*, London: Verso, 1985.
——, 'Post-Marxism Without Apologies', *New Left Review*, 166 (1987), pp. 79–106.

Laclau's major writings

Laclau, Ernesto, *Politics and Ideology in Marxist Theory: Capitalism, Fascism, Populism*, London: NLB, 1977.
——, *New Reflections on the Revolution of Our Time*, London and New York: Verso, 1990.
——(ed.), *The Making of Political Identities*, London and New York: Verso, 1994.

——, *Emancipation(s)*, London and New York: Verso, 1996.
——, *On Populist Reason*, London and New York: Verso, 2005.
Butler, Judith, Ernesto Laclau and Slavoj Žižek, *Contingency, Hegemony, Universality: Contemporary Dialogues on the Left*, London and New York: Verso, 2000.

Mouffe's major writings

Mouffe, Chantal, *The Return of the Political*, London and New York: Verso, 1993.
——(ed.), *The Challenge of Carl Schmidt*, London and New York: Verso, 1999.
——, *The Democratic Paradox*, London and New York: Verso, 2000.
——, *On the Political*, London and New York: Routledge, 2005.

References and further reading

Aronowitz, Stanley, 'Theory and Socialist Strategy', *Social Text*, 1986/7, pp. 1–16.
Beck, Ulrich, *The Reinvention of Politics: Rethinking Modernity in the Global Social Order*, Cambridge: Polity Press, 1997.
Forgacs, David, 'Dethroning the Working Class?', *Marxism Today* 29(5) (May 1985), p. 43.
Geras, Norman, 'Post-Marxism?', *New Left Review*, 163 (May/June 1987), pp. 40–82.
Giddens, Anthony, *Beyond Left and Right – The Future of Radical Politics*, Cambridge: Polity Press, 1994.
Hartmann, Heidi, 'The Unhappy Marriage of Marxism and Feminism: Towards a More Progressive Union', in L. Sargent (ed.), *The Unhappy Marriage of Marxism and Feminism: A Debate on Class and Patriarchy*, London: Pluto Press, 1981, pp. 1–41.
Howarth, David, 'Ethos, Agonism and Populism: William Connolly and the Case for Radical Democracy', *British Journal of Politics and International Relations*, 10(2) (2008), pp. 171–93.
Lyotard, Jean-François, *The Postmodern Condition: A Report on Knowledge* [1979], trans. Geoff Bennington and Brian Massumi, Manchester: Manchester University Press, 1984.

DAVID LYNCH (B. 1946)

A highly respected and critically acclaimed filmmaker, Lynch is probably best known to the general public through his television series *Twin Peaks*. This became a cult success in both America and Europe in the early 1990s, and is still regularly cited, and studied, as a prime example of postmodern television. His films vary from the early arthouse-style *Eraserhead* through big-budget, mainstream studio-backed projects like *Dune*, to dark and edgy exposes of the underside of American suburban and small-town life such as *Blue Velvet*, and then latterly some strange projects implying that we are mere playthings of the supernatural, as in *Lost Highway* and *Inland Empire*. *Twin Peaks* is very much in that latter category, with the supernatural playing a critical role in the unfolding of the narrative. A director of numerous television commercials, Lynch also works as an artist and craftsman (furniture maker in the main), and, somewhat to the bemusement of critics of late, as a singer and musician. A CD released in 2011, entitled 'Crazy Clown Time', was described by one critic as a 'nightmarish' album delivered in a 'strangled, high' voice by the director (Tyler 2011). He has even gone into the club business, opening one designed in typically esoteric style by himself in Paris in 2011, Club Silencio.

Twin Peaks can be made to sound like a fairly straightforward story, a murder mystery in which the murderer is sought by the local police force, backed up by an FBI agent, Agent Cooper, assigned to help out with the case. Yet it turns out to be a deeply strange and disturbing world that is pictured, possibly connected to the supernatural (or even cruelly manipulated by it, a theme Lynch keeps returning to in his later work) and in which evil is a very real presence. It is set in a small logging town in the Pacific North-West of America, peopled by a cast of oftentimes quite bizarre characters like the Log Lady, who carries a log around in her arms everywhere she goes but otherwise acts in a fairly normal manner. Pretty well everyone we come across in the town has some odd quirk, or quirks, to their character. Agent Cooper, for example, initially seems like a stereotypically clean-cut American professional lawman, and went on to become something of a cult hero in his own right, with much-repeated catchphrases such as 'damned fine cup of coffee'; but as the series progresses he reveals himself to be a channeller for the supernatural and apparently to believe in magic, bringing these exotic talents to bear in his search to discover the murderer of the young student Laura Palmer that kicks off the story.

There is often a dream-like quality to the narrative, particularly evident in the, presumably supernatural, Red Room scenes, where the characters speak in very distorted voices created by the process of having them read their lines backwards, recording that, and then dubbing these in to the scene having reversed the original recording. That dream-like, spooky, quality is a recurrent feature of Lynch's work, and the editor of a book of interviews with the director, *Lynch on Lynch* (Chris Rodley), suggests that the line between dreams and real life is for Lynch 'a badly guarded checkpoint where no one seems to be stamping passports' (Rodley 2005: 267). It is an observation that very neatly describes *Twin Peaks*, where it is never very clear what is real and what is imaginary, particularly since the real itself can seem so weird. Rodley, rightly enough, emphasises the importance of the 'uncanny' in Lynch's work, asserting that it 'lies at the very core' (Rodley 2005: ix) of his filmmaking.

The plot of *Twin Peaks* keeps going off at angles seeming to have nothing to do with the main narrative, and there are many red herrings and loose ends to be noted along the way. By the end of the work's run it could sometimes seem as if Lynch and his collaborators (he employed several writers and directors over the course of the series, not directing every episode himself) were trying to see just how far they could push narrative credibility without losing their audience altogether on what was for many critics 'a postmodern train to nowhere' (Rodley 2005: 156). In fact, the American network buying the series, ABC, cancelled it after its second year, much to both Lynch's and its devoted following's dismay. He was to respond to the frustration of fans in the aftermath of the cancellation by putting together a prequel film, *Twin Peaks: Fire Walk With Me*. Although not very well received by the critics, at least this filled in some of the gaps left by the aborted television series by providing a back story, if often a confused and meandering one (which admittedly was entirely consonant with the narrative to follow).

Taking those kind of risks with narrative credibility is a characteristic of Lynch's work which is evident as early as *Eraserhead*, a highly fragmented and disconnected series of images rather than a coherent story as such, and they can pose considerable problems for his audience, as in the later films *Lost Highway* and *Inland Empire*. Nothing he has done since *Twin Peaks* has attracted anything like the same degree of public attention or critical approval (although *Mulholland Drive* did win Lynch the best director award at the Cannes Film Festival). For many critics *Twin Peaks* remains the quintessential example of postmodern television: a work where the murder mystery succeeded in engaging the attention of the general television audience (if not quite enough of them to please its host network, unfortunately enough), while its stylistic and thematic quirks left wide scope for critical and intellectual debate.

Blue Velvet posits all sorts of unsavoury behaviour going on behind the façade of the American Dream, beginning with the lead character – played by Kyle MacLachlan, later to be cast as Agent Cooper – discovering a severed ear. There is an undercurrent of menace in the film, much of it set at night, which is particularly conveyed through the character of Frank, played by Denis Hopper at his most manic and malevolent, who in one of the film's most notorious scenes brutally makes love to his apparently masochistic mistress while inhaling noisily through an oxygen mask. *Wild at Heart* proves to be another typically tangled narrative involving runaway lovers (played by Nicolas Cage and Laura Dern, the latter a Lynch regular), drug–dealing, crime and references to *The Wizard of Oz*. If there is an underlying moral message to either of these films it remains well hidden.

Mulholland Drive was originally conceived as a television series but was cancelled by the commissioning network and so turned into a film for general release by the director. It featured most of the trademarks of the style Lynch had honed in *Twin Peaks*, with multiple plots, an array of bizarre characters, many apparent loose ends (some of which would no doubt have been worked out more fully if it had gone on as a series as intended, although with Lynch one never quite knows), and a general air of mystery and often menace. It is an intriguing piece of work which may well have developed into a cult like *Twin Peaks*, but the mainstream media will always be wary of maverick figures like Lynch. Lynch has in fact had a troubled relationship with the American TV networks since *Twin Peaks*, with various projects going adrift.

Arguably Lynch's most daring film is *Lost Highway*, which falls into two distinct parts, each of which makes sense in its own terms of reference but which have only the most tenuous of connections, leading to one of the director's most oblique endings. This is thanks to a somewhat less than credible turn of plot in the middle of the narrative in which a suspected murderer is transformed into a completely different character overnight while imprisoned in his police cell, an incident which, not surprisingly, completely throws the authorities, who then have no choice but to turn him free. Again, there is a sense of supernatural intervention and the pervasive sense of evil's presence – an atmosphere that Lynch is a master at creating. His own description of the first section of the film between the characters Fred and Renée is worth pondering on in that respect:

It's about a couple who feel that somewhere, just on the border of consciousness – or on the other side of that border – are bad,

bad problems. But they can't bring them into the real world and deal with them. So this bad feeling is just hovering there, and the problems abstract themselves and become other things. It just becomes like a bad dream.

(Rodley 2005: 225)

That is, however, just about as far as Lynch will ever go in 'explaining' his films. When asked about 'The Mystery Man' in the film, an unnamed character who appears in both parts of the narrative, Lynch is characteristically unforthcoming: 'I don't wanna say what he is to me, but he's a hair of an abstraction' (Rodley 2005: 229).

Inland Empire also takes many liberties with narrative line in its story concerning the misfortunes that befall an American remake of a European film that was never completed because the two leads were murdered. In consequence, the project itself seems to be cursed. As with *Twin Peaks* the plot can be made to sound straightforward, but the film comes across as disjointed and often wilfully obscure, destined for the arthouse circuit rather than the commercial mainstream. Although played with considerable conviction by the actors, how the different narrative strands hang together is not at all clear. After establishing its basic narrative premise, *Inland Empire* proceeds to cut rapidly between the making of the American film, the heroine's private life, subtitled episodes in Poland and even scenes between actors dressed as giant rabbits. Neither does the ending clarify things much, with the heroine wandering off the film set after her death scene to find herself apparently still within the film's narrative. Closure and resolution are not really primary Lynchean concerns, however, which is possibly why his films elicit so much critical interpretation.

So convoluted have Lynch's narratives become that he can confuse critics if he ever chooses not to indulge in these, as apparently is the case in the film *Straight Story*, which came between *Inland Empire* and *Mulholland Drive* in his canon. As some critics remarked, *Straight Story* gave the impression of being just that, a straightforward tale (based on a documented real-life event of an American pensioner who journeyed to see his ill brother on a motor-powered lawnmower) with no buried subtext. If so, it is something of a first for Lynch, although it could just be that it is even more well-hidden than usual: the rest of Lynch's output makes one wary of taking anything he does at face value, and the actual event itself is strange enough in its own right to encourage metaphorical readings.

Lynch's major works

Lynch, David (dir.), *Eraserhead*, David Lynch, in association with the American Film Institute Center for Advanced Film Studies, 1976.

——(dir.), *Dune*, Dino De Laurentiis/Universal, 1984.

——(dir.), *Blue Velvet*, De Laurentiis Entertainment Group, 1986.

——(dir.), *Twin Peaks*, ABC TV Network, 1990.

——(dir.), *Wild at Heart*, Propaganda Films for Polygon, 1990.

——(dir.), *Twin Peaks: Fire Walk With Me*, Twin Peaks Productions, 1992.

——(dir.), *Lost Highway*, CIBY-2000, Asymmetrical Productions, 1997.

——(dir.), *Straight Story*, Asymmetrical Productions, Canal+, *et al.*, 1999.

——(dir.), *Mulholland Drive*, Canal, 2001.

——(dir.), *Inland Empire*, Studio Canal, Camerimage, Asymmetrical Productions, 2007.

References and further reading

Rodley, Chris (ed.), *Lynch on Lynch*, 2nd edition, London: Faber and Faber, 2005.

Tyler, Kieron, 'CD: David Lynch – Crazy Clown Time', *The Arts Desk*, http://www.theartsdesk.com/new-music/cd/david-lynch-crazy-clown-time, 2011 (accessed 11 July 2012).

JEAN-FRANÇOIS LYOTARD (1924–98)

Lyotard is generally taken to be one of the major figures of postmodern thought, although he saw himself as more of a commentator on it and could be highly critical of it on occasion, regarding it as ultimately somewhat superficial and not always engaged enough with politics in the way that he thought of as necessary. Lyotard himself was political to the core and considered this to be an essential requirement for being a philosopher, although he could also be critical of philosophy itself as a discipline, as well as professional philosophers in general. The latter were all too prone to become defenders of some particular ideological system (in Lyotard's lifetime communism or liberal democracy, for example), whereas for Lyotard philosophers should strive to avoid becoming identified with the ruling class and always maintain a sceptical bias towards the dominant ideology. Their goal ought to be to develop a 'philosophical politics' (Lyotard 1988a: xiii) that would enable oppressed groups to find their voice and participate meaningfully within the political process, rather than being imposed on by those more powerful. Support for those marginalised by political systems remains an abiding concern of Lyotard (a characteristic he shares with Michel Foucault), and he adopts a consistently anti-establishment stance throughout his writings.

The work of Lyotard's most sympathetic in tone towards post-modernism is *The Postmodern Condition*, which turned out to be one of the most influential works of cultural theory of the later twentieth century, promoting the 'little narrative' approach to politics and announcing the emergence of a distinctively 'postmodern science' (Lyotard 1984: 60, 53) which generated paradox rather than certain knowledge. The postmodern condition was where grand narratives (or metanarratives, as they are also known) ceased to attract support and found their authority, their powers of 'legitimation' as Lyotard conceived of it, draining away: 'We no longer have recourse to the grand narratives – we can resort neither to the dialectic of Spirit nor even to the emancipation of humanity as validation for postmodern scientific discourse' (Lyotard 1984: 60). Instead, he encouraged us to cultivate an attitude of 'incredulity toward metanarratives' (Lyotard 1984: xxiv) and to participate in anti-establishment oriented 'little narratives' seeking to contest the abuses of those in power. Little narratives were to be temporary groupings with no ambition to develop into permanent political forces, which would run the risk of turning into the establishment as their power grew. They were designed to correct the excesses of grand narratives rather than to become yet another example of those themselves.

Lyotard's conception of 'postmodern science' is very contentious. Picking up on developments in physics such as catastrophe theory and chaos theory, Lyotard concludes that science is no longer producing knowledge but a series of paradoxes calling into question existing scientific theories. Few scientists would accept this vision of their subject, however, regarding paradox as a temporary phase on the way to greater refinement of their theories. Paradox is to a scientist a motivation to look for new explanations, not an end to his or her enquiries. Lyotard's use of scientific theory has been particularly attacked by Alan Sokal and Jean Bricmont in *Intellectual Impostures*, the argument being that it represents a gross misunderstanding of the theories involved: 'The theories cited by Lyotard of course produce new knowledge, but they do so without changing the meaning of the word' (Sokal and Bricmont 1998: 128).

One of the most important aspects of Lyotard's thought is his attempt to find a rationale for making value judgements, particularly moral ones, in the aftermath of the relativism intrinsic to so much poststructuralist and postmodern thought. Lyotard is one of the few thinkers in the postmodern camp to confront this issue head on, as in

Just Gaming (co-authored with Jean-Loup Thébaud) and *Heidegger and 'the Jews'*. In the former he takes inspiration from Aristotle's ethics, whereas in the latter he addresses the thorny problem of how to judge historical events like Auschwitz from a relativistic standpoint. Lyotard's reading of Aristotle is as an arch-pragmatist who invites us to judge all cases on their merits, without reference to previous judgements. We are to be as pragmatic as possible rather than to rely on universal rules or principles. This is the condition that Lyotard refers to as 'paganism', and for him it represents the ideal form of political organisation. Whether it would be possible to construct a legal system on the basis of paganism is more questionable, but Lyotard is mainly concerned with making sure that we stay clear of the influence of any grand narrative, which would to a large extent predetermine any judgement that was made, thus reinforcing that narrative's authority.

Auschwitz poses a more intractable problem in this respect, since it is analysed by most commentators in terms of its violation of an Enlightenment-derived notion of a code of human rights. Lyotard, however, is more interested in the larger historical dimension, whereby the Jews become symbolic of the tendency of grand narratives to marginalise those who do not conform to their system, those who are unmistakably different from the norm. It is taken to be a characteristic of grand narrative to treat the different as 'other' and so to exclude them from the rights and privileges accorded to the mass. Lyotard suggests that we regard 'jews' as a category including all those who come to be considered 'other' in their society. The defence of difference is another abiding concern of Lyotard's, as it is for post-structuralists and postmodernists in general, who feel that modernity promotes a homogenisation of human experience.

Lyotard is particularly critical of the way that so many Germans turned a blind eye to the treatment of the Jews under the Nazi regime, becoming complicit in the scheme to render them all but non-existent – in effect, to erase them from history as if they had never been, thus contriving to erase the very notion of difference itself. The eminent German philosopher Martin Heidegger is singled out as a high-profile example of this collective act of 'forgetting', which to Lyotard becomes the ultimate sin one can commit against the other: difference must never be denied in this way. Heidegger was a critical influence on postwar French philosophy from existentialism onwards, and the issue of his Nazi sympathies became a very controversial topic amongst poststructuralist and postmodernist thinkers in France in the 1980s, leading to the so-called 'Heidegger Affair', where sides were taken for and against in what became a bitter dispute played out in public. Whereas Jacques Derrida offered a guarded defence of Heidegger's philosophy, Lyotard was deeply critical, particularly of what he considered to be totalising aspects in his philosophical concepts.

The issues raised by difference figure prominently in another of Lyotard's major works, *The Differend*. The differend is an irreconcilable difference between two parties that all too often is 'resolved' by one party imposing its will on the other through an act of sheer power. What we should be doing is respecting such differences, which for Lyotard are the product of using different 'phrase regimens', each with its own set of prescribed moves which, crucially, cannot be applied outside its own sphere. Lyotard conceives of phrase regimens as being in the nature of an archipelago, where each island is separate from the other but it is possible to move between them, as long as the traveller respects the rules and regulations applying in each case and does not import rules from his or her own regimen. Differends occur when someone is not playing the game by failing to respect each regimen's integrity.

Lyotard lays a lot of store by the notion of the 'event', which for him symbolises the openness and unpredictability of history, as well as the inability of any philosophical or socio-political theory to determine how the future will work out. Again, it is that sense of there being no universal rule dictating our conduct, no grand narrative whose dictates we are duty bound to follow. Events have their own internal logic which we are powerless to control, Lyotard describing them in dramatic fashion as 'the impact, on the system, of floods of energy such that the system does not manage to bind and channel this energy' (Lyotard 1993b: 64).

Lyotard also emphasises the importance of the sublime in human affairs, taking its existence to be yet more evidence of our inability to exert control over events: 'Sublime violence is like lightning. It short-circuits thinking with itself. … [T]he sublime is a sudden blazing, and without future. Thus it is that it acquired a future and addresses us still, we who hardly hope in the Kantian sense' (Lyotard 1994: 54–5). The sublime undermines our Enlightenment-derived notion that we can be masters of our destiny, forcing us to recognise the sheer contingency of human existence – another staple feature of the postmodern outlook. Lyotard has a range of terms to denote the forces that lie beyond our control, with the 'figure' being another important one, as in his doctoral thesis, only recently translated into English as *Discourse Figure*.

The anti-deterministic cast of postmodern thought comes out very strongly at such points, with the 1968 Paris *événements* constituting a particularly cogent example of the event in action. The shameful role of the French Communist Party (PCF) in supporting the government spurred Lyotard on to take an increasingly hostile attitude to Marxism, a prime example of the grand narratives that he so detested. It is a hostility that comes to a head in *Libidinal Economy*, which features a spectacularly hysterical attack on Marxism for its failure to encompass the factor of desire in human affairs.

Like most other thinkers included under the heading of the postmodern, Lyotard is a proponent of fluidity as regards political commitment, in his case defining this as the state of 'svelteness':

> Stendhal already said at the beginning of the nineteenth century that the ideal is no longer the physical force of ancient peoples; it is flexibility, speed, metamorphic capacity (one goes to the ball in the evening, and one wages war the next day at dawn). Svelteness, wakefulness, a Zen and an Italian term.
>
> (Lyotard 1993b: 28)

To be svelte is to have the ability to change roles, and political positions, quickly if circumstances demand this, with Lyotard playing on the fashion-world connotation of the word as 'slender'. The more slender one's beliefs the better (the notion is very similar to Deleuze and Guattari's 'nomadism'): what is to be avoided at all costs is any regression to dogmatism. Thought in general has this fluidity for Lyotard, who describes it as being like the movement of clouds, a series of unpredictable events unfolding into the future and thus not really in the control of any one individual (see *Peregrinations*). Svelteness and fluidity remain central to his conception of philosophy, which refuses to be trapped into defending set positions; and that is to be considered a hallmark of postmodern thought.

For all his suspicion of postmodern thought, therefore, Lyotard has to be regarded as one of the major sources of what we now call postmodernism: a tireless defender of difference and critic of absolutist and totalitarian theories, both hallmarks of the postmodern ethos.

Lyotard's major writings

Lyotard, Jean-François, *The Postmodern Condition: A Report on Knowledge* [1979], trans. Geoff Bennington and Brian Massumi, Manchester: Manchester University Press, 1984.
——, *The Differend: Phrases in Dispute* [1983], trans. Georges Van Den Abbeele, Manchester: Manchester University Press, 1988a.

——, *Peregrinations: Law, Form, Event*, New York: Columbia University Press, 1988b.

——, *Heidegger and 'the Jews'* [1988], trans. Andreas Michel and Mark Roberts, Minneapolis, MN: University of Minnesota Press, 1990.

——, *The Inhuman: Reflections on Time* [1988], trans. Geoffrey Bennington and Rachel Bowlby, Oxford: Blackwell, 1991.

——, *Libidinal Economy* [1974], trans. Iain Hamilton Grant, London: Athlone Press, 1993a.

——, *Political Writings*, trans. Bill Readings and Kevin Paul Geiman, London: UCL Press, 1993b.

——, *Lessons on the Analytic of the Sublime* [1991], trans. Elizabeth Rottenberg, Stanford, CA: Stanford University Press, 1994.

——, *Discourse, Figure* [1971], trans. Anthony Hudek, Minneapolis, MN: University of Minnesota Press, 2011.

Lyotard, Jean-François and Jean-Loup Thébaud, *Just Gaming* [1979], trans. Wlad Godzich, Manchester: Manchester University Press, 1985.

References and further reading

Sokal, Alan and Jean Bricmont, *Intellectual Impostures: Postmodern Philosophers' Abuse of Science*, London: Profile Books, 1998.

BRIAN McHALE (B. 1954)

McHale is a critic and theorist whose importance to postmodernism lies in his work putting together a classification system for postmodern fiction that differentiates it from the modernist canon. In McHale's scheme postmodern fiction is marked by a shift to the ontological from the epistemological, and that is a shift entailing a distinctively different way of perceiving the world; although he emphasises that it is possible for writers to operate on both sides of the divide over the course of their career, and provides examples of those who have. Appropriating some ideas outlined in Dick Higgins's book *A Dialectic of Centuries*, McHale proceeds to formulate a 'general thesis' about both modernist and postmodernist fiction:

> [T]he dominant of modernist fiction is *epistemological*. That is, modernist fiction deploys strategies which engage and foreground questions such as those mentioned by Dick Higgins in my epigraph: 'How can I interpret this world of which I am a part? And what am I in it?' ... [T]he dominant of postmodernist fiction is *ontological*. That is, postmodernist fiction deploys strategies which engage and foreground questions like the ones Dick Higgins calls

'post-cognitive': 'Which world is this? What is to be done in it? Which of my selves is to do it?'

(McHale 1987: 9, 10)

McHale's goal in *Postmodernist Fiction*, therefore, is to come up with a workable postmodern poetics for fiction, and to that end he examines the work of a clutch of authors he feels have made the transition from modernist to postmodernist poetics during their career; namely, Samuel Beckett, Alain Robbe-Grillet, Carlos Fuentes, Vladimir Nabokov, Robert Coover and Thomas Pynchon. McHale sets out to determine the common features we would expect to find in postmodern fiction: 'what this book primarily aspires to do is to construct the repertory of motifs and devices, and the system of relations and differences, shared by a particular class of texts' (McHale 1987: xi). Identify those motifs and devices, relations and differences, and one has the dominant of the age, and thus a method for classifying and then analysing texts.

In *Constructing Postmodernism*, on the other hand, McHale sets out to provide 'multiple, overlapping and intersecting inventories and multiple corpora; not *a* construction of postmodernism, but a plurality of constructions; constructions that, while not necessarily mutually contradictory, are not fully integrated, or perhaps even integrable, either' (McHale 1992: 3). The point he is making here is that postmodernism has no set boundaries, nor is there general agreement as to what it involves, or even should involve as a theory, but that it certainly 'exists discursively, in the discourses we produce *about* it, and *using* it' (McHale 1992: 1). The book is designed to be more flexible in its approach to postmodernist texts than *Postmodernist Fiction* was, and to that end analyses a very wide range of narratives, going as far back in literary history as James Joyce's *Ulysses*. (This is not too surprising a historical reach, given that authors as far back as Laurence Sterne have been claimed for the postmodern by some commentators (see, for example, Pierce and de Voogd, *Laurence Sterne in Modernism and Postmodernism.*)) Part of the reason for the whole exercise is to answer critics of *Postmodernist Fiction*, who complained of the lack of actual textual readings to test the model of the postmodern literary aesthetic being floated, and in the process of doing so in *Constructing Postmodernism* McHale makes adjustments along the way.

For McHale the presence of ontological concerns is what defines a postmodern text, rather than the widely touted theory of double-coding derived from Charles Jencks, and in fact McHale is careful to distance himself from that school of thought: 'Jencks is not the only version of postmodernism, nor is it the one I endorse. I prefer to construct a postmodernism with an ontological orientation, that is, a poetics subordinated to an ontological dominant' (McHale 1992: 206). This emphasis on the ontological means that McHale is still thinking in classificatory terms, so any recent texts that do not meet his criterion are defined as 'late modernist' instead, such as Joseph McElroy's novel *Women and Men* (McHale 1992: 206). While one can see the rationale behind this decision, it does demonstrate one of the drawbacks of any classification process, that it can become a game between rival checklists. However, it is a fair point to make that double-coding should not be thought of as enough on its own to make a text postmodern, and indeed it is a feature that is by no means unique to the postmodern age – hence the tendency to claim earlier writers such as Laurence Sterne for the postmodern canon. It all depends on how one wants to define double-coding, and that too can soon decline into a game of questionable usefulness in critical terms.

A very obvious criticism to make of McHale is that he is operating with a binarist interpretation of postmodernism and modernism, with texts being allocated to one or the other side, even though he tries to be as flexible about the classification process as possible, admitting that many texts are difficult to pin down in that way. The irony is that binarism is precisely what postmodern thought is concerned to challenge, with figures like Jacques Derrida arguing strongly against it (see his *Writing and Difference*, for example). While it is McHale's stated objective to provide a poetics of postmodernism, it is also a possible criticism that his vision of postmodernism is so formalistic, with little attention being paid to the world outside literature, a world which saw the emergence of the kind of social and political changes Jean-François Lyotard considered to be so vital to the construction of the post-modernist worldview. McHale was writing in the 1980s, and much has happened since then in social and political terms that has affected postmodern thought. He could hardly have foreseen such changes, but his formalistic approach does tend to exclude the possibility that, as Pat Waugh has suggested, postmodernism is as much a 'mood', or attitude of mind, as anything else (Waugh 1992: 1), and that it need not be reduced to a question of formal properties alone when it comes to the arts. Any writer who self-consciously responds to that 'mood' could be described as postmodern.

Something was happening in the literary world of the time that was worth pondering on, however, a definite change of direction in both style and themes, and McHale is still worth consulting when it comes to the fiction of the 1980s, particularly in its American guise. There was a recognisably 'ontological turn' on the American literary scene, although that has not necessarily remained a defining feature of postmodern writing since. The major European postmodernist writers have shown a greater concern with establishing a dialogue with the past, and with double-coding their texts: Eco is an excellent example of this tendency in *The Name of the Rose*, as well as his various other works of fiction, as is Peter Ackroyd in novels like *Hawksmoor*. In comparison to them, many of the authors McHale is dealing with in *Postmodernist Fiction* can seem rather mannered, and many have struggled to find much of an audience. This is not to say that one group is more truly postmodern than the other, rather that post-modernism in fiction is arguably far more diverse than McHale seems to be allowing. There are none of the practical suggestions offered by John Barth here either, such as an encouragement to reintroduce plots, storylines and credible characterisation into the novelist's practice (see Barth 1997).

McHale regards science fiction 'as postmodernism's noncanonized or "low art" double' (McHale 1987: 59), given that it has an emphatically foregrounded ontological dominant. Characters in sci-ence fiction are routinely placed in worlds not their own which force them into interpreting them if they are to survive there. Detective fiction, on the other hand, is to be considered the quintessentially modernist 'double', with its epistemological dominant. This too can be questioned, and a strong case can be made for including much detective fiction of the last three decades or so under the post-modernist heading. Authors like James Ellroy are very much in dia-logue with the moral attitudes of their society, and present authority in their works as unworthy of popular support given the degree of corruption that lies under its surface (see Ellroy's *LA Confidential*, for example). Detective fiction in general in the later twentieth/early twenty-first century has been particularly successful in portraying the 'incredulity toward metanarratives' (Lyotard 1984: xxvi) that Lyotard saw as the hallmark of the postmodern era. Institutional authority in this fiction has long since lost any credibility it may have had with the general public, and individuals have to take the law into their own hands if they wish to see anything like justice done. Postmodern detective fiction of the Ellroy kind does not offer us the neat resolu-tion to moral dilemmas that its classic counterpart invariably does (evil overcome by the forces of good, closure achieved), and in that sense might be described as being every bit as much the '"low art" double' of postmodernism as its science fiction rival.

McHale has also engaged with postmodernist poetry in *The Obligation Toward the Difficult Whole*. Looking at poets such as James Merrill, John Ashbery and Susan Howe, McHale strives again to identify common themes and strategies that differentiates their work from that of their modernist forerunners, while admitting that the notion of a shift to an ontological dominant is not as applicable in this case. Nevertheless, he does feel he can speak of 'poems, which, on the one hand, do have aspirations to a kind of unity, but also exhibit resistance or skepticism toward unity' (McHale 2008), and thus can be grouped under the heading of the postmodern.

Ultimately, rather than trying to pin postmodernism down as an aesthetic classification, it might be better to speak of writers and artists working within a postmodern era, and, as suggested earlier, self-consciously responding to the 'mood' that applies there. Some will respond to the socio-political changes taking place around them more directly than others will, and their work may well show signs of the shared 'motifs and devices' that McHale is seeking out; but they can still be discussed under the heading of the postmodern even if they do not exhibit precisely the characteristics that McHale has decided go to define its literary expression.

McHale's major writings

McHale, Brian, *Postmodernist Fiction*, New York and London: Methuen, 1987.

——, *Constructing Postmodernism*, London and New York: Routledge, 1992.

——, *The Obligation Toward the Difficult Whole: Postmodernist Long Poems*, Tuscaloosa, AL: University of Alabama Press, 2004.

——, 'On the Obligation toward the Difficult Whole: Interview with Brian McHale', *Hortus Semioticus*, 3 (2008), http://www.ut.ee/hortussemioticus/1_2008/mchale.html (accessed June 5, 2012).

McHale, Brian and Randall Stevenson (eds), *The Edinburgh Companion to Twentieth-Century Literatures in English*, Edinburgh: Edinburgh University Press, 2006.

References and further reading

Ackroyd, Peter, *Hawksmoor*, London: Hamish Hamilton, 1985.

Barth, John, 'The Literature of Replenishment' [1980], in *The Friday Book: Essays and Other Non-Fiction* [1984], Baltimore, MD and London: Johns Hopkins University Press, 1997, pp. 193–206.

Derrida, Jacques, *Writing and Difference* [1967], trans. Alan Bass, Chicago: University of Chicago Press, 1978.

Eco, Umberto, *The Name of the Rose* [1980], trans. William Weaver, London: Secker and Warburg, 1983.

Ellroy, James, *LA Confidential*, New York: Grand Central Publishing, 1990.

Higgins, Dick, *A Dialectic of Centuries: Notes Towards a Theory of the New Arts*, New York: Printed Editions, 1978.

Lyotard, Jean-François, *The Postmodern Condition: A Report on Knowledge* [1979], trans. Geoff Bennington and Brian Massumi, Manchester: Manchester University Press, 1984.

Joyce, James, *Ulysses* [1922], Harmondsworth: Penguin, 1969.

McElroy, Joseph, *Women and Men*, New York: Alfred A. Knopf, 1987.

Pierce, David and Peter de Voogd (eds), *Laurence Sterne in Modernism and Postmodernism*, Amsterdam and Atlanta, GA: Editions Rodopi, 1996.

Waugh, Patricia (ed.), 'Introduction', *Postmodernism: A Reader*, London: Edward Arnold, 1992, pp. 1–10.

BENOIT B. MANDELBROT (1924–2010)

A mathematician who worked both in industry (IBM, for many years) and academe, Mandelbrot was one of the major theorists behind chaos theory, and his work on phenomena such as fractals has been highly influential not just within various fields in science but also within the world of the arts. Posters containing fractal images had a particular vogue in the later twentieth century, and can still be found on sale today. Mandelbrot himself drew attention to the artistic potential of computer-generated fractal graphics, as in the illustrations for his seminal work on the subject *Fractals: Form, Chance and Dimension*, calling them 'examples of semi-abstract "art"' (Mandelbrot 1977: 25). The landscape architect Charles Jencks, one of the key theorists of postmodern aesthetics, has alluded to fractal geometry in some of his recent creations (see Jencks, http://www.charlesjencks.com?#!projects (accessed 27 July 2012)), indicating the continuing interest in the phenomenon within the creative arts. Jean-François Lyotard even managed to draw some socio-political conclusions out of Mandelbrot's work in his highly influential study *The Postmodern Condition*, claiming that it reinforced his belief that 'postmodern science' offered a challenge to our conception of knowledge.

Fractal geometry is designed to cover all those instances in the natural world that cannot be covered by classical, Euclidean, geometry. As Mandelbrot notes, 'no surface in Euclid represents adequately the boundaries of clouds or of rough turbulent wakes' (Mandelbrot 1977: 1), and nature is just full of similar cases. It is observations such as this that have led to the formulation of chaos theory, which is concerned with the behaviour of non-linear systems in general. Mandelbrot is famous for his claim that we can never measure precisely the length of a coastline, because of the fractal formation that lies embedded beneath any point we reach on the trajectory. Thus he can provocatively title chapter II of his book *Fractals: Form, Chance and Dimension*, 'How Long is the Coast of Britain?' (Mandelbrot 1977: 27). No coastline is a smooth continuous curve, which would be easily enough measurable using Euclidean geometry. Instead, to a greater or lesser degree, coastlines are rugged and irregular, leading Mandelbrot to 'the conclusion that the final estimated length is not only extremely large but in fact so large that it is best considered infinite' (Mandelbrot 1997: 27). The fractal formation of a coastline goes down as far as our microscopes can reach, revealing a series of 'self similar' patterns as it goes, and has to be presumed to go on even beyond that for future generations of technology to explore.

As the science writer James Gleick has put it: 'The mind cannot visualize the whole infinite self-embedding of complexity. But to someone with a geometer's way of thinking about form, this kind of repetition of structure on finer and finer scales can open a whole new world' (Gleick 1988: 100). What Mandelbrot and various other experimenters in the field found as they scaled down to lower and lower levels was 'that all the scales had similar patterns, yet every scale was different' (Gleick 1988: 231): self similarity with a twist, as it were. Mandelbrot sets, as they came to be known, have proved to be particularly appealing to the artistic community, who find the patterns that emerge out of the scaling-down process productive of very striking images.

The conclusion to be reached from this observation about coastlines, and all other phenomena that do not respond to Euclidean geometry (and they are many and various), is that we can never form a complete picture even from objects that are familiar to us, indeed objects that are part of our everyday experience and apparently not mysterious. Both scientific enquiry and human knowledge have built-in limits, and postmodern theorists can adapt such findings to reinforce their own claims about the nature of human ability. Within the known lurks an unknown which must forever lie beyond our skills to reveal. This is a conclusion which postmodernist thinkers have been only too happy to embrace, fitting in as it does with their revival of interest in the notion of the sublime, a catch-all term for that realm permanently inaccessible to our understanding (see particularly the work of Lyotard, as in *Lessons on the Analytic of the Sublime*).

Chaos theory also features the 'Butterfly Effect', which describes how small, apparently insignificant, actions in a dynamic, non-linear system, such as the weather, can have very large-scale effects at a later point in the system's development as the action progressively magnifies: 'the notion that a butterfly stirring the air today in Peking can transform storm systems next month in New York' (Gleick 1988: 8). One of the theory's other somewhat perplexing features to the layperson is the 'strange attractor', the point towards which the pattern of a non-linear system is drawn: 'Nature was *constrained*. Disorder was channelled, it seemed, into patterns with some common underlying theme' (Gleick 1988: 152). What that theme was, however, lay beyond our understanding; as does the notion of a system being both unpredictable and deterministic simultaneously. Again, postmodernists like to play up such paradoxes, their counter-intuitive quality providing further proof to them of the limits of human control and human reason.

Mandelbrot's *Fractals and Scaling in Finance* is a work that takes on more significance since the credit crash of 2007–8 (parts of the book had been published in article form as long ago as the early 1960s). One of the main reasons for that crash was the belief amongst the financial industry that various new economic 'products' that had been developed in recent years had greatly minimised the risk factor in financial trading. Another belief was that the more rational investors were in making their stock choices the more stable the market would be. Whether investors do act in a rational manner is a moot point; various psychological studies would suggest the opposite much of the time, with herd-like activity coming to the fore in both booms and busts, and emotions being more of a factor than is generally admitted. But Mandelbrot's researches into fractals led him to warn that even 'rational behavior on the part of the market may lead to "wild" speculative bubbles' (Mandelbrot 1997: 471) on occasion.

All that Mandelbrot is doing is reminding us that probability and chance play very large parts in the market and that risk will therefore always be present to some degree – meaning that the threat of discontinuity will always be present too. These are uncontroversial points to make, one might think, but the financial industry felt it had succeeded in largely removing risk from the trading process through the impact of products like 'derivatives' and 'credit swaps' (even if these remained mysterious entities to many in the business itself, most notably at higher management levels); hence the widely touted political reaction in the early twenty-first century that the days of 'boom and bust' economy were now a thing of the past. Ironically, this belief led to greater and greater risks being taken, with all the disastrous consequences for the global economy that we have witnessed since the credit crash. Mandelbrot's warning in 1963 that 'one should expect to find nonsense moments and nonsense periodicities in economic time series' (Mandelbrot 1997: 396) looks all the more disturbingly prescient in hindsight. Whether market traders and investors have learned much of a lesson from the latest episode of 'nonsense moments' is much more doubtful.

It is all the more ironic to find Mandelbrot reflecting in the preface to *Fractals and Scaling* in 1997 that although 'Stock Market "chartists" ... believe that charts embody everything needed to predict the future and devise winning strategies', the market was nevertheless proving worryingly prone to 'near-*discontinuities*' that suggested we needed 'new statistical tools' (Mandelbrot 1997: 1, 9) to make market analysis more rigorous. A decade later, however, we were to find out what a really 'wild' discontinuity could be like. The stock market would certainly seem to qualify as a non-linear system, so the extent to which this particular discontinuity represented a 'Butterfly Effect' in the workings of some unknown – and possibly unknowable as far as even the most rigorous of 'Stock Market chartists' are concerned – strange attractor is intriguing to speculate upon.

What emerges from Mandelbrot's work that is of particular interest to postmodernists is a sense of indeterminacy and undecidability within physical reality – and he emphasises that 'the power of chance is widely underestimated' (Mandelbrot 1977: 84) in the workings of the natural world. Chaotic processes do not just occur at the mysterious sub-microscopic level of quantum physics, they are also widespread at a level where we can all experience them (the weather, most notoriously). To postmodernists this is further proof of the limitations of human knowledge and reason, and any evidence they can glean from science to bolster this view, as Mandelbrot does seem to be offering up, is gratefully appropriated; although Alan Sokal and Jean Bricmont were quick to point out any looseness in such appropriations in their book *Intellectual Impostures*, where they went after such figures as Lyotard (a fan of Mandelbrot's ideas), Jean Baudrillard and the writing duo of Gilles Deleuze and Félix Guattari. Lyotard's use of fractal geometry is criticised for generalising from specific instances such as coastlines and clouds to the evolution of science itself. Sokal and Bricmont further criticise him for claiming that 'postmodern science', as Lyotard dubbed it in *The Postmodern Condition* (Lyotard 1984: 53), is the search for the unknown for its own sake rather than merely the periodic discovery of the unknown. Standard scientific practice would indicate that when something unknown is generated by their research, scientists will then go on to do their best to bring it within the field of knowledge by further exploration and refinement or revision of the relevant theories.

Lyotard can be criticised as well for confusing the unpredictable with the unknowable. Sokal and Bricmont's point is that unpredictability about non-linear sequences does not mean unpredictability about potentially all series, and it is a well-taken one. But there is a certain amount of hair-splitting going on in terms of the difference between unpredictability and unknowability – and, as far as Mandelbrot is concerned, between randomness and chance in the field of physics (see Mandelbrot 1977: 84). Neither is it surprising that philosophers would be drawn to speculate on the implications of natural phenomena featuring infinity within what to us in the everyday world is a finite shape: the work of Mandelbrot and chaos theorists in general remains very suggestive in that respect.

Mandelbrot's major writings

Mandelbrot, Benoit B., *Fractals: Form, Chance and Dimension*, San Francisco: W. H. Freeman, 1977.
——, *The Fractal Geometry of Nature*, New York: W. H. Freeman, 1982.
——, *Fractals and Scaling in Finance: Discontinuity, Concentration, Risk*, New York: Springer, 1997.

References and further reading

Gleick, James, *Chaos: Making a New Science*, London: Cardinal, 1988.
Jencks, Charles, http://www.charlesjencks.com?#!projects (accessed 27 July 2012).
Lyotard, Jean-François, *The Postmodern Condition: A Report on Knowledge* [1974], trans. Geoff Bennington and Brian Massumi, Manchester: Manchester University Press, 1984.
——, *Lessons on the Analytic of the Sublime* [1991], trans. Elizabeth Rottenberg, Stanford, CA: Stanford University Press, 1994.
Sokal, Alan and Jean Bricmont, *Intellectual Impostures: Postmodern Philosophers' Abuse of Science*, London: Profile Books, 1998.

STEVE REICH (B. 1936)

Reich is a key figure in the development of minimalism, one of the most distinctive contributions to the canon of classical music to come out of the postmodern era; although minimalists have also made a particular point of trying to break down the barrier between classical and popular musical expression, regarding this as the product of an outmoded form of society. He is widely regarded as one of the most influential composers of his time. In his early career Reich is amongst the purest of minimalist composers, reducing music largely to the element of rhythm, as is particularly well displayed in works like *Clapping Music* and *Drumming*, which consist of precisely those elements, stretching over a considerable length of time. The former work consists of two musicians clapping in and out of phase with each other's rhythm; the latter has nine percussion instruments plus singers and a whistler, again making use of phasing techniques (although it allows for this number to be increased if desired), but it is the insistent beat of the drumming that dominates the score and tends to leave the most lasting impression on listeners. *Drumming* can also vary quite considerably in length, since it is left up to the performers how long to keep repeating the phrases in each section. These scores have a tendency to divide critical opinion quite sharply, as one might expect, but they certainly do represent a rejection of the Western classical music metanarrative, where melody, harmony and rhythm are all involved, and manipulated in a process of development of thematic ideas. Neither can the scores strictly be described as modernist, since they steer clear of such staples of the modernist repertoire as serial (or twelve-tone) music, with its complex and highly intellectualised compositional procedures.

Reich seems to have stripped music down to its barest essentials in the works just mentioned, much of the music's interest lying in the way he applies the technique of 'phase shifting'. This is where melodies (which in the case of *Drumming* and *Clapping Music* are little more than rhythmic patterns with periodic slight variations in pitch) are repeated, as in medieval canons or rounds, but are allowed to move out of phase with the previous round on re-entry into the composition, and so on until its conclusion. Reich explains that compared to such older forms of the 'infinite canon' figure, in his version of it, in 'the *phase shifting process* the melodies are usually much shorter repeating patterns, and the imitations, instead of being fixed, are variable' (quoted in Mertens 1983: 48). The result is a subtly shifting texture which can be very engrossing, despite the simplicity of the underlying material. It is a method Reich deploys consistently in his compositions, but as his career has progressed he has turned to much larger ensembles than in the earlier works, from his own band to the full symphony orchestra and chorus in *The Desert Music*, an ambitious setting of poetry by William Carlos Williams. K. Robert Schwarz sees a movement from minimalism to 'maximalism' (Schwarz 1996: 78) in

Reich's work in this respect (a distinction he also makes as regards Philip Glass's compositional career).

In his early career, no doubt reflecting a musical education which emphasised such a style of composition at the time, Reich did dabble briefly in serialism, but eventually he was drawn into a general reaction amongst younger American composers against that style. We can note a rejection by that generation of what could be called the 'modernist paradigm' in the twentieth-century serious music world, where composers like Pierre Boulez were still involved in developing serial techniques, despite the lack of any ready audience for that kind of music. That paradigm was particularly being called into question by such composers as Lamont Young and Terry Riley.

The nature of the experiments taking place, and how composers were turning their backs on traditional norms of what classical music was deemed to be, can be gauged by works like Riley's *In C*, which very much set the tone for what became the minimalist style. *In C* proves to be exactly that: a piece which involves a group of musicians (the composer does not specify how many, leaving this up to the performers) playing a series of phrases in the key of C, while a piano relentlessly plays C major chords throughout. There is no real development of ideas, as there is in both traditional tonal music and abstract serialism (although their respective methods of constructing this are very different). Experiments like Riley's were a part of the New York arts scene in the 1960s and 1970s (the 'Downtown' scene, as it came to be known), when ideas from poststructuralism and postmodernism were beginning to filter in, particularly amongst artists, as Peter Halley's *Collected Essays* go on to record (Halley 2000). The effect of such ideas on any given individual is hard to determine, but at the very least a general questioning of the various established modes of working throughout the arts was very much in the air in this period, with the legacy of modernism beginning to be seen as oppressive. Reich's version of minimalism emerges from that rebellious, counter-modernist, milieu, as does Philip Glass's. Both musicians formed their own bands in early career (Steve Reich and Musicians in the former case), in order to give concerts of their works at a point when minimalism was attracting little interest from the musical establishment, and they have continued to perform with them on occasion.

Early works such as *Clapping Music* and *Drumming* can have a hypnotic effect on the audience, although not all will be attracted to the lack of variety in the pieces, which reduce music to its basics. Especially in its early days, as Riley's *In C* clearly demonstrates, development is a fairly rudimentary notion in minimalist composition, being restricted to slight shifts in rhythm and pitch, often over quite extended periods of time, and Reich is one of the most accomplished exponents of this style. Phase shifting effectively fills in for development in Reich's music. The fact that he also trained as a jazz drummer in his youth might go some way towards explaining Reich's ongoing fascination with rhythm, and he has also studied African drumming in Ghana – one of the sources of inspiration for *Drumming*. Reich does expand the ensemble in *Music for Eighteen Musicians*, which features more variety in sound and timbre than *Clapping Music* or *Drumming* in that there are periodic climaxes, although they still emerge from phase shifting patterns. *Music for Eighteen Musicians* still relies very heavily on the hypnotic effect of its insistent rhythms, however, which does make an appeal to followers of other musical genres such as jazz or rock; in fact, the work of musicians like Reich and Glass has had a notable influence on those musical styles, with minimalism even having a brief vogue in jazz circles, which has a long history of using repeated rhythmic patterns. One of Reich's compositions, *Electric Counterpoint*, was specifically written for the jazz guitarist Pat Metheny. Reich himself has denied wanting to create a hypnotic effect through his music, saying that what he is hoping for is for the listener 'to be wide awake and hear details you've never heard before' (Interview in sleeve notes to recording of *The Desert Music*).

Scored for string quartet and tape loop (the latter a technique frequently used by minimalist composers), *Different Trains* makes use of snatches of recorded interviews throughout the score, these being repeated in the manner of musical phrases. Using direct speech in this way is something found in the work of other minimalist composers such as John Adams. The interviews are about America before World War Two, Europe during the war, and then the postwar period, these making up the three sections of the piece. The middle section includes samples taken from interviews with Holocaust survivors, discussing the trains that went to concentration camps. Others sampled include Reich's ex-governess and a retired Pullman porter from the transcontinental lines across America. In his notes to a recording of the piece, Reich recalls making regular rail journeys from New York to Los Angeles during the war, and this putting him in mind of the fact that, as a Jew, had he been in Europe at the time he might well have been in a train transporting him to a concentration camp. The work also uses recorded train sounds from the 1930s and 1940s. Spoken text, this time a phrase derived from the philosopher Ludwig

STEVE REICH (B. 1936)

Wittgenstein, 'How small a thought it takes to fill a whole life!', also features in the later work *Proverb*.

The Desert Music sets to music texts taken from three poems by the American poet William Carlos Williams, and is scored for a large orchestra and a chorus of twenty-seven voices. In an interview in the sleeve notes to its recording, Reich says that he was reflecting on various deserts when composing the piece, such as the Sinai Desert which the Jewish people had to traverse after their exodus from Egypt, as well as his own memories of travelling across the Mojave Desert in the American South-West. Amongst the extracts from Williams is one that goes, 'It is a principle of music / to repeat the theme. Repeat / and repeat again, / as the pace mounts', which, as Reich points out, is particularly appropriate to his compositional style.

It is a fair point to make about minimalists like Reich that their music has tended to become more traditional over time: fairly consistently tonal, building in more in the way of development of ideas, extending the harmonic palette. No one would mistake such work for traditional classical composition, but it does not seem to alienate audiences to the extent that serial music plainly did, nor is it anything like as quirky as the work of such other rebels against the system as John Cage, as in his 'composition' *4'33"*, where absolutely nothing is played over that specified length of time by the designated piano and soloist. While Cage is admired by many in the world of music, and experiments like *4'33"* are thought-provoking and did influence early minimalist composers, he has hardly had any impact at all on the wider public, for whom he is at best a figure of notoriety because of *4'33"*. Although it could be quite uncompromising in its early works, minimalism eventually represents a reaction to attitudes of that sort, and clearly has been successful in widening the audience for serious music. Reich has to be considered one of the most important figures in this turn back to connecting with the audience, and apart from inspiring other minimalists his work has been very influential on musicians throughout the rock world, giving minimalism even greater contact with the general public as elements of the style are adapted to that and various other genres.

Reich's major works

Reich, Steve, *Drumming*, 1970.
——, *Clapping Music*, 1972.
——, *Music for Pieces of Wood*, 1973.
——, *Six Pianos*, 1973 (later recast as *Six Marimbas*, 1986).

——, *Music for Eighteen Musicians*, 1974–6.
——, *The Desert Music*, 1983.
——, *New York Counterpoint*, 1985.
——, *Electric Counterpoint*, 1987.
——, *Different Trains*, 1988.
——, *Proverb*, 1995.

References and further reading

Halley, Peter, *Collected Essays 1971–1987* [1988], Zurich and New York: Bruno Bischofberger Gallery and Sonnabend Gallery, 2000.
Mertens, Wim, *American Minimal Music* [1980], trans. J. Hautekeit, London: Kahn and Averill, 1983.
Riley, Terry, *In C*, 1964.
Schwarz, K. Robert, *Minimalists*, London and New York: Phaidon Press, 1996.

RICHARD RORTY (1931–2007)

Rorty's philosophy has a strongly pragmatic bias, and this helps to explain his sympathy towards poststructuralism and postmodernism, which one might call ultra-pragmatic philosophical styles, steering well clear as they do of fixed positions and the notion of absolute truths. One commentator, Jonathan Ree, has gone so far as to describe Rorty as 'the only post-modernist anyone can understand, or the poor-person's Derrida' (Ree 1990: 37), and Rorty is indeed a lucid stylist by the standards of so much modern and postmodern philosophical writing. Rorty counters the charge of relativism that tends to be made of pragmatist philosophy by arguing that no one really thinks 'that every belief on a certain topic, or perhaps on *any* topic, is as good as every other' (Rorty 1982: 166). The issue only arises if one insists, as non-pragmatist philosophers do, that the notion of truth has to be grounded in some universal theory. If that is not the case, then pragmatists suggest that what we should do is to debate each belief 'in terms of the various concrete advantages and disadvantages it has' (Rorty 1982: 168), and that we shall always be able to specify these even in the absence of some universal theory of what constitutes truth. Rorty also suggests, more than somewhat provocatively as most of his peers in the world of American and English philosophy are concerned, that the discipline has much to learn from literary studies in this respect, since this is much more a matter of differing inter-pretations of the world than the establishment of lasting truths. For

Rorty, this is more attractive to the general public than philosophical disputation, and his own preference is for a post-philosophical culture (as philosophy is currently practised, anyway).

In *Philosophy and the Mirror of Nature* Rorty disputes the notion, widely held within the discipline, that '[p]hilosophy can be foundational in respect to the rest of culture because culture is the assemblage of claims to knowledge, and philosophy adjudicates such claims' (Rorty 1980: 3). What the work of Ludwig Wittgenstein, Martin Heidegger and John Dewey reveals to us, however, is that such a belief is no longer tenable, enabling Rorty to call the bulk of modern philosophy into question. This will prove to be a recurring motif of his writing. Rorty goes on to explore instead 'the possibility of a post-Kantian culture, one in which there is no all-encompassing discipline which legitimizes or grounds the others' (Rorty 1980: 6). It is a quest that immediately puts Rorty on the same wavelength as poststructuralist and postmodernist philosophers like Jacques Derrida and Jean-François Lyotard, both of whom adopt a defiantly antifoundational stance in their work. Rorty has a radical agenda to pursue, and it is 'to undermine the reader's confidence in "the mind" as something about which one should have a "philosophical" view' (Rorty 1980: 7). In postmodern fashion, the critique that follows is designed to demonstrate the flaws in foundational philosophy, and Rorty is unapologetic that he is offering no new theories to replace it, or on any of the supposedly 'perennial' problems and topics of Western philosophy that he discusses over the course of the book. Even to engage in debate over these perennials is to compromise oneself as a pragmatist, with Rorty's attitude towards these being much like that of an atheist towards religion.

Rorty's view of what he is doing is that it is designed to be 'therapeutic rather than constructive' (Rorty 1980: 7), which neatly – if too neatly, his detractors would claim – sidesteps the issue of what it is that he is grounding his own critique on. They can only regard this as another instance of the relativism they find so widespread, and so unacceptable, in poststructuralist and postmodernist philosophy. Rorty freely concedes that he has no foundational concept for his own work, nor does he believe it is necessary to have one; but that does of course go against the grain of philosophical history. However, that does not necessarily undermine what such figures as Rorty, Derrida and Lyotard are saying, it just means that they are thrown back on rhetorical techniques of persuasion to make their case – even if Rorty does try to make himself sound as kindly disposed as possible towards the reader by the use of the word 'therapeutic'. The implication behind that word is that there really is no problem to be dealt with, so we have no need to tax ourselves trying to find a solution. All we can do is explore how it is that we have reached a situation where there appears to be a problem, and we can then see how to avoid it in future. This is to be the antidote to all those philosophers who 'have given their subject a bad name by seeing difficulties nobody else sees' (Rorty 1989: 12). In Rorty's view, philosophers have a bad habit of posing 'unanswerable questions' (Rorty 1982: 36), and we should simply ignore them from now on. Critics of postmodernism, however, will continue to demand something more 'constructive' from a movement with such iconoclastic intent.

Rorty takes issue with the notion that the mind is the mirror of nature, and that there is such a clear distinction between the realms of the mental and the physical as has been assumed in modern times – roughly from the time of René Descartes's theory of mind–body dualism onwards. Such a concern with boundaries is a very characteristic feature of postmodern thought, the general drift of which is to find these more permeable than we have been led to believe: mind–body is yet another dualism inviting deconstruction. Rorty contends that the mind–body problem demands that we have a clear sense of what 'mental' means, only to conclude that its use merely signals our ability to play a particular 'philosophical language-game'; a game with no relevance 'outside of philosophy books, and which links up with no issues in daily life' (Rorty 1980: 22).

In *Consequences of Pragmatism*, Rorty is in typically provocative form in attempting to revive pragmatism as a philosophical style, arguing that this is the only way to overcome the mistakes of mainstream philosophy. On the subject of pragmatism and truth, for example, he blithely asserts that 'truth is not the sort of thing one should expect to have a philosophically interesting theory about. For pragmatists, "truth" is just the name of a property which all true statements share' (Rorty 1982: xiii). It is only when one tries to find some general feature(s) common to all such statements that makes them 'true' that problems begin: unfortunately, that is what much of the history of philosophy seems to Rorty to have been about – all to no point, as he sees it. Pragmatists, on the other hand, think it is misguided to look for a definitive theory of 'Truth', or any such capitalised term harking back to Platonic idealism: 'Pragmatists are saying that the best hope for philosophy is not to practise Philosophy' (Rorty 1982: xv). Pragmatism is for Rorty a means of identifying false problems, and 'Philosophy' is just full of these. 'A post-Philosophical culture', however, 'would be one in which men and women felt themselves alone, merely finite, with no links to something beyond' (Rorty 1982: xlii–xliii). Philosophy is based on an illusion, and Rorty feels we should be able to grow out of this.

Contingency, Irony, and Solidarity puts the case for an ironic world-view which acknowledges that we have no universal theories to fall back upon. The irony is that so much of our cultural history has been predicated on the belief that there are such universal theories by which human actions can be judged, whether these be religious or philosophical. While we might react with despair to such a realisation, Rorty recommends an attitude of irony as being more appropriate, and specifically what he refers to as one of 'liberal ironism'. Liberal ironists recognise that there is no universal theory, whether meta-physical or theological, to appeal to when seeking to justify actions, no 'central beliefs and desires [that] refer back to something beyond the reach of time and chance' (Rorty 1989: xv). Rorty wants us to strive instead towards a culture that is both postmetaphysical and postreligious, where we try our best to create a sense of human solidarity, devel-oping an 'imaginative ability to see strange people as fellow sufferers' (Rorty 1989: xvi). This will not be achieved by philosophical debate of the old style, but by 'a general turn against theory and toward narrative' (Rorty 1989: xvi). Literature in particular is to be a major source of the cultural change Rorty seeks, and he recommends var-ious authors such as Charles Dickens, Vladimir Nabokov and George Orwell towards that end. The point of literature, of course, is that it is not a matter of truth or falsehood, but of its impact on the imagination, its ability to make us perceive the world differently.

Rorty consistently refuses to engage with traditional philosophy on its own grounds throughout *Contingency, Irony, and Solidarity*, and shrugs off charges of relativism, claiming that '[a] liberal society is one whose ideals can be fulfilled by persuasion rather than force, by reform rather than revolution, by the free and open encounters of present linguistic and other practices with suggestions for new prac-tices' (Rorty 1989: 60). He concedes that his outlook is utopian, and we can note the same problem arising here as in so much postmodern thought: by what agency do we achieve the desired socio-political state where universal theories have been jettisoned and everyone is open to 'persuasion'? Chantal Mouffe's theory of 'agonistic' politics (see *The Democratic Paradox*) can be criticised on the same basis.

Although he can be critical of certain aspects of 'Continental' phi-losophy of the poststructuralism/postmodernism persuasion, Rorty finds its goals more congenial than those of the analytical tradition that has been so dominant in the Anglo-American world. He shares with the Continentals an abiding suspicion of authority and of universal theories, and similarly regards the search for foundations as little more than a wild-goose chase. Taking sides, however, merely perpetuates misunderstandings of what philosophy is about: 'If we put aside wistful talk of bridge-building and joining forces, we can see the analytic–Continental split as both harmless and permanent. We should not see it as tearing philosophy apart. There is no single entity called "philosophy" which once was whole and now is sundered' (Rorty 1982: 226). What both sides are guilty of is assuming that their arguments demolish the other's position, and for Rorty this is to remain stuck in a pointless game that does little to improve the human lot. As a pragmatist, he feels that 'what matters is our loyalty to other human beings clinging together against the dark, not our hope of getting things right' (Rorty 1982: 166). Somewhat sentimental though this sounds, it is very much in the spirit of the postmodern to see no point in identifying with the cause of metanarratives any longer.

Rorty's major writings

Rorty, Richard, *Philosophy and the Mirror of Nature*, Oxford: Blackwell, 1980.
——, *Consequences of Pragmatism*, Brighton: Harvester, 1982.
——, 'Habermas and Lyotard on Postmodernity', in Richard J. Bernstein (ed.), *Habermas and Modernity*, Cambridge: Polity Press, 1985, pp. 161–75.
——, *Contingency, Irony, and Solidarity*, Cambridge and New York: Cambridge University Press, 1989.
——, *Objectivity, Relativism and Truth: Philosophical Papers, Vol. 1*, Cambridge and New York: Cambridge University Press, 1991a.
——, *Essays on Heidegger and Others: Philosophical Papers, Vol. 2*, Cambridge and New York: Cambridge University Press, 1991b.
Rorty, Richard, J. B. Schneewind and Quentin Skinner (eds), *Philosophy in History*, Cambridge: Cambridge University Press, 1984.

References and further reading

Mouffe, Chantal, *The Democratic Paradox*, London and New York: Verso, 2000.
Ree, Jonathan, 'Timely Meditations', *Radical Philosophy*, 55 (1990), pp. 31–9.

EDWARD W. SAID (1935–2003)

Said's *Orientalism* is one of the most influential contributions to the literature on postcolonialism, and has helped to set the terms of reference for debate in that area for quite some time now. His thesis was that the West had constructed an image of the Middle East as the antithesis to Western society, the 'Orient', its irrational, emotionally based and exotic other. Whereas modern Western society was socially and politically progressive, the 'Orient' was pictured as backward, reactionary and essentially childish in nature, lacking the dynamism and technological sophistication that we have long since come to associate with Western culture. It was an idea that developed from the increasing contact between the West and the Arabic/Islamic world over the course of the eighteenth and nineteenth centuries, and was used as an excuse for extensive colonisation of the area by the European powers, ostensibly bringing order and modern civilisation to a pre-modern culture which had been stagnating for several centuries. Eventually, the Orient came to signify not just that particular geographical area but the so-called 'Third World' (now characterised as 'developing') in general.

Orientalism was a cast of mind which just assumed the innate superiority of Western culture, and saw modernisation as a necessity for all others, the ideal to which they should be helped actively to aspire. Knowledge very much equalled power in this case, the power – indeed, as Western nations saw it, the duty – to override local customs and ways of life. It would not be until the mid-twentieth century that many of the nations involved managed to break free of colonialism and take charge of their own destiny, although that sense of being inferior to the West, and its 'grand narrative' of economic and technological power, continues to haunt them right up to the present day. Indeed, many of them now stand in what could only be called a neo-colonial relationship to the West, with the added complication of having a Westernised state with powerful Western allies, Israel, established in the Middle East in the post-World War Two period. The tensions generated by this act have never been resolved, and are still festering several decades later, posing a permanent threat to global security.

Said is a scholar who can be said to lack a grand narrative himself, being born a Christian Palestinian, meaning that he had no state to treat as 'home' for the greater part of his life after the creation of Israel, and then spending most of his academic career in New York City at Columbia University. As he notes in *Culture and Imperialism*, 'I grew up as an Arab with a Western education. Ever since I can remember, I have felt that I belonged to both worlds, without being completely *of* one or the other' (Said 1994a: xxx). Said examines the effect of these factors on his life and work in detail in *Out of Place: A*

Memoir and *Reflections on Exile and Other Literary and Cultural Essays*. Apart from anything else, his consistent support for the Palestinian cause (expressed in works like *The Politics of Dispossession: The Struggle for Palestinian Self-Determination, 1969–1994* and *Covering Islam: How the Media and the Experts Determine How We See the Rest of the World*) made him a controversial figure in American life, where support for Israel is politically very strong – particularly so in New York City, with its large Jewish population. There was not, as he sadly notes, an equivalent 'Palestinian lobby' (Said 1994a: xix) for those of his background to fall back on for support.

Aside from *Orientalism*, Said has also written some fairly standard works of literary criticism, such as the early *Joseph Conrad and the Fiction of Autobiography*, *Beginnings: Intention and Method* and then *The World, the Text, and the Critic*. In *Beginnings* he emphasises the importance of difference in writing, whether critical or creative, arguing that 'beginning is *making* or producing *difference*; but – and here is the great fascination in the subject – difference which is the result of combining the already-familiar with the fertile novelty of human work in language' (Said 1975: xiii). If this seems to nod in a poststructuralist direction – and Said does regard the issue of 'beginnings' that he is concerned with in the book as intrinsic to this movement, a 'central problem' (Said 1975: 283) of our age intellectually – then he nevertheless proceeds to express quite strong reservations about both structuralism and poststructuralism before the book is over. Foucault, for example, is a thinker 'obsessed with the inescapable fact of ontological discontinuity' (Said 1975: 285), who projects this condition back onto the past in order to be able to make his, often highly contentious, historical generalisations. We are enjoined always to remember with Foucault that this is an author who 'writes neither philosophy nor history as they are commonly experienced' (Said 1975: 288); although Said clearly has a lot of respect for the verve and originality of Foucault's 'archaeologies' (*The History of Sexuality*, for example), which at the very least offer a new perspective on social and intellectual history.

Structuralism as a whole does not come out too well from Said's critique, which makes him at least sympathetic to what Jacques Derrida is doing in *Writing and Difference*, although he complains that Derrida somewhat overdoes his deconstruction of the structuralist enterprise. Eventually, the 'nihilistic radicality' of Derrida's writing (Said 1975: 343) appears to constitute something of a dead end to Said, for whom Foucault succeeds in opening up more lines of enquiry for the cultural commentator. It is Foucault's notion of 'discourse' that underpins *Orientalism*, where Said defines Orientalism as 'a *distribution* of geopolitical awareness into aesthetic, scholarly, economic, sociological, historical, and philological texts' (Said 1995: 12), that invite analysis on that basis.

The World, the Text, and the Critic offers an overview of the critical enterprise as it is practised in the later twentieth century, with Said arguing that it has taken a wrong turn in the academy, referring to 'a cult of professional expertise whose effect in general is pernicious' because it has led away from everyday social and political concerns:

> We tell our students and our general constituency that we defend the classics, the virtues of a liberal education, and the precious pleasures of literature even as we also show ourselves to be silent (perhaps incompetent) about the historical and social world in which all these things take place.
>
> (Said 1983: 2)

The kind of historical consciousness that lies behind *Orientalism* is very much in play here: this is a critic for whom social and political context must always be taken into account when discussing texts, and who feels that literary theory is progressively failing to meet its obligations to its audience in this respect. In a withering assessment of what is happening in humanities departments in the academy in the 1980s, Said asserts that '[i]t is not practising criticism either to validate the status quo or to join up with a priestly caste of acolytes and dogmatic metaphysicians' (Said 1983: 5).

It is undoubtedly *Orientalism* that has made Said's name, however, and it has proved to be a book which arouses strong passions: as Vinay Lal has said in a recent assessment of Said's work, the text 'continues to elicit an equal measure of adulation and vitriolic criticism' (Lal 2012: 247). 'The Orient was almost a European invention', Said asserts in his opening paragraph to the book, 'one of its [Europe's] deepest and most recurring images of the Other' (Said 1995: 1). The Orient, therefore, has served an important socio-political purpose in Europe, particularly since the Enlightenment period when the process of colonisation began to gather pace. So powerful has Orientalism been that the Orient cannot to our own time be considered 'a free subject of thought or action' (Said 1995: 3), and Said proceeds to demonstrate how the discourse that expedited this condition came about. In terms of the Middle East, the main players in the creation of that discourse are in the first instance Britain and

France in their imperialist guises, with America an increasingly important influence since the end of World War Two (as in its unstinting support for the state of Israel). For Said, this is to mean a close study of 'the dynamic exchange' (Said 1995: 14) that took place between various writers and intellectuals and the socio-political order brought about by Orientalism, an exchange that played a key role in maintaining the latter's credibility and authority. It is the fact that Orientalism is still with us, still informing Western attitudes and political decisions, that Said wants above all to draw to our attention. For him this is most clearly seen in the way that the Arab population in his own homeland is treated as if it were 'the disrupter' (Said 1995: 286) of Israeli statehood: in effect, a mere nuisance.

Said turns his attention to Western culture in *Culture and Imperialism*, which set out to build on *Orientalism* by describing 'a more general pattern of relationships between the modern metropolitan West and its overseas territories' (Said 1994a: xi) that can help us to understand the phenomenon. Placing narrative at the centre of this exercise, Said covers a wide range of fiction from Jane Austen onwards, but his concern is as much to show how local resistance developed to imperialism in the colonised countries as how Western authors represented the imperialist ethic in their work. Said's anger is addressed against a Western world order, as portrayed in so much nineteenth- and twentieth-century European fiction, 'whose representatives seem at liberty to visit their fantasies and philanthropies upon a mind-deadened Third World' (Said 1994a: xxi) as if the latter had no culture of its own that was worth preserving.

The Politics of Dispossession and *Covering Islam* constitute Said in openly polemical mode concerning his lost homeland, attacking both Western governments' policies over the years and the image that the Western media present of the Islamic world in general. The overall problem, as Said sees it, is that '"Islam" is not what it is generally said to be in the West today' (Said 1997: 172), but the more it is misrepresented there the greater the chance that, out of sheer desperation at this distorted picture, it will turn into a force as reactionary and violent as the Western media and public apparently believe it to be. Were this to happen, the blame could be laid squarely with the discourse of Orientalism.

Said's major writings

Said, Edward, *Joseph Conrad and the Fiction of Autobiography*, Cambridge, MA: Harvard University Press, 1966.

——, *Beginnings: Intention and Method*, Baltimore, MD and London: Johns Hopkins University Press, 1975.

——, *The World, the Text, and the Critic*, London and Boston, MA: Faber and Faber, 1983.

——, *Culture and Imperialism*, London: Vintage, 1994a.

——, *The Politics of Dispossession: The Struggle for Palestinian Self-Determination, 1969–1994*, London: Chatto and Windus, 1994b.

——, *Orientalism: Western Conceptions of the Orient* [1978], 2nd edition, Harmondsworth: Penguin, 1995.

——, *Covering Islam: How the Media and the Experts Determine How We See the Rest of the World* [1981], 2nd edition, London: Vintage, 1997.

——, *Out of Place: A Memoir*, Cambridge, MA: Harvard University Press, 2000.

——, *Reflections on Exile and Other Literary and Cultural Essays*, London: Granta, 2001.

——, *Humanism and Democratic Criticism*, New York and Chichester: Columbia University Press, 2004.

References and further reading

Derrida, Jacques, *Writing and Difference* [1967], trans. Alan Bass, Chicago: University of Chicago Press, 1978.

Foucault, Michel, *The History of Sexuality: Volume I. An Introduction* (1976), trans. Robert Hurley, Harmondsworth: Penguin, 1981.

Lal, Vinay, 'Assessment: Edward Said', *Critical Muslim*, 2 (2012), pp. 247–60.

CINDY SHERMAN (B. 1954)

An artist whose primary medium is photography, Sherman has also worked as a film director (*Office Killer*), done some film acting and produced advertising material. She has put herself at the centre of her art, in a series of different poses suggesting different identities, often based on, or echoing, scenes in films – particularly the Hollywood 'noir' genre of the 1940s and Italian neo-realism, as in her classic series *Untitled Film Stills*, the work she made her reputation with back in the 1980s. A sense of a dialogue with the past is very much in evidence in Sherman's work, therefore, which also suggests the post-modern belief in our ability to change roles, and arguably identities, at will – as in Jean-François Lyotard's concept of 'svelteness' (Lyotard 1993) or Gilles Deleuze and Félix Guattari's 'nomadism' (Deleuze and Guattari 1988). Sherman's photographic work since the stills has largely been in the pose form, as in her series *Fairy Tales*, *Disasters*, *Centerfolds*, *Fashion* and *History Portraits*, featuring herself again in most cases. In the *Sex* series, however, she used medical dummies set in pornographic situations to create images with feminist implications; while the *Disgust* series concentrates on shots of objects.

Sherman's photographs of herself, with their evocation of genres like noir and neo-realism, are also excellent examples of the notion of simulacra (see Baudrillard 1983), since they have no proper 'original' lying behind them (with a few exceptions, such as an early photo-booth shot of her made up to look like the television star Lucille Ball, of *I Love Lucy* fame). If they are in the style of film noir, then they are not specific, merely reminiscent and resonant of the genre, and the genre itself is fiction of course, so any copy of it would be a copy of something merely imitating real life anyway – or even, just to complicate matters further, other works in the same genre. Douglas Crimp, an influential art critic who wrote extensively on the postmodern turn in the New York art scene in the 1970s and 1980s, spoke of there being 'an unbridgeable distance from the original, from even the possibility of an original' (Crimp 2006: 28) in the art then being produced by younger artists, an assessment which is particularly appropriate to Sherman's photographic shots.

Sherman has spoken of herself in her early career as deciding 'to do a group of imaginary stills all from the same actress's career' (Sherman 2003: 5), and then the process simply taking off from there. In Crimp's view, what the stills reveal above all is 'the fiction of the self', which becomes 'nothing other than a discontinuous series of representations, copies, and fakes' (Crimp 2006: 34). Sherman has stated, in an interview with the film director John Waters, that one of the main motivations behind her art was that 'I had the desire to transform myself' (in Respini 2012: 69), and she does so dramatically over the course of her career through her various series. Interestingly enough, Waters describes her as 'a female female impersonator' (Respini 2012: 69), an observation which captures some of the complexity her work raises over the issue of identity.

The Complete Untitled Film Stills catalogues Sherman in her various poses over the period 1977–80. There are seventy stills, all arbitrarily numbered so that they actually go up to number 84 in the collection. There is a feminist dimension to this work (as there is in many of the series), foregrounding issues about the male gaze, with women being reduced to the status of mere images with no power to remove themselves from becoming objects of spectatorship. Women are very much objects in her shot, which suggests a feminist agenda of some sort. There is also a sense of loneliness and isolation communicated through the stills, with Sherman often pictured alone in deserted settings: Untitled 48, for example, portraying her as a hitchhiker, looking backwards down the road with a suitcase standing alongside; or Untitled 44, where she is caught across the tracks all alone in a deserted railway station in Flagstaff, Arizona. In other shots she can look emotionally wrought (Untitled 30); or, in arguably her best-known shot (Untitled 21, the camera looking up from below to her head and shoulders framed against tall city buildings, in typically noir fashion), wary, as if waiting for something dramatic to happen. All of the shots imply a narrative behind them, but one that viewers will have to supply themselves from the period and genre details included – the black-and-white image, the clothes of the 1940s and 1950s that the actress is wearing. The fact that Sherman uses the 'Untitled' label in all her series gives little away, inviting speculation on the part of the audience.

Centerfolds is another even more direct exploration of the male gaze, featuring Sherman in a series of erotic poses of the kind found in soft porn magazines. These attract the male gaze, but simultaneously challenge it to examine the attitudes that lie behind it, because Sherman is merely acting out being a centrefold. There are layers of complexity in these images, since in real centrefolds the model is acting out the role asked of her by the magazine as the sexually provocative woman deliberately courting male attention, while behind that there is Sherman in her role as 'the female female impersonator'. Women are even more reduced to objects by shots of this nature, which ought to make the male audience question just what it is looking for in such cases. Although the series was commissioned by the journal *Artforum*, they rejected it, worried at what their readers' reaction might be. The series turns into a critique of the centrefold genre, and more importantly the entire history of gender relations that generates it. *Fashion* started as a commission from French *Vogue* magazine, Sherman being asked to produce shots of herself wearing Balenciaga designer clothes, and working up a series from this that effectively becomes a critique of the vapidity of the fashion industry.

In *Disgust* Sherman focuses on scenes of repulsive objects, lurid shots of rubbish, decaying food and vomit, with discarded objects strewn around, such as Untitled 175 and 179; even insects crawling round a body sprawled on the ground (Untitled 173). She describes herself, somewhat enigmatically, as someone who has 'a juvenile fascination with things that are repulsive. It intrigues me why certain things are repulsive. To think about why something repulses me makes me that much more interested in it. I feel I have to explore it' (in Lichtenstein 2012). Increasingly as her career goes on, there is also a noticeable leaning towards the grotesque, with Sherman donning outlandish, occasionally clown, costumes (Untitled 411 and 414, for example). She has indicated that she felt the need to challenge her audience more after the critical acclaim awarded her early work, telling John Waters that her sudden popularity made her feel 'nervous' (Respini 2012: 69), so she deliberately turned her attention to more disgusting and disturbing images, giving her 'juvenile fascination' free rein.

Sherman's work broadens in scope to encompass not just images from fairy tales but even Old Master paintings, as in the Virgin and Child shots in Untitled 216 and 223. Work like this also communicates a strong sense of dialogue with the past, since many of the Old Master scenes she portrays reference medieval and Renaissance art which itself is often referencing even older times, as in its religious subjects. Increasingly over her career, too, Sherman explores the topic of ageing, an emotive subject in a society which places so much value on youthfulness, and in which women in particular are judged on their looks: the kind of actors she is capturing in the *Film Stills* series, for example, soon find work drying up as they get into their thirties and forties and lose their youthful glamour. The heavily made-up and lined faces in Untitled 465 and 468 suggest older society women of a city like New York, struggling to keep ageing at bay.

Sex represents another investigation of sexuality, pornography and censorship, using prosthetic body parts from mannequins in place of live models and arranging them in a series of highly provocative poses. Sherman comments that 'I would hope that these images would make people confront their own feelings about sex, pornography, or erotic images and their own bodies' (in Lichtenstein 2012). There is certainly a shock value attached to the series, which Sherman concedes made many of the audience at its first exhibition 'very uncomfortable' (in Lichtenstein 2012), as if they were actually viewing shots of live models rather than latex mannequins. Lichtenstein remarks that although the body in the shots 'is obviously a simulacrum', nevertheless 'the effect is human as well as artificial' (in Lichtenstein 2012), thereby increasing the overall disturbing quality of the work. At least part of that disturbing quality derives from the fact of the work appearing during a period when the AIDS epidemic was becoming so widely known.

Sherman has created an impressive body of work which invites theoretical speculation; 'at the crossroads of diverse theoretical discourses – feminism, postmodernism, and poststructuralism, amongst others' (Respini 2012: 13), as Eve Respini has noted in the introductory essay to a Sherman retrospective exhibition catalogue. Sherman expresses a somewhat ambivalent attitude towards theory, writing in one of her notebooks that 'I can't seem to keep from making everything have a sexual, "political", or "heavy" edge, which I don't exactly want here' (in Cruz and Smith 1998: 184); but by presenting herself in a series of roles she does raise very awkward questions about the nature of female identity and how our culture constructs and perceives this. Questions about the male gaze can hardly fail to come to mind either; as she says of the *Centerfolds* series, she 'wanted to make people feel uncomfortable' (Respini 2012: 73) in viewing them. The fact that in some series Sherman is posing either as a boy or a man merely adds a further layer of complication to her work, suggesting perhaps that sexual identity too is no more than a mere simulacrum.

Sherman's major works

Sherman, Cindy, *Murder Mystery People*, 1976.
——, *Centerfolds*, 1981.
——, *Fashion*, 1983.
——, *Fairy Tales*, 1985.
——, *Disgust*, 1986–7.
——, *Disasters*, 1986–9.
——, *History Portraits*, 1988–90.
——, *Sex*, 1992.
——(dir.), *Office Killer*, Good Machine, Good Fear and Kardana-Swinsky Films, 1997.
——, *The Complete Untitled Film Stills* [1977–80], 2nd edition, New York: Museum of Modern Art, 2003.

References and further reading

Baudrillard, Jean, *Simulations*, trans. Paul Foss, Paul Patton and Philip Beitchman, New York: Semiotext(e), 1983.
Crimp, Douglas, 'The Photographic Activity of Postmodernism', in Joanna Burton (ed.), *October Files: Cindy Sherman*, Cambridge, MA and London: MIT Press, 2006, pp. 25–38.
Cruz, Amanda and Elizabeth A. T. Smith (eds), *Cindy Sherman: Retrospective*, Museum of Modern Art, Chicago and Museum of Modern Art, Los Angeles: Chicago and Los Angeles, 1998.
Deleuze, Gilles and Félix Guattari, *A Thousand Plateaus: Capitalism and Schizophrenia* [1980], trans. Brian Massumi, London: Athlone Press, 1988.

Lichtenstein, Therese, 'Interview with Cindy Sherman', *Journal of Contemporary Art*, http://www.jca-online.com/sherman.html (accessed 30 September 2012).

Lyotard, Jean-François, 'A Svelte Appendix to the Postmodern Question', in *Political Writings*, trans. Bill Readings and Kevin Paul Geiman, London: UCL Press, 1993, pp. 25–9.

Respini, Eva (ed.), *Cindy Sherman*, New York: Museum of Modern Art, 2012.

GAYATRI CHAKRAVORTY SPIVAK (B. 1941)

Spivak is a cultural theorist and translator, of both theoretical and fictional texts, who makes an important contribution to post-structuralist and postmodern thought with her work on the concept of the 'subaltern', which has resonated throughout the fields of both postcolonialism and feminism (although it is worth noting that she is not happy about the idea of conflating poststructuralism and post-modernism, as is the practice of this volume). The translator of Jacques Derrida's *Of Grammatology*, she has been significantly influenced by deconstruction. This has given her an abiding concern with issues such as difference and plurality, which she has read back into postcolonial theory, often to question the assumptions made there by others. Despite the impact deconstruction has had on her work, she claims that 'I'm not really a deconstructionist because I can't do those meticulous yet playful (literary criticism) or scholarly yet audacious (philosophy) readings' (Spivak 1990: 155). She also disclaims the idea that she is a 'real' Marxist or feminist too, conceiving of herself as being on the outside of most such discourses and thus able to make strategic interventions into them.

The concept of the subaltern was originally conceived by the Italian Marxist theorist Antonio Gramsci to refer to those groups in society living under the hegemony of the ruling elite, whereby the elite had managed to impose its system of values on them; but it was developed in terms of postcolonialism within the Subaltern Studies Group, founded by Ranajit Guha (see Guha and Spivak 1988). As outlined by Spivak in the essay 'Can the Subaltern Speak?', a subaltern is in a subordinate position to a powerful ruling authority, as is the case with native subjects under a colonial regime, where they become the 'Other' to the ruling colonial class. Everything about the subaltern's culture is marginalised by the colonial power and assumed to have little intrinsic value compared to the systems, institutions and ideas that are brought in by the colonisers. In the manner of cultural imperialism, the colonial grand narrative is considered to have pre-cedence over the existing native one, no matter how venerable the latter's history may be: colonialism is taken to equal social and tech-nological progress, and to be the means by which nations are brought into the modern world from a pre-modern past. As Spivak points out, the subaltern is silenced by the conquering power's discourse in a situation analogous to that defined as a 'differend' by Jean-François Lyotard (see Lyotard 1988). This is particularly the case with the female subaltern, who is silenced by patriarchal as well as colonial power; as Spivak puts it, 'If, in the context of colonial production, the subaltern has no history and cannot speak, the subaltern as female is even more deeply in shadow' (Spivak 1993a: 82–3). This is still the case when the colonial power leaves, as native patriarchal power simply steps into the breach.

The primary example Spivak uses in the essay is that of 'sati', the Indian custom of the ritual burning of a wife at her husband's funeral, which eventually was outlawed by the British colonial administration. Spivak delves into the history of sati to demonstrate that it was a custom beginning to fall out of use by the time of British rule, as well as a contested one anyway in terms of its translation from ancient texts. In one particular case, in Bengal, it often resulted from male pressure to commit the act because local law allowed widows to inherit property at the expense of other surviving male relatives, giving those relatives an incentive to invoke tradition. The situation became more complicated when the British rulers made the assump-tion that sati was considered all but mandatory in Hindu law and felt obliged to legislate against it as abhorrent to the Western mentality. What Spivak's analysis reveals is a chain of misunderstandings which point up the failings of colonial imperialism as much as anything.

The essay is also notable for Spivak's spirited attack on Gilles Deleuze and Michel Foucault for what to her is their negative effect on postcolonial discourse. Although both theorists emphasise differ-ence and pluralism throughout their work, Spivak identifies an essentialism at work in some of their main concepts that has since crept into the analyses of many postcolonial theorists. 'Desire', for example, is assumed to have a universal application, and is also, and unforgiveably for Spivak, detached from any ideological considera-tions: 'In the name of desire, they reintroduce the undivided subject into the discourse of power' (Spivak 1993a: 69). Difference is erased when this happens. Both theorists are held guilty of generalising from a Western perspective, such that the concept of the 'Other' becomes homogeneous as well. In postcolonial terms this can mean that Other is made to stand for the whole non-Western world, with no differentiation between countries, histories and, importantly here in Spivak's analysis, the differences within particular cultures – as expressed, for example, in gender and class. Neither is she persuaded by such theorists' apparent identification with the cause of the Other, regarding this as merely another example of ingrained cultural imperialism: 'It is impossible for contemporary French intellectuals to imagine the kind of Power and Desire that would inhabit the unnamed subject of the Other of Europe' (Spivak 1993a: 75).

Derrida is taken to be a corrective to such views as these, with his work on language (as in *Of Grammatology*, for which Spivak also provides an extensive Introduction) demonstrating how we fall into such traps, and counselling constant awareness of this on our part. There is a consistently anti-essentialist message in Derrida's work, that, as someone always concerned to challenge totalising assumptions, Spivak finds a far more productive basis from which to undertake cultural analysis: 'I must here acknowledge a long-term usefulness in Jacques Derrida which I seem no longer to find in the authors of *The History of Sexuality* and *Mille Plateaux*' (Spivak 1993a: 104). Spivak is always on the lookout for the tendency to totalise, criticising it repeatedly also when it is applied to 'Woman' as a category.

Spivak has given many interviews, and *The Post-Colonial Critic* puts together a collection of these to help situate her in the discourse of theory in general and postcolonialism in particular. She consistently emphasises the political implications of her work as both theorist and teacher. Questioned about her view of the relationship between textuality and politics, for example, she makes it very clear that she is against the study of textuality as a self-contained practice on its own, separate from politics. This is to lose sight of the social context within which textual study takes place, the institutional establishment and the role it plays in its culture, which for a theorist like Spivak cannot be separate from politics. Postcolonialism alone would make that point, being an inherently political theoretical position within the institution. Spivak is always aware, too, of her own rather ambivalent position within the Western educational system, and the politics that go along with being '[t]he post-colonial diasporic Indian who seeks to decolonize the mind' (Spivak 1990: 67).

Outside in the Teaching Machine looks closely at the concept of 'marginality', noting that it had become something of a buzzword in the humanities in the later twentieth century, to the extent that there had been 'an explosion of marginality studies in college and university teaching in the United States' (Spivak 1993b: ix). She cautions against this becoming a superficial method of analysis, another example of erasing difference rather than keeping it foregrounded: 'When a cultural identity is thrust upon one because the center wants an identifiable margin, claims for marginality assure validation from the center' (Spivak 1993b: 55). The centre is thus in control of the discourse that results, and the implications of that in an area like postcolonial theory, where marginality is a heavily used concept, become obvious; the West as centre is continuing to impose its values on the non-Western world, in a manner that could be seen as neo-colonial. Marginality then becomes a term with universal application, whereas for Spivak '[t]here can be no universalist claims in the human sciences' (Spivak 1993b: 53). Feminism, too, she firmly points out, can be guilty of this trait: 'The way in through French feminism defines the third world as Other. Not to need that way in is, paradoxically, to recognize that indigenous global feminism must still reckon with the bitter legacy of imperialism transformed in decolonization' (Spivak 1993b: 141).

Despite the struggle that an academic with her background – marginal, postcolonial – has to go through in contesting the tendency to universalise from within the Western educational system itself (Spivak teaches mainly in America), she still insists it is necessary to engage with Western theoretical discourse if we are going to address the politics of postcolonialism: 'I have long held that in the arena of decolonization proper, the call to a complete boycott of so-called Western male theories is class-interested and dangerous. For me, the agenda has been to stake out the theories' limits, constructively to use them' (Spivak 1993b: x). That becomes a consistent refrain in her work, to appropriate theory in order to work against it from within; in the process demonstrating how even apparently counter-cultural theories can have blind spots, and can fail to shake off their heritage of assumed cultural superiority. The technique is unmistakably deconstructionist in both approach and intent.

The influence of deconstruction means that Spivak remains a committed proponent of difference and plurality, and she has queried whether postcolonial thought has always given these their due. In *Other Asias* she suggests that there might have been a tendency amongst theorists to see the postcolonial experience as similar throughout the world, whereas she holds to the view that 'the expanding versions of postcolonial theory would have to "pluralize" Asia', on the grounds that we could not regard 'our own corner of the continent as exemplary' (Spivak 2008: 8) of the rest. The notion of hybridity, as theorised by Homi K. Bhabha (see *The Location of Culture*), can seem to marginalise difference, and when that happens 'the subaltern is once again silent for us' (Spivak 1993b: 255). Spivak's interventions into theory are designed to show how such negative effects can be avoided.

Spivak's major writings

Spivak, Gayatri Chakravorty, *In Other Worlds: Essays in Cultural Politics*, New York and London: Routledge, 1988.

——, *The Post-Colonial Critic: Interviews, Strategies, Dialogues*, ed. Sarah Harasym, New York and London: Routledge, 1990.

——, 'Can the Subaltern Speak?', in Patrick Williams and Laura Chrisman (eds), *Colonial Discourse and Post-Colonial Theory: A Reader*, Hemel Hempstead: Harvester Wheatsheaf, 1993a, pp. 66–111.

——, *Outside in the Teaching Machine*, New York and London: Routledge, 1993b.

——, *A Critique of Postcolonial Reason: Towards a History of the Vanishing Present*, Cambridge, MA: Harvard University Press, 1999.

——, *Death of a Discipline*, New York and Chichester: Columbia University Press, 2003.

——, *Other Asias*, Oxford and Malden, MA: Blackwell, 2008.

——, *Nationalism and the Imagination*, Chicago and London: University of Chicago Press, 2010.

——, *An Aesthetic Education in the Era of Globalization*, Cambridge, MA: Harvard University Press, 2012.

Guha, Ranajit and Gayatri Chakravorty Spivak (eds), *Selected Subaltern Studies*, New York: Oxford University Press, 1988.

References and further reading

Bhabha, Homi K., *The Location of Culture* [1994], 2nd edition, London and New York: Routledge, 2004.

Deleuze, Gilles and Félix Guattari, *A Thousand Plateaus: Capitalism and Schizophrenia* [1980], trans. Brian Massumi, London: Athlone Press, 1988.

Derrida, Jacques, *Of Grammatology* [1967], trans. Gayatri Chakravorty Spivak, Baltimore, MD and London: Johns Hopkins University Press, 1976.

Foucault, Michel, *The History of Sexuality: Volume I. An Introduction* [1976], trans. Robert Hurley, Harmondsworth: Penguin, 1981.

Lyotard, Jean-François, *The Differend: Phrases in Dispute* [1983], trans. Georges Van Den Abbeele, Manchester: Manchester University Press, 1988.

QUENTIN TARANTINO (B. 1963)

Tarantino is one of the most controversial filmmakers of his generation, whose body of work bears many of the hallmarks of the postmodern aesthetic, such as a self-conscious dialogue with the past, a deliberate blurring of the line between high and popular art, and an extensive use of pastiche. He is very much influenced by the B-movie and exploitation movie culture that tended to be looked down on by the major Hollywood studios (not to mention the critical fraternity); filmmakers such as Roger Corman, for example, with whom Tarantino briefly worked in his early career. As well as that, however, he also acknowledges the influence of many other directors and film traditions ranging from Hollywood to the avant-garde, Nicholas Ray to Jean-Luc Godard. His list of favourite films includes both Martin Scorsese's *Taxi Driver* and Charles Barton's *Bud Abbott and Lou Costello Meet Frankenstein*. Such eclectic taste gives Tarantino's work a rich layer of intertextuality which appeals to the more knowledgeable film audience, while his use of genre can draw in a popular audience as well. It is a powerful combination that certainly qualifies as double-coding, although Tarantino does like to play around with the conventions of any genre that he works in – 'fucking up the breadcrumb trail' (Peary 1998: 110) as he colourfully describes his approach. Tarantino's dialogue, too, with its copious references to popular culture but also heavily mannered style, adds to the pervasive sense of intertextuality in his work, and is one of the most distinctive features of his films.

As both writer and director of his own films, Tarantino can lay stronger claim to being an *auteur* than many of his peers in the American film industry: this is someone who is clearly fascinated with the entire process of filmmaking and keen to be involved in every last aspect of it. He even took over the role of cameraman on one of his own films, *Death Proof*, giving further evidence of his complete immersion in the filmmaking process. As well as writing scripts, and acting as producer, for other directors, Tarantino has also worked as an actor, on both stage and screen, although without establishing all that much of a reputation in that guise, mostly receiving rather lukewarm notices from the critics.

Tarantino's first feature was *Reservoir Dogs*, a 'heist genre' film with some extremely violent scenes – and Tarantino does seem to be very drawn to graphic depictions of violence throughout his oeuvre. As the critic Camille Nevers observed in an interview with Tarantino in the French film journal *Cahiers du Cinéma*: 'They say his film is violent. Indeed it is, a dense violence, in itself and for itself, and without a trace of self-consciousness' (Peary 1998: 6). Tarantino's position on this aspect of his work is that '[i]f violence is part of your palette, you have to be free to go where your heart takes you' (Peary 1998: 29). He is also capable of making remarks in interviews, such as 'I don't take the violence very seriously. I find violence funny' (Peary 1998: 59), which suggests that a desire to shock is an important part of his character. Interviewers do tend to keep quizzing him about his apparent obsession with violence, and it continues to feature strongly in his films. One suspects, however, that whereas some directors would concern themselves with the meaning behind portraying violence on screen, Tarantino's interest lies primarily in its visual impact and the colours that it releases. He does regard violence as simply a part of everyday life and feels quite free to present it as such. It could be argued that as violence *is* more a part of everyday life in America than in Europe there is an element of realism to Tarantino's continued portrayal of it in his work.

Pulp Fiction is often regarded as Tarantino's finest achievement, a series of interlinked stories that jump back and forward in time in a technically very assured manner (even Tarantino's critics agree that his technique is impressive). It contains some of Tarantino's most celebrated dialogue, particularly in the scenes between the two gangsters, Jules and Vincent, played by Samuel L. Jackson and John Travolta respectively. The former holds forth about various matters from popular culture on several occasions, even in scenes that then erupt in explicit violence: as his character puts it, 'I have this speech I give before I kill somebody'. The juxtaposition of the mundane and the violent, 'the talk–talk, bang–bang' style, as one interviewer, J. Hoberman, described it (Peary 1998: 153), is a Tarantino characteristic and it renders the violence even more shocking when it does arrive, by the disparity between the two registers.

Jackie Brown, adapted from an Elmore Leonard novel, *Rum Punch*, features another Tarantino characteristic that could also be defined as a gesture towards double-coding, and that is the casting of film actors from previous generations after their career has gone into decline. In this case it is Pam Grier, star of some of the best-known 'blaxploitation' films of the 1970s. Tarantino clearly knows his film history, particularly in terms of its popular genres, and is always happy to pay homage to it. Yet another somewhat forgotten actor, Robert Forster, is also given a significant role in the film, and even John Travolta's career was in the doldrums until Tarantino resurrected it by casting him as a gangster hitman in *Pulp Fiction*. *Jackie Brown* is also somewhat notorious for the free use of the word 'nigger' by one of its main characters, Ordell Robbie, played by Samuel L. Jackson. Although it is true to say that the word has to some extent been reclaimed by the black community in America in recent times, it still has considerable shock value in a film context – particularly when used by a white writer-director. As so often with his films, there is a sense of Tarantino exploring just how far he can push the boundaries of taste, and he does seem very self-consciously to cultivate the image of Hollywood's bad boy director.

Kill Bill I and *II* draw heavily on martial arts films of the kind made popular by Hong Kong and Japanese cinema, and even include an animated scene (*anime*) in the Japanese style, so there is quite a mix of genres going on here, as well as yet another example of genre homage on the part of the director. The *Grindhouse* double-bill, however, co-directed by Robert Rodriguez, has met with less approval by the critical fraternity, which was less impressed with the appeal to past genres displayed in this instance, finding the final pro-duct if anything too reminiscent of the rather slapdash quality of the originals (exploitation genres such as 'slasher' films). The overall package consisted of two films, one by Rodriguez (*Planet Terror*) and the other by Tarantino (*Death Proof*), complete with fake trailers for supposedly 'forthcoming' films, although each segment was later released separately under the respective director's name with extra material added. Tarantino was also credited as 'special guest director' on a scene in Rodriguez and Frank Millar's film *Sin City*.

Inglourious Basterds, Tarantino's foray into the war-film genre, drew a certain amount of criticism for taking liberties with historical reality, in a plot-line that had an American secret service team acting behind German lines in order to take revenge for the treatment of Jews by the Nazi regime. Once again there was no lack of violence on view, which is standard for such a genre of course. In his most recent film, *Django Unchained*, Tarantino has turned his attention to the Western, imposing his own style and concerns onto this most stylised of film genres, with its jealously guarded mythology and long list of cine-matic heroes like John Wayne. Gavin Smith remarked of Tarantino's first two films, *Reservoir Dogs* and *Pulp Fiction*, that the director seemed to be testing how far he could 'push genre convention towards dissonance' (Peary 1998: 98) without losing the audience on the way, and he continues on in that vein with the Western in *Django Unchained*. The main genre influence here is the spaghetti-Western of such directors as Sergio Leone, meaning that Tarantino is paying homage to a genre which was already designed to be a homage to a genre: double-coding squared, one might almost say. One of the primary characteristics of the spaghetti-Western was its extreme vio-lence (often verging on the cartoonish), something that Tarantino has shown himself to be only too willing to punctuate his films with, right from the beginning.

A standard criticism of Tarantino's work is that it is all too knowingly postmodern, and that it bears little resemblance to real life, preferring instead to be in dialogue with earlier films. Thus interviewers for the French magazine *Positif* can query if he 'is just making borrowed, post-modern, self-reflexive art with no connection to reality, just a kind of formalist game.' (Peary 1998: 87). Tarantino's response is that even if he is deliberately alluding to other films in his own, his first concern is always 'to tell a story that will be dramatically captivating' (Peary 1998: 87). Gavin Smith's suggestion that '[o]n one level your movies are fictions, but on another level they're movie criticism, like Godard's films' (Peary 1998: 109) is more to Tarantino's liking, although he is quick to point out that he does not regard this as an intellectual exercise and that for him the key point of filmmaking is storytelling. He also thinks that the intertextuality for which he is so famed is simply a matter of responding non-judgementally to the ubiquitous media culture that is all around us nowadays, which means that, for instance, the bulk of film history is now available to pretty well anyone who wants to access it, by means of television and DVDs. So saturated have we become in media and popular culture that audiences are far more attuned to intertextuality than earlier generations were, and Tarantino feels he is simply playing to what is now a well-established sensibility. It is a sensibility which he finds very congenial himself – Tarantino is above all a film fan, with a voracious appetite for the medium's products, from B-movies through to the avant-garde. This means that he fulfils yet another criterion of the postmodern aesthetic, and that is the confident way that he sets about blurring the boundary between popular and high art.

Tarantino's major works

Tarantino, Quentin (dir.), *Reservoir Dogs*, Momentum, 1992.
——(dir.), *Pulp Fiction*, Jersey Films, A Band Apart, Miramax Films, 1994.
——(dir.), *Jackie Brown*, A Band Apart, Miramax Films, 1997.
——(dir.), *Kill Bill, I*, A Band Apart, Miramax Films, Super Cool Manchu, 2003.
——(dir.), *Kill Bill, II*, A Band Apart, Miramax Films, Super Cool Manchu, 2004.
——(dir.), *Grindhouse* (double-bill, *Planet Terror* and *Death Proof*, with Robert Rodriguez), Dimension Films, Troublemaker Studios, *et al.*, 2007.
——(dir.), *Death Proof* (extended version of *Grindhouse* version), Troublemaker Studios, 2007.
——(dir.), *Inglourious Basterds*, Universal Pictures, A Band Apart, *et al.*, 2009.
——(dir.), *Django Unchained*, Columbia Pictures, *et al.*, 2012.

References and further reading

Barton, Charles (dir.), *Bud Abbott and Lou Costello Meet Frankenstein*, Universal Studios, 1948.

Leonard, Elmore, *Rum Punch*, New York: Delacorte, 1992.

Peary, Gerald (ed.), *Quentin Tarantino: Interviews*, Jackson, MS: University Press of Mississippi, 1998.

Rodriguez, Roberto and Frank Millar (dirs), *Sin City*, Dimension Films and Troublemaker Studios, 2005.

Scorsese, Martin (dir.), *Taxi Driver*, Bill/Phillips, Italo/Judaeo Productions, 1976.

RENÉ THOM (1923–2002)

René Thom was a mathematician, whose work on topology (the study of the shapes of systems) and morphogenesis (the study of forms) helped to generate catastrophe theory, which provided new insights into the workings of complex systems – particularly their propensity to reach crisis points at certain stages of their development. Topological models mapped out where such discontinuities were most likely to occur. Along with its successors chaos theory and complexity theory, catastrophe theory has exerted a powerful influence on the postmodern mind, since in each case there is a sense of there being events in the physical world lying beyond all human efforts to exert meaningful control over them. Postmodernists are always hunting to find evidence to reinforce this worldview, with Jean-François Lyotard, for example, drawing heavily on such theories in *The Postmodern Condition*, where he references Thom at various points to suggest that systems can never be considered to fall entirely within our power. Thus we have his comment that '[i]t is not true that uncertainty (lack of control) decreases as accuracy goes up: it goes up as well' (Lyotard 1984: 56). In other words, the more complex a system becomes, the more vulnerable to breakdown it also becomes simultaneously; the irony being that our technology is geared towards improving the accuracy of all its products, that being a cornerstone of our culture.

Catastrophe theory holds that we can map out the discontinuities and ruptures that will occur within systems as they develop over time, and all complex systems will feature such breakdowns at some point: as Alexander Woodcock and Monte Davis have noted, '[d]iscontinuity is as much the rule as the exception' (Woodcock and Davis 1978: 14) in our universe. It is the relationship between stability and instability that fascinates Thom, and that raises the issue of the 'succession of form':

> One of the central problems studied by mankind is the problem of the succession of form. Whatever is the ultimate nature of reality (assuming that this expression has meaning), it is indisputable that our universe is not chaos. We perceive beings, objects, things to which we give names. These beings or things are forms or structures endowed with a degree of stability; they take up some part of space and last for some period of time.
>
> (Thom 1975: 1)

The universe as we experience it normally exhibits this kind of stability; yet we are also aware of change, so 'we must concede that the universe we see is a ceaseless creation, evolution, and destruction of forms and that the purpose of science is to foresee this change of form and, if possible, explain it' (Thom 1975: 1). Such changes do not, however, fall into a 'single well-defined pattern' (Thom 1975: 1), which means that both determinism and indeterminism feature in them. This is the point at which postmodern philosophers start to become really interested, since it brings paradox into play and that can be used to undermine systems of thought. A statement such as 'the same local situation can give birth to apparently different outcomes under the influence of unknown or unobservable factors' (Thom 1975: 2) suggests there are limits to our ability to impose our will on events, and to postmodernists it is evidence to back up their theories. Thom regards it as ironical that indeterminism arises in such instances, since science is in the main concerned with trying to deny its existence and providing a firm basis for prediction.

Thom goes on to speak of 'ambiguous or catastrophic situations where the evolution of phenomena seems ill determined' (Thom 1975: 2), and it is here that we can see where some of the problems emerge in the appropriation of his theory for other purposes. 'Ambiguousness' sounds far less dramatic than 'catastrophic', but of course it is the latter which has passed into more general currency. Since the ability to predict how processes will develop plays such a large part in both science and everyday affairs, Thom notes that the tendency is to use 'local models' (Thom 1975: 2) to remove indeterminacy as much as possible, thus enabling prediction to take place. We then have what he calls a 'formalizable' process, although since it 'is not necessarily deterministic' it cannot be considered 'entirely satisfactory' (Thom 1975: 2, 3) by scientists. That opens up just enough of a gap to attract postmodern philosophers like Lyotard into calling into question our assumptions about the predictive powers of metanarratives.

Thom puts forward a model designed 'to parameterize the local states of a system' called 'the catastrophe set' (Thom 1975: 7), and as first characterised by him it does not sound unduly dramatic: 'the space of observables M contains a closed subset K, called the *catastrophe set*, and as long as the representative point m of the system does not meet K, the local nature of the system does not change' (Thom 1975: 7). When m does meet K, a discontinuity occurs which alters the previous state of the form in question. Thom is careful to point out, however, that by close analysis of K's local nature it is possible to predict discontinuities to some degree. There are many of these '*elementary catastrophes*', as Thom calls them (Thom 1975: 8), but it is not until these manifest themselves as a series of accidents at a local level that we have a significant change in the overall form. It is a fair criticism that postmodern theorists tend to emphasise the factor of unpredictability more than Thom appears to be doing here. He does wonder, however, whether his theory might also be applied to everyday, ostensibly unformalisable, experiences to some beneficial effect: 'for example, the cracks in an old wall, the shape of a cloud, the path of a falling leaf, or the froth on a pint of beer' (Thom 1975: 9); that is precisely what chaos theory has gone on to do.

Thom's work on morphogenesis rapidly becomes densely mathematical, but he keeps dropping in intriguing asides of the kind that inspire philosophical reflection. He asks us to suppose, for example, that we could isolate a natural process in a box (B), and then observe it for a specified period (T, that being the time axis) such that we could investigate all of its points; if we found no difference between a given point (x) and any other in its neighbourhood, then it would be a 'regular point' rather than a 'catastrophic point' (Thom 1975: 38). However, he concedes that this distinction 'is obviously somewhat arbitrary because it depends on the fineness of the observation used. One might object, not without reason, that each point is catastrophic to sufficiently sensitive observational techniques. This is why the distinction is an idealization, to be made precise by a mathematical model' (Thom 1975: 38). Even if this is no more than a possibility, it is enough to suggest to the more active philosophical imagination that we are always on the cusp of discontinuity – and that is a world-picture to which many postmodernists subscribe. It is an obvious criticism of such an interpretation, however, that it seems obsessed with the discontinuity at the expense of the more general stability within which it occurs.

Catastrophe theory is another of the scientific theories that Alan Sokal and Jean Bricmont feel has been badly misunderstood, and thus misappropriated, by postmodern philosophers. Their objections to Lyotard's work are worth considering, because they raise some important issues about the relationship between the sciences and philosophy, particularly the extent to which practitioners in the latter field can extrapolate material from the former to advance socio-political theories. Noting that Lyotard takes both fractal geometry and catastrophe theory as instances of 'postmodern science', they agree that these mathematical theories are interesting and that they have proved to have applications in areas like physics, but, contrary to Lyotard's claim to that effect, 'they have in no way called into question traditional scientific epistemology' (Sokal and Bricmont 1998: 127). They go on to criticise Lyotard for using concepts from catastrophe theory to construct a picture of the evolution of science itself; Lyotard asserting that 'postmodern science … is theorizing its own evolution as discontinuous, catastrophic, nonrectifiable' (Lyotard 1984: 60). Granted that there are different resonances between these terms in mathematical and philosophical contexts, there is nevertheless still some correspondence, and what Lyotard is describing sounds very much like one of Thomas Kuhn's paradigm shifts (see *The Structure of Scientific Revolutions*). Lyotard's conclusion that postmodern science 'is producing not the known, but the unknown' (Lyotard 1984: 60) is worth questioning, however, as Sokal and Bricmont proceed to do; but even here he could be given the benefit of the doubt in that science is becoming increasingly aware that it has limits, that there are aspects of the universe which will always remain hidden from us. Where Lyotard is right is that recent science (such as Thom's) has succeeded in altering our world-picture, and that does have socio-political implications.

It would be a great pity if only scientific specialists were thought to be qualified to comment on scientific theories, as that would further increase the gap between science and the general public. Thom himself seems to be reaching out to other fields in his opening sentence to the 'Preface' of *Structural Stability and Morphogenesis*: 'This book, written by a mathematician, is hopefully addressed to biologists and specialists of other disciplines whose subjects have so far resisted mathematical treatment' (Thom 1975: xxiii). He even recommends to non-mathematicians to skip the more complex technical sections of the book, and warns against mathematics becoming too rarefied and self-contained for public understanding: 'I am certain that the human mind would not be fully satisfied with a universe in which all phenomena were governed by a mathematical process that was coherent but totally abstract' (Thom 1975: 5). For all the abstraction of his own work, it does encourage us to find wider-ranging applications of its theories.

Catastrophe theory has been widely applied to many areas of the physical world, including human and animal behaviour, although its findings have been the subject of considerable debate. Thom himself, as we have noted, felt it had particular relevance to biology, and that it could help to correct what he regarded as certain misconceptions that had crept into this field. He argued, for example, that biologists tended to use the term 'information' in too simplistic a manner, and that in most cases 'form' would be more appropriate. To a large extent catastrophe has been superseded by chaos theory and complexity theory, which provide even more sophisticated models as to the inner workings of complex systems. Thom's work clearly has laid much of the groundwork for these, and at the very least he has also provided much food for philosophical thought.

Thom's major writings

Thom, René, *Structural Stability and Morphogenesis: An Outline of a General Theory of Models* [1972], trans. D. H. Fowler, Reading, MA: W. A. Benjamin, 1975.
——, *Mathematical Models of Morphogenesis* [1980], trans. W. M. Brookes and D. Rand, Chichester: Ellis Horwood, 1983.
——, *Semio Physics: A Sketch*, Reading, MA: Addison-Wesley, 1990.

References and further reading

Kuhn, Thomas, *The Structure of Scientific Revolutions* [1962], 2nd edition, Chicago and London: University of Chicago Press, 1970.
Lyotard, Jean-François, *The Postmodern Condition: A Report on Knowledge* [1979], trans. Geoff Bennington and Brian Massumi, Manchester: Manchester University Press, 1984.
Sokal, Alan and Jean Bricmont, *Intellectual Impostures: Postmodern Philosophers' Abuse of Science*, London: Profile Books, 1998.
Woodcock, Alexander and Monte Davis, *Catastrophe Theory*, Harmondsworth: Penguin, 1978.

ROBERT VENTURI (B. 1925)

Venturi is a prominent architect and architectural theorist, most famous for his provocative, co-authored study *Learning from Las Vegas*, which makes an impassioned case for the value of the playful vernacular architecture associated with that city (mere 'kitsch' as critics generally dismissed it), as opposed to the seriousness and severity of the modernist project, with its penchant for social engineering. It was a book that, as the Marxist commentator on postmodernity David Harvey aptly summarised it, provided a 'powerful cutting edge' (Harvey 1990: 40) to the rise of architectural postmodernism. What modernist architects had lost, according to Venturi, was a sense of the functional quality of most buildings, preferring to make aesthetic statements instead – based on an aesthetic for which he and his associates had little sympathy. A gulf had opened up between architects and the public because '[a]rchitects are out of the habit of looking nonjudgmentally at the environment[.] ... Architects have preferred to change the existing environment rather than enhance what is there' (Venturi 1977a: 3). It is this 'progressive' attitude, the impulse to change and if necessary destroy what is already there, that Venturi is concerned above all to challenge, informing us that '[a]s an architect I try to be guided not by habit but by a conscious sense of the past – by precedent, thoughtfully considered' (Venturi 1977b: 13). What this leads to in Venturi's case is the championing of 'complexity and contradiction' (see Venturi 1977b) in architecture, instead of the fetish for formal purity and apparent simplicity of meaning in the modernist movement.

Venturi and his collaborators found in Las Vegas a style of architecture that was the very antithesis of modernism, a style designed to speak directly to the popular consciousness using humour and garish colours, as well as an array of decorative elements that brashly drew attention to themselves in a manner that modernism would reject utterly. The aesthetic involved in a city like Las Vegas was apparently chaotic and far more concerned with making an immediate impact on the passer-by than modernism, with its high ideals of architectural purity and social engineering, ever was. Vegas was unashamedly commercial, and its buildings positively revelled in this state of affairs, opting for kitsch in their efforts to grab the attention of the passing general public, in the hope that they would then take the bait of the services or goods being offered by the establishment in question rather than those of any of their competitors: 'stop here' was the unmistakable message they conveyed. Issues of aesthetics did not come into the transaction at all, and for Venturi and his associates this was to be applauded rather than, as was usually the case with their peers in the architectural profession, criticised as a professional failing.

Whereas modernist architects, with their obsessively purist approach, 'rejected the combination of fine art and crude art'

(Venturi 1977a: 6), Venturi sets out to reinstate this method of proceeding, pointing out that it is regularly to be found in the architecture of the Italian Renaissance and Counter-Reformation, where
grand palaces and more humble dwellings, often housing everyday
trades, are to be found cheek by jowl – something that any visitor to
Italy's old towns and cities can hardly help noticing. The unity sought
by modernist architects is singularly missing in such cases, and Venturi
is to draw his inspiration from such models as these rather than from
modernist icons such as Le Corbusier, who once memorably suggested demolishing most of central Paris and starting again to achieve
just such a sense of unity. If order was to be identified in Las Vegas's
architecture, it would have to be a product of its specific, workaday,
function.

In going into Las Vegas in such detail, Venturi's aim is to make the
study of the existing urbanism in America 'a socially desirable activity'
in the hope that will make inner-city regeneration 'less authoritarian'
(Venturi 1977a: 6) than it currently is. He posits some interesting
parallels between Las Vegas and Rome that he feels hold some very
important lessons for his architectural peers, challenging them to
recognise that 'Las Vegas is to the Strip what Rome is to the Piazza',
and that there are 'violent juxtapositions of use and scale in both
cities' (Venturi 1977a: 18) that will repay close attention for what
they reveal about constructing a public-friendly environment. The
main lesson is that architects ought to be fitting their buildings in
with how cities are actually being, and have been, used rather than
wishing to redesign them according to some aesthetic metanarrative.
In Las Vegas this means adhering to a scheme that makes it easy to
move from one casino to another by car – that requirement shaping
how the Strip has developed as the city's gambling industry has
grown.

There is a unity of function to be noted on the Strip too, in that
the hotel-casinos are close enough to the road to be seen from passing
cars, but with a reasonable amount of parking space to be found at
the front and sides of the building (car transport being assumed to be
the norm). It is also noticeable that all the attention has been paid to
the front of the buildings, the 'business end' as it were, with the back
generally being 'styleless' (Venturi 1977a: 35) because it is of no
commercial importance; the same principle goes for each casino's
signs, which very deliberately 'inflect toward the highway' (Venturi
1977a: 51), where new trade is to be found. Inside, casinos follow a
similar pattern in having dimly lit gambling rooms with no windows,
causing clients to lose their sense of time, which is all to the benefit of

the casino owners of course, since the lack of distraction is likely to induce their clients to keep on gambling. Venturi does make the point, however, that he is not concerned with the morality of Las Vegas, just with the way that it works as an urban phenomenon.

Venturi moves on from Vegas to consider the more general issue of how he can encourage 'a new but old direction in architecture' (Venturi 1977a: 87), which sounds an admirably postmodern attitude to adopt. In keeping with the anti-modernist tenor of the book, it is made clear that Venturi and his associates will not be proceeding from aesthetic considerations, the authors boldly declaring instead that 'we shall argue for the symbolism of the ugly and ordinary in architecture ... for architecture as shelter with symbols on it' (Venturi 1977a: 90). Thus are we introduced to the concept of 'the decorated shed', which constitutes for Venturi *et al.* what architecture should henceforth take as its primary model. As an example of how this works in practice they choose a building of their own, Guild House, an apartment block in Philadelphia, which they contrast with another apartment block from the 1960s, Crawford Manor in New Haven, built by the architect Paul Rudolph. The symbolism of the buildings is 'ugly and ordinary' and 'heroic and original' (Venturi 1977a: 93), respectively. The latter approach, with its relative austerity of manner (decoration-free, for example) recalling the 'reformist-progressive' (Venturi 1977a: 103) agenda of high modernism, is dismissed as being irrelevant to the way society is developing nowadays. As the authors uncompromisingly declare, 'this is not the time and ours is not the environment for heroic communication via pure architecture' (Venturi 1977a: 163). Guild House is claimed to be more attuned to people's everyday lives and what they actually want from the buildings they live in (bearing in mind that Guild House is designed for elderly residents).

Venturi concludes *Learning from Las Vegas* by pointing out that their theories on architecture have grown out of the kind of commissions that the Venturi and Rauch practice has been receiving over the years – small scale, low budget in the main. Critics described the buildings that resulted as 'ugly' and 'ordinary', but the firm decided to embrace these notions, happy with the 'humbler role for architects' that they signalled, on the grounds that this was 'artistically a more promising one' (Venturi 1977a: 129) than modernism offered.

Venturi's commitment to the vernacular and popular taste remains undimmed throughout his architectural career, as in his presentation of *Iconography and Electronics Upon a Generic Architecture* as '[a] gentle manifesto that acknowledges the demise of a universal architecture defined as expressive space and industrial structure' (Venturi 1996: 3). Venturi has a very different vision of what architecture ought to be doing in the later twentieth century in the aftermath of the 'demise' of modernism and the 'International Style' that it relentlessly promoted: 'Let us acknowledge architecture for now that is not ideologically correct, rhetorically heroic, theoretically pretentious, boringly abstract, technologically obsolete. Let us acknowledge the elemental quality of architecture as shelter and symbol – buildable and usable shelter that is also meaningful as a setting for living' (Venturi 1996: 3). It is just this practical quality that is missing from so much of modernist architecture, a recognition that to their inhabitants buildings are in the first place dwellings where they will spend their everyday lives, whether at home or at work.

Neither is Venturi necessarily happy with everything that has replaced modernism under the heading of the postmodern, as his dismissal of 'the parvenu historicism of Postmodernism, and now sado-masochistic expressionist applications of Deconstructionism as complexity and contradiction gone rampant' (Venturi 1996: 8) clearly reveals. The target is probably architects like Rem Koolhaas and the Deconstructivist School, who do work under the influence of such theories. The point being made is that postmodernism, too, can have its version of ideological correctness, and that this is always to be avoided. Venturi remains an iconoclastic voice within the profession, always willing to query the consensus view.

There are some similarities to be noted between Venturi's view of what architecture should be and those of Charles Jencks, more generally known as the major voice of postmodern architectural theory. Venturi's call to take the past into account, as well as to keep the needs of the general public in mind when designing buildings, is certainly consistent with what Jencks went on to theorise as 'double-coding' in *The Language of Post-Modern Architecture* (Jencks 1991: 12). While Jencks may not emphasise the vernacular to the extent that Venturi does, they are in many ways engaged in much the same campaign against modernist severity and authoritarianism, and in calling for a more pragmatic, indeed more human, approach to architecture. Venturi's championing of popular taste is also very much in tune with how postmodern aesthetics subsequently has developed. Perhaps most importantly, both Venturi and Jencks force architects to rethink their relationship to the public, and the need to do that has been a cornerstone of postmodernism across the arts.

Venturi's major writings

Venturi, Robert (with Denise Scott Brown and Steven Izenour), *Learning from Las Vegas: The Forgotten Symbolism of Architectural Form*, 2nd edition, Cambridge, MA and London: MIT Press, 1977a.

——, *Contradiction and Complexity in Architecture*, 2nd edition, London: Butterworth Architecture, 1977b.

——, *The Architecture of Robert Venturi*, Albuquerque, NM: University of New Mexico Press, 1989.

——, *Iconography and Electronics Upon a Generic Architecture*, Cambridge, MA and London: MIT Press, 1996.

——(with Denise Scott Brown), *Architecture as Signs and Systems: For a Mannerist Time*, Cambridge, MA: Belknap Press, 2004.

References and further reading

Harvey, David, *The Condition of Postmodernity: An Enquiry into the Origins of Cultural Change*, Cambridge, MA and London: Blackwell, 1990.

Jencks, Charles, *The Language of Post-Modern Architecture* [1975], 6th edition, London: Academy Editions, 1991.

GRAHAM WARD (B. 1955)

Ward is one of the main figures in the Radical Orthodoxy movement in religious studies, a group who regard postmodernism as a symptom of a crisis in secularism that it can take advantage of in order to reintroduce a theological dimension into Western culture. In the edited collection of essays entitled *Radical Orthodoxy: A New Theology*, the editors (Ward among them) picture secularism as being 'soulless, aggressive, nonchalant and nihilistic', and argue that it has left a spiritual vacuum within society that offers a 'supreme opportunity' (Milbank *et al.* 1999: 1) for the new theological project its advocates are proposing. While insisting that it is true to 'credal Christianity and the exemplarity of its patristic matrix', Radical Orthodoxy also declares itself aware of the need 'to rethink the tradition' (Milbank *et al.* 1999: 2) of Christianity that it has inherited, and that means engaging with the various intellectual currents of the modern and postmodern worlds rather than just restating old dogma and dismissing all criticisms out of hand.

Ward's own essay in this collection, 'The Displaced Body of Jesus Christ', rejects the notion that it is possible to reach an understanding of Christ's nature or body by treating him from a human perspective as a gendered Jew. For Ward, questions such as 'Can a male Saviour save women?' and modern investigations into the sexuality of Jesus, which simply continue the nineteenth-century rational search for the historical Jesus, fail to discern the nature of corporeality in Christ. For these approaches take the human to be the measure of the Christic.

(Milbank *et al.* 1999: 163)

Behind such a search lies the Enlightenment worldview that reason can uncover the mysteries of the world, including those associated with divinity. Enlightenment thought is not willing to accept what goes against reason, and of course so much of religious thought does so in the guise of miracles and their like. Ward's line, echoing certain aspects of deconstructive thought, is that the body of Jesus is subject to a 'series of displacements' such that we can speak of 'the deferred identity of the body of the Messiah' (Milbank *et al.* 1999: 163). Christ's ascension, which is the aspect Ward chooses to concentrate on in his analysis of Christ's corporeality, is then to be interpreted as 'the final stage in the destabilized identity of the body of the Messiah' (Milbank *et al.* 1999: 163). And that destabilised identity is to be considered 'multi-gendered' rather than simply male, a conclusion which runs counter to any rational analysis of the situation. Even if deconstructionists would not necessarily take this as proof of Christ's divinity, the concepts that are being brought into play by Ward are certainly not alien to them: at the very least there is a family resemblance here to their conception of identity as very fluid and flexible.

Ward offers a new approach to religious language in *Barth, Derrida and the Language of Theology* that establishes links between the work of the German theologian Karl Barth and Jacques Derrida's deconstruction – by way of the Lithuanian-French philosopher Emmanuel Levinas. Derrida's critique of logocentricity is of particular interest to Ward, since it enables him to counter the Enlightenment-derived tendency to rationalise Christian belief by moving it firmly into the domain of philosophy. In consequence, as Ward complains, 'concern with the historical Jesus focussed upon his ethical relevance, not his metaphysical claims' (Ward 1995: 6). It is precisely those metaphysical claims, and the mystery that inevitably accompanies them, that Ward wishes to resurrect, thereby to make us aware of '[t]he wholly other of the incarnation, the divinity of Christ' (Ward 1995: 6). These are topics which cannot be fully explained in human terms, or in the language of human understanding. Derrida's concept of *différance* becomes theologically very significant for Ward, therefore, providing a means to mark the way out to the construction of 'a new theology of the Word' (Ward 1995: 10).

Ward emphasises the importance of the factor of 'negotiation' in Derrida's work (as when he is writing of Levinas), arguing that '[n]egotiation suggests suspicion of intentionality (one's own and the other's)' (Ward 1995: 174). There is always some form of negotiation going on within textuality, Ward claims, and by examining the nature of Derrida's negotiation with Levinas we can apply the lessons learned to the work of Barth and thus move 'towards a postmodern Christology' (Ward 1995: 175). To question metaphysics in the radical manner that Derrida does, to argue that meaning is continually being deferred by the operation of *différance*, is for Ward to pose what are at base theological problems, such as the recurrent one 'of needing to speak of that which cannot be spoken about' (Ward 1995: 206). In fact, Ward even goes so far as to say that '*différance* can only define itself within the theological' (Ward 1995: 233).

Postmodernism is the world of the net and cyberspace, and it is there we must explore if we want to work out the nature of the postmodern God, as Ward proceeds to do in his Introduction to the collection of essays in *The Postmodern God*. Taking on board the theories of both Fredric Jameson (*Postmodernism, or the Cultural Logic of Late Capitalism*) and David Harvey (*The Condition of Postmodernity*) that posit a close bond between postmodernism and late capitalism, Ward suggests that when we treat 'cyberspace as a cultural metaphor for postmodernism' we can recognise 'that modernism is linked to specific conceptions of time, space, and substance, and that postmodernism explodes the myths and ideologies constructing these conceptions' (Ward 1997: xvii). The thrust of modernism is away from the religious to the secular, but in Ward's reading of recent cultural history '[t]he emergence of the postmodern has fostered post-secular thinking – thinking about other, alternative worlds' (Ward 1997: xxii). The world of theology has been able to reassert itself, therefore, especially with 'the development of cyberspace – a spatiality which is only virtually real and within which time and materiality (as conceived by the project of modernity) disappear' (Ward 1997: xxii). That is a type of context in which theology feels entirely at home, although it would have to be said that postmodernism did not necessarily envisage pluralism as encouraging a return of metanarratives – it takes a highly selective interpretation of postmodernism's commitment to both pluralism and difference to see them as designed to sanction that. The status of religion as a metanarrative is not really something that Ward addresses.

Ward goes on to make the rather startling claim that 'only theology can complete the postmodern project' (Ward 1997: xxxiv), pointing out that if postmodernists are keen to bring about the 'death of the subject', then theology, which 'cannot conceive of … an autonomous subject' at all (Ward 1997: xlii), can provide the best model. He also claims that there is no problem with foundations in theology, because '[i]t cannot think its own origin; it seeks and desires among the consequences of that which always remains unthought' (Ward 1997: xlii). It could be objected, however, that this is to take refuge in the good old Christian standby of the mysteriousness of God; since the existence of God is not being held up to question, then God, mysterious or not, is functioning as the ground of a metanarrative at such points. Ward effectively calls for a takeover of the postmodern by theology, encouraging it to 'subsume postmodernism's cyberspace, writing through and beyond it, in order to establish its own orders' (Ward 1997: xlii); but that would be to obliterate the postmodern as most of its major theorists understand it.

It does sound as if Ward is trying to reduce the 'other, alternative worlds' opened up by postmodern thought to the one true way of Christian theology, especially when he closes his essay by arguing that we have come 'to a forking of the ways' (Ward 1997: xliii) and must choose which to take. The reference to *The Pilgrim's Progress* sends out an unequivocal message in that regard. On the one side lies nihilism and on the other faith, which hardly seems like a very pluralistic, or difference-supporting, worldview.

Cities of God explores how to make theology resonate more fully with the new urban culture that developed in the West in the later twentieth century, a world of 'unprecedented social atomism and the deepening of virtual reality' (Ward 2000: ix). Ward feels this is a world just waiting for a theological response in order to restore a sense of purpose to people's lives, and that postmodernism is failing to deliver this, being implicated instead with late capitalism in the creation of 'cities of endless desire' that are 'primed with fantasy, hyped with ecstasy, dazzling in the allure of promised, sybaritic pleasures' (Ward 2000: 52, 53). Again, Ward seeks to turn the net and cyberspace to account, using them to generate a sense of community rather than to stimulate our desires, although his tone on these will strike many as over-judgemental and even wildly exaggerated. Not every non-Christian in the contemporary city lives a life of fantasy, ecstasy and sybaritic pleasures – or wants to.

As with the work of John Caputo (see *What Would Jesus Deconstruct?*, for example), one can acknowledge the ingenuity that goes into the analysis of problem areas in Christian theology using the tools of deconstruction and the postmodern while being sceptical of a system of belief that requires such theoretical ingenuity to be expended on it in order to render it credible and keep criticism at bay. Our attention is continually being drawn to what we cannot know and what we cannot say, and this does not exactly facilitate debate – theological or otherwise. Pragmatist philosophers like Richard Rorty would be particularly harsh on such a form of discourse, regarding it as little more than a language-game that consistently refers 'back to something beyond the reach of time and chance' (Rorty 1989: xv). From that perspective, there is no problem to resolve, and for the pragmatist whatever it is that 'remains unthought' need not concern us.

Ward's major writings

Ward, Graham, *Barth, Derrida and the Language of Theology*, Cambridge: Cambridge University Press, 1995.
——, *Theology and Contemporary Critical Theory*, Basingstoke and London: Macmillan, 1996.
——, 'Introduction, or, A Guide to Theological Thinking in Cyberspace', in Graham Ward (ed.), *The Postmodern God: A Theological Reader*, Oxford and Malden, MA: Blackwell, 1997.
——, *Cities of God*, London and New York: Routledge, 2000.
——(ed.), *The Blackwell Companion to Postmodern Theology*, Oxford: Blackwell, 2001.
——, *True Religion*, Oxford: Blackwell, 2002.
——, *Christ and Culture*, Oxford: Blackwell, 2005a.
——, *Cultural Transformation and Religious Practice*, Cambridge: Cambridge University Press, 2005b.
——, *The Politics of Discipleship: Becoming Postmaterial Citizens*, Ada, MI: Baker Academic, 2009.
Milbank, John, Catherine Pickstock and Graham Ward (eds), *Radical Orthodoxy: A New Theology*, London and New York: Routledge, 1999.

References and further reading

Bunyan, John, *The Pilgrim's Progress* [1678], ed. James Blanton Wharey, rev. Roger Sharrock, Oxford: Clarendon Press, 1960.
Caputo, John, *What Would Jesus Deconstruct?: The Good News of Postmodernity for the Church*, Grand Rapids, MI: Baker Academic, 2007.
Harvey, David, *The Condition of Postmodernity: An Enquiry into the Origins of Cultural Change*, Cambridge, MA and Oxford: Blackwell, 1990.
Jameson, Fredric, *Postmodernism, or the Cultural Logic of Late Capitalism*, London: Verso, 1991.

Rorty, Richard, *Contingency, Irony, and Solidarity*, Cambridge and New York: Cambridge University Press, 1989.

HAYDEN WHITE (B. 1928)

White has been one of the most important figures to develop a postmodern line on history, emphasising that history must always be seen as the result of particular ideological viewpoints, and that it can never be objective in character. Instead, it constitutes a series of narratives, none of which can claim superiority over the others in terms of truth-value (this will depend on your particular ideological perspective) and all of which have some claim on the historian's attention. 'I treat the historical work as what it most manifestly is: a verbal structure in the form of a narrative prose discourse' (White 1973: ix), and that should indicate to us that it is shaped in a particular way from a particular viewpoint, and with particular goals in mind. There cannot be assumed to be any grand narrative of history by which all historical writing can be judged, and that of course is a long-running tradition in the discipline in the West, with Western culture being given the central role in how world history has unfolded (a recent high-profile instance of this tendency would be Niall Ferguson's *Civilization: The West and the Rest*, which unashamedly starts from the premise that West is best). White is quite explicit about this: 'it is possible to view historical consciousness as a specifically Western prejudice by which the presumed superiority of modern, industrial society can be retroactively substantiated' (White 1973: 2). Colonialism, after all, was entirely predicated on just such a belief, and the attitudes behind it die hard.

Metahistory, White's most important publication, sets out to present 'a formal theory of the historical work' (White 1973: ix) so that we can determine how to assess any particular example against its competitors in the field. White identifies three strategies by which historians go about their business of explanation: formal argument, emplotment and ideological implication. These strategies are then broken down further into four types of articulation each: if we take formal argument, for example, these constitute 'Formism, Organicism, Mechanism, and Contextualism' (White 1973: x). Further to that, White posits four main modes of historical consciousness behind history writing: 'Metaphor, Synecdoche, Metonymy, and Irony' (White 1973: xi). He emphasises that for him history is, at a deep level, essentially an exercise in poetics, and that its 'scientific' side has tended to be overplayed by recent generations of historians (with professional status in mind no doubt, given the high profile science has been granted in contemporary culture). From that position it follows that no one mode can be claimed as more realistic than any of the others, and that the choice we make between modes should be considered as 'aesthetic or moral rather than epistemological' (White 1973: xii). We are enjoined as well to recognise the important role that invention plays in history writing, with White pointing out how '[t]he same event can serve as a different kind of element of many different historical stories' (White 1973: 7) depending on the role it is assigned by any particular historian. The historian is someone who employs 'narrative tactics' (White 1973: 7) no less than the writer of fiction does, and has just as much scope for interpretation.

Emplotment works by using the structure of either Romance, Tragedy, Comedy or Satire, and the one adopted by the historian will shape the narrative according to the expected conventions of each type. As an example of how explanation by means of formal argument works, White cites Karl Marx. Formal argument operates in a syllogistic fashion: a major premise outlining some kind of 'universal law of causal relationships'; a minor premise detailing 'the boundary conditions within which the law is applied'; and then a conclusion in which 'the events that actually occurred are deduced from the premises by logical necessity' (White 1973: 11). In Marx this universal law involves the base/superstructure relation, in which the economic circumstances obtaining in the former determine the character of the institutions and social relations in the latter, but not the other way round. Base equals universal law, superstructure the boundary conditions, and from that Marx can deduce events such as the economic depressions of his own era. Capitalism dictated certain kinds of social institutions and relationships between that society's classes, but its contradictions as a theory occasioned periodic economic downturns. This is what Marx explains at length in *Capital*.

Equally, Marx can be seen as an example of argument by ideological implication in that he espouses a 'Radical' vision of history which is oriented towards revolution to achieve its aims (the other main ideological positions White lists are Anarchism, Conservatism and Liberalism). This is what Marx is propounding in *The Communist Manifesto*, on the basis that history has developed in such a way as to make a revolution to bring about a new social order entirely viable: for Marx in 1848, revolution's time had come. Marx's narrative tactics are much in evidence in both these examples, and, as White has suggested, whether one finds such arguments persuasive will be a moral or aesthetic decision on the individual reader's part.

Marx is a particularly telling illustration of White's point that there is 'an elective affinity between the act of prefiguration of the historical field and the explanatory strategies used by the historian in a given work' (White 1973: 427), and it is a condition to be noted in all of the various schools of historical writing and historical consciousness that he picks out for study in *Metahistory*. White's various case studies enable him to argue that the distinction between standard history writing and philosophy is somewhat notional: each must be seen to contain elements of the other. Marxist historians, for example, cannot help but incorporate Marx's philosophy of history approach into their assembling and presenting of their material: their finished work is, after all, intended to demonstrate the superior validity of the Marxist worldview and its universalist claims. Ultimately, White's argument is that all we can do is to identify the interpretative strategies at work in any given historian's work, without assuming that there is some meta-level by which it can be judged; as he summarises it, '*on historical grounds alone* I have no basis for preferring one conception of the "science" of history over the other. Such a judgment would merely reflect a logically prior preference' (White 1973: 432–3).

White's emphasis on narrative is something that he shares with many postmodern thinkers. For Jean-François Lyotard in *The Post-modern Condition*, for example, the act of narration is basic to social existence and needs no metanarrative to justify it: 'Narration is the quintessential form of customary knowledge' and narratives 'are legitimated by the simple fact that they do what they do' (Lyotard 1984: 19, 23). Structuralism, too, has repeatedly referred to the critical role played by narrative in human affairs. As Roland Barthes put it in 'Structural Analysis of Narratives', we are confronted with narratives wherever we look in our culture: 'The narratives of the world are numberless. Narrative is first and foremost a prodigious variety of genres, themselves distributed amongst different substances[.] ... [N]arrative is present in every age, in every place, in every society' (Barthes 1977: 79).

White looks more broadly at the nature of discourse in *Tropics of Discourse*. The use of tropes is at the very heart of discourse for him, and what they signal is that discourse is always delivered from a par-ticular position, that it can never be the only possible way of viewing or reporting events:

> [T]roping is both a movement *from* one notion of the way things are related *to* another notion, and a connection between things so that they can be expressed in a language that takes account of the

possibility of their being expressed otherwise. Discourse is the genre in which the effort to earn this right of expression, with full credit to the possibility that things might be expressed otherwise, is preeminent.

(White 1978: 2)

And history is very much a discourse to White, where the particular historian's narrative, whatever it may be, can always be expressed otherwise: one has only to consider the difference between history written by colonisers and those they have colonised to appreciate the force of that argument. So there is no definitive interpretation of any historical event, as theories such as Marxism like to claim of their own. Marxism is only one discourse amongst many, and White rejects the notion of false consciousness on which so much of the theory's vision of history is based, arguing that 'it is not a matter of choosing between objectivity and distortion, but rather between different strategies for constituting "reality" in thought so as to deal with it in different ways' (White 1978: 22). The idea that Marxism is a series of strategies rather than a science would, of course, be anathema to its adherents.

In *Content of the Form* White continues his exploration into the nature of historical narrative, identifying it as a particularly modern form of history writing, such that 'the official wisdom has it that however objective a historian might be in his reporting of events … his account remains something less than a proper history if he has failed to give to reality the form of a story' (White 1987: 5). The tendency now is to regard older kinds of historical writing like annals and chronicles as inferior to narrative, but for White it is more a case of these being forms representing a different conception of reality than we now have. Narrative allows greater scope for interpretation, which is going to make it attractive to a culture in which various ideologies are competing for control.

It is a criticism often made of postmodernism that it leads to a destabilising relativism where we cannot judge between one argument and another, one position and another. White might appear to be laying himself open to just such an objection by rejecting the very possibility of a metahistory, but he nevertheless makes it clear that none of us will find all historical accounts equally persuasive. We still discriminate between historical narratives on aesthetic or moral grounds, and no matter how deeply held these are, they are always up for discussion. Ultimately, we are taken back to ideology; the concept of metahistory is ideologically motivated and used to exert power, and that is what White is concerned to warn us against as much as anything. His theories are designed to enable us to recognise when historical narrative is trying to manipulate us by closing off alternative approaches to interpretation, and constitute a model for constructing resistance to such a discourse.

White's major writings

White, Hayden, *Metahistory: The Historical Imagination in Nineteenth-Century Europe*, Baltimore, MD and London: Johns Hopkins University Press, 1973.

——, *Tropics of Discourse: Essays in Cultural Criticism*, Baltimore, MD and London: Johns Hopkins University Press, 1978.

——, *Content of the Form: Narrative Discourse and Historical Representation*, Baltimore, MD and London: Johns Hopkins University Press. 1987.

——, *Figural Realism: Studies in the Mimesis Effect*, Baltimore, MD: Johns Hopkins University Press, 1999.

——, *The Fiction of Narrative: Essays on History, Literature and Theory, 1957–2007*, ed. Robert Doran, Baltimore, MD: Johns Hopkins University Press, 2010.

References and further reading

Barthes, Roland, *Image-Music-Text*, ed. and trans. Stephen Heath, Fontana: London, 1977.

Ferguson, Niall, *Civilization: The West and the Rest*, London: Allen Lane, 2011.

Lyotard, Jean-François, *The Postmodern Condition: A Report on Knowledge* [1979], trans. Geoff Bennington and Brian Massumi, Manchester: Manchester University Press, 1984.

Marx, Karl, *Capital*, I–III, trans. Ben Fowkes, Harmondsworth: Penguin, 1976, 1978, 1981.

Marx, Karl and Frederick Engels, *The Communist Manifesto* [1848], ed. Frederick L. Bender, New York and London: W. W. Norton, 1988.

SLAVOJ ŽIŽEK (B. 1949)

Žižek is widely regarded as a maverick figure in the field of philosophy and cultural theory, and his work is not always easy to pin down in terms of its politics. He is one of the most marketed celebrities on the academic circuit, much given to making provocative and extreme statements which can often clash with what he says in his written works. He is capable of defending Marxism on occasion, even though in his early works there is a distinctly post-Marxist bias, including a particularly effective argument against the concept of false consciousness in *The Sublime Object of Ideology*, which represents a direct threat to Marxist orthodoxy and its theory of hegemony. Žižek has taken particular inspiration from the work of the post-Freudian psychoanalyst Jacques Lacan, and has used Lacan's theories to make important contributions to the critical literature on the director Alfred Hitchcock, amongst others.

The Sublime Object of Ideology comes up with an intriguing theory as to why systems like communism had managed to survive as long as they had despite their shortcomings being almost painfully obvious to the citizens of the communist bloc. Žižek himself had first-hand knowledge of this resilience as a citizen of the former Yugoslavia, when it still contained his native Slovenia. Drawing on the work of both Lacan and the contemporary German philosopher Peter Sloterdijk (see his *Critique of Cynical Realism*), Žižek argued that we were very prone as individuals to develop a condition he dubbed 'enlightened false consciousness' (Žižek 1989: 29), whereby we were able simultaneously both to believe and not believe in particular theories or states of affairs. This meant that we developed a selective blind spot to knowledge that we had difficulty coming to terms with or simply found too painful to face up to, either psychologically or ideologically. Žižek gave as an example the case of a man who is able to put the fact of his wife's sudden death from breast cancer out of his mind, until his wife's pet hamster, which forms a living link back to her, dies also; at which point he breaks down and subsides into acute depression.

For Žižek enlightened false consciousness is an entirely understandable reaction to a situation where individuals have very little control over their destiny, as was the case in communist states in general. In such conditions inhabitants develop a 'fetish' that enables them to continue on an everyday basis, despite harbouring considerable reservations about having to do so somewhere deep within their mind. It was no secret in such states that the economy was not really delivering on its promises, with shortages of basic consumer goods (including foodstuffs) being all too evident on a regular basis. Doing anything about this, however, was rendered all but impossible by the power of the totalitarian state, therefore the fetish was felt by Žižek to be an entirely realistic response to the situation.

The impact of this theory is to make us see that false consciousness could also apply in communist countries, despite the fact that Marxist orthodoxy ascribes it to the non-communist world only, holding that authentic consciousness means to be actively engaged in the struggle for the dictatorship of the proletariat, which was assumed to have been successful in any state under communist rule. False consciousness is what underpins the Marxist theory of hegemony, so such a reading of it calls it into question in no less powerful a way than does Ernesto Laclau and Chantal Mouffe's critique of it in *Hegemony and Socialist Strategy*, the book that launched post-Marxism as a theoretical position. To describe the condition as enlightened also carries a particular sting: that it is a recognition that one has no choice but to go along with the situation one finds oneself in, that it must even be embraced against one's better interests. That is hardly a conclusion likely to commend itself to classical Marxist theorists, since it suggests that Marxism, too, is capable of peddling a false picture of reality, one geared towards serving the interests of those in power no less than in a capitalist society. Yet another disjunction between rulers and ruled is brought to light, and much to the discredit of the communist world, which is being held guilty of leaving individuals with no option but to develop their own particular fetish in order to cope with everyday existence under such a regime.

Žižek's writings on film have a similarly psychoanalytical bias, as can be seen in works like *Enjoy Your Symptom!*, where Lacanian concepts are applied to a wide range of Hollywood films, from the work of Charlie Chaplin onwards. What psychoanalysis enables us to recognise, Žižek insists, is 'the contours of fetishism' (Žižek 2008: x), that lie behind our ideological system – and the products of that system, such as films. Hollywood films become a way of demonstrating a series of questions that arise out of Lacanian psychoanalysis, such as: 'Why Does a *Letter* Always Arrive at its Destination?', 'Why is *Woman* Always a Symptom of Man?' or 'Why is *Reality* Always Multiple?' (Žižek 2008: 1, 35, 221). In the first case, Chaplin's *City Lights* answers the question because it is a film that is 'structured in a strictly "teleological" manner, all its elements point toward the final moment, the long-awaited culmination' (Žižek 2008: 3). Without the touching, if also highly sentimental, final scene, when the once-blind flower-seller recognises her benefactor in the shabby tramp by pressing a coin into his hand, the film would have little point: it is a letter which, from the point of view of the narrative conventions of the time and the artform, just *must* arrive. In the latter case, it is Alfred Hitchcock who provides the answer. Hitchcock's films, Žižek argues in an edited collection of essays on that topic, contain elements of realism, modernism and postmodernism over the course of the director's long career, and help us to understand the differences in interpretation that each style demands. The main difference between modernism and postmodernism for Žižek is that in the former we are trying to tease meaning out of something 'incomprehensible' (Žižek 1992: 1), whereas the latter invites us to read complex meanings into something apparently straightforward.

Žižek is arguably at his most maverick in his book *In Defence of Lost Causes*, where he argues the case for a return to revolutionary terrorism on behalf of the world's oppressed in order to bring down the current neoliberal political order. The fact that so many leftist-oriented revolutions went wrong and declined into repression in the past is not, Žižek insists, to be taken as proof that any future attempt inevitably will go the same way, although it would have to be objected that the track record is not good on that score. The extent to which Žižek thinks such a revolution is likely remains, at best, unclear.

Along with Lacan, Hegel has always formed a major influence on Žižek's thought, and in *Less Than Nothing: Hegel and the Shadow of Dialectical Materialism* he suggests that the book might be thought of as *The Imbecile's Guide to Hegel*, before launching into a typically off-centre discussion about what differentiates imbeciles from idiots or morons.

Books like these display a nostalgia for communism that seems at odds with the post-Marxist tendencies of Žižek's earlier work, and confirms the sense his writing increasingly conveys of a thinker who is hard to pin down – who may, in fact, have no central core to his beliefs. If we can posit such a thing as a postmodern communist, then Žižek would appear to have created the template for it. He seems above all these days to be a defender of lost causes, and in so doing he is isolating himself from most of the critical socio-political debates of his time. You could say that Žižek can go to the extremes he does because such views pose no particular threat to the status quo; there is no longer much of a constituency around for pro-communist arguments, even in post-credit crisis times.

Žižek's maverick persona and calculatedly outrageous assertions cannot disguise something deeply problematical about postmodern thought, and that is its failure to have any really substantial impact on political life. He has stated in an interview that 'I think the task of people like me is not to provide answers but to ask the right questions' (Aitkenhead 2012: 9), and while that is a valid enough point in its way, it could be objected that this is ultimately something of an admission of defeat for any politically motivated cultural commentator or philosopher to make. Postmodern thought is highly effective at asking the right questions, and has been doing so for quite some time now, but in the absence of anything more positive being offered, as critics like Fredric Jameson have pointed out (Jameson 1991), that leaves our culture stuck in the default position of late capitalism/ neoliberalism. While not everyone would want to go as far as Jameson and say that postmodernism therefore qualifies as late capitalism's 'cultural logic' and can therefore be regarded as one of the main props of the system, one can nevertheless see some point in his assessment. Even when some answers are provided, as in the work of Jean-François Lyotard ('little narrative' (Lyotard 1984: 60), 'paganism' (Lyotard and Thébaud 1985: 19)) or Ernesto Laclau and Chantal Mouffe ('radical democracy'), there is invariably an element of 'institutional deficit' involved: how do we get to the stage where such ideas can be made to work on the large scale rather than at a local level? Neither does Žižek's defence of revolutionary terrorism seem any more than a romantic notion nowadays after the collapse of the Soviet empire and the history of repression that went along with it from its earliest days onward. Rather as with the Marxist theory of hegemony (see Laclau and Mouffe 1985), we come away from Žižek so aware of how successful capitalism is at deflecting dissent that we might wonder how a revolutionary situation can ever come about.

Žižek's major writings

Žižek, Slavoj, *The Sublime Object of Ideology*, London and New York: Verso, 1989.

——(ed.), *Everything You Always Wanted to Know about Lacan (But Were Afraid to Ask Hitchcock)*, London and New York: Verso, 1992.

——, *Welcome to the Desert of the Real*, London and New York: Verso, 2002.

——, *How to Read Lacan*, London: Granta, 2006.

——, *Enjoy Your Symptom!: Jacques Lacan in Hollywood and Out* [1992, 2001], London and New York: Routledge, 2008.

——, *In Defence of Lost Causes*, London and New York: Verso, 2009a.

——, *Violence: Six Sideways Reflections*, London: Profile, 2009b.

——, *First as Tragedy, Then as Farce*, London and New York: Verso, 2009c.

——, *Living in the End Times*, London and New York: Verso, 2010.

——, *Less than Nothing: Hegel and the Shadow of Dialectical Materialism*, London and New York: Verso, 2012.

References and further reading

Aitkenhead, Decca, 'Humanity is OK, but 99% of People Are Boring Idiots', *Guardian*, G2 Section, 11 July 2012, pp. 6–9.

Jameson, Fredric, *Postmodernism, or the Cultural Logic of Late Capitalism*, London: Verso, 1991.

Laclau, Ernesto and Chantal Mouffe, *Hegemony and Socialist Strategy: Towards a Radical Democratic Politics*, London and New York: Verso, 1985.

Lyotard, Jean-François, *The Postmodern Condition: A Report on Knowledge* [1979], trans. Geoff Bennington and Brian Massumi, Manchester: Manchester University Press, 1984.

Lyotard, Jean-François and Jean-Loup Thébaud, *Just Gaming* [1979], trans. Wlad Godzich, Manchester: Manchester University Press, 1985.

Sloterdijk, Peter, *Critique of Cynical Realism* [1983], trans. Michael Eldred, London: Verso, 1988.

INDEX